WHAT
OTHERS REJECT,
God Accepts

WHAT OTHERS REJECT,
God Accepts

A Pastor's Journey Toward Wholeness

I arrived in September 1940

REV. CAROLYN CAMMENGA

XULON PRESS ELITE

Xulon Press Elite
2301 Lucien Way #415
Maitland, FL 32751
407.339.4217
www.xulonpress.com

Paperback ISBN-13: 978-1-6628-1900-1
eBook ISBN-13: 978-1-6628-1901-8

Contents

Preface

*T*his is the story of a child who was born out of wedlock to a mother who would eventually give her up for adoption. A child who, in spite of four and a half years of loving care by her maternal grandparents, faced the rejection of being given away. Why, she did not know nor understand. She only knew she was not wanted.

She was adopted by wonderful parents who loved her and gave her all the support, affirmation and opportunities imaginable, yet through it all the fear of rejection persisted. But God had a very special plan for her life and year by year, as she began to trust Him, her fear of rejection and failure began to dissipate.

She not only came to trust Jesus as her personal Savior, but allowed Him to direct her life, one step at a time, into full time Christian service.

During her forty years as a female pastor in two male-dominated denominations, she experienced many challenges, disappointments, and failures, yet through it all God was faithful and this book is the result of that faithfulness.

For you see, I was that child.

Blessings always,
Carolyn Jean Cammenga (Rev. Mrs.)

Chapter One:
The Journey Begins

I looked all around and all I saw was darkness. Then I looked a bit closer and saw a small trickle of light emerging from under the closed door. I pulled the blanket up closer and tried to remain calm. After all, I was only three and this was a new experience. Always before, my grandma and grandpa had been there to comfort and protect me. Now I was alone and scared. As I look back on that night years later, that's all I can remember. I must have been somehow rescued because here I am, an adult, trying to piece together a life that had a rather blurred beginning.

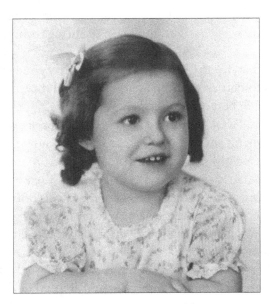

Carolyn at 2 years old

I lived with my Grandma and Grandpa Simmons, my birth mother's parents, in an upstairs apartment in Oak Park, Illinois quite close to West

Suburban Hospital. Memories of my first four years are scattered. There were always the decorative ornaments on the Christmas tree, the retelling of the "Night Before Christmas" with a special note that it was written by Clement Clark Moore, my great-great grandfather. This story was mixed with other stories of ship builders in Delaware and a seminary professor in New York City. I especially remember grandma noting that Dr. Moore actually wrote other poems; however, most of his life was spent as an ancient language professor at the General Theological Seminary in New York City.

My grandparents were wonderful people. They loved me dearly and made sure that I always knew just how special I was. Grandpa worked for Webcor; in fact, I was told that he was the person who invented the record changer for them. Grandma stayed home and took care of me.

One weekly event, the vacuuming of the living room carpet, found me gathering up my one and only doll and escaping to the sofa, feet tucked securely under my trembling body. I did not like the vacuum cleaner! Although my doll was my favorite toy, I also enjoyed playing with Lincoln Logs. I remember one night, with my logs spread out on the living room floor, I commented to my grandparents that I smelled smoke. They were certain that it was just the newness of the logs. When I persisted, they proceeded to the dining room and looked out the window toward the neighboring apartment. Sure enough, smoke was pouring from their windows. I was later praised as a "first responder".

I remember that, for the most part, I was a pretty good eater. One exception was stewed tomatoes; grandma suggested that I mix them with mashed potatoes: not much better but doable!

My secure world took a tumble when my birth mother, whom I had rarely seen, and her husband entered my life. For some unknown reason my stepfather took an extreme disliking of me. He punished me repeatedly, mostly verbally, for things that in his eyes were wrong. I especially remember his standing over me while I brushed my teeth, insisting that I was doing it wrong. One memorable bright spot occurred when I was taken to my grandparents' bedroom to catch a glimpse of my new baby brother. He looked so small lying on that bed. The memory of that brief visit would stay with me for years to come.

In September of 1940 I was four and a half. My grandparents could no longer take care of me and my mother and stepfather did not want me. Actually, I am not sure I even realized that she was my mother nor what a mother was really like. My grandparents had always functioned as my "parents" and I was confused as to just who this other woman was. In any case, at that point in my life I felt like a "Box Marked Reject." No one wanted me, or so I thought. A decision was made that I would be adopted. I did not understand exactly what that meant, only that I was leaving the only home that I had ever known and going to a new, totally unknown place. I remember standing at the window of our apartment that last day, waving goodbye to grandpa as he left for work, just as I had always done, not realizing, of course, that this would be my last "goodbye." He turned, caught my eye and waved just as always. Then he was gone. He was leaving for work, just as he did every weekday. He was leaving for the day; I was leaving for good. Adoption? What did that mean? Why? Had I done something wrong? Was I really a bad little girl like my stepfather kept saying? What about grandma and grandpa? Couldn't they continue to take care of me? I looked at the little black suitcase by the door and the doll beside it. These were the sum of my treasures...all I had accumulated in four and a half years. The doll's name was Suzie. Her clothes were in the little black bag, all handmade by grandma.

Was my little brother going too, I wondered? Where was he now? I had only seen him one time and he had seemed so very small—only a bit larger than Suzie. I had never actually held him—I guess they were afraid I'd hurt him.

I looked back one last time through the window. Nothing there. The next thing I remember was getting out of a car in Riverside, Illinois with my Suzie doll and small suitcase and walking up a pathway to where two strangers were waiting for me, smiling. I was not frightened—only puzzled. Who were these people and why did they want me? No one else did. They greeted me with hugs and escorted me up to their second-floor apartment. My new life had begun.

Carolyn with new parents

3

My new mother made me a coat and hat for the special occasion of creating an announcement of my arrival to share with their friends and family. In the photo, on the book cover, I am holding my only two possessions: my Suzie doll and my small suitcase.

Those next few months were just a vague memory. Our apartment was small with only one bedroom. I slept there and my parents slept on a hide-a-bed in the living room. One of the first tasks was changing my first name. I did not like my name "Gayle" and was eager to change it. After an evening's discussion we decided on "Carolyn Jean," and a new birth certificate was issued.

I was later to learn the conditions of my adoption. My new parents, realizing that my birth grandparents had lovingly cared for me for four and a half years, agreed to keep them an active part of my life with the understanding that they would never try to connect me with my birth mother. All holidays after that included either our visiting their apartment or their coming to spend time with us.

That first Christmas was spectacular! We went to Grandma Brainerd's, my mother's mother, in Sharon, Pennsylvania, for a large family gathering. I discovered that I had five pairs of aunts and uncles plus six cousins. My grandma loved to bake! I eagerly watched her bake pies and then was overjoyed when she let me make "piggy-wiggies" with the leftover dough. I carefully rolled out the dough, put butter, cinnamon and sugar on top, rolled it up, cut it into small pieces and put it in the oven to bake. What an accomplishment for a four-year-old! Someone thought I was special enough to spend time with me! Then there was the Christmas tree. It was even bigger than the one my birth grandparents had had; but there was one main difference. Underneath this tree were lots of boxes, many of which had my name on them.

Christmas morning arrived and I found to my utter delight that under the tree were presents for me: dolls and a doll bed, stuffed animals, and a small piano, to name only a few. A movie my father took shows me so delighted that I kept dancing around and around the gifts, even before picking one up!

During that first year in the apartment, I remember having my first set of paper dolls, standing on the back porch licking egg beaters following a cake-baking event and going to the dentist for the first time. The reward for enduring that latter event was an ice cream cone.

As the months passed, I earned the trust of my "parents", who were no longer my "new parents" any more. One weekly event was being allowed to walk alone to the local bakery. This involved walking from our apartment, crossing one street, crossing the railroad tracks and one other street before arriving at my destination. I carried a dime which in those days bought one loaf of sliced bread. My treat was getting to eat the crust on the way home. Today I am shocked that my parents had that much faith in their now five-year old child to allow her to traverse two streets and the railroad tracks alone!

For the most part I was a pretty compliant daughter. My parents and I did come to one impasse however: liver! We had a rule that you always had to clean your plate before leaving the table. That was before liver was introduced! I remember sitting at the table way past 10 p.m., refusing to eat liver. My parents finally gave up and sent me to bed. As the years passed, they finally agreed that if eating liver was the only problem they had to face with me, they were indeed lucky!

That first summer went by quickly as our family enjoyed many trips to Lake Michigan to swim and to the Brookfield Zoo which recently had acquired two pandas, Sue Lynn and Mae Lynn.

Fall of 1941 arrived, ushering in two very special events: a new house and a new experience—school! It had become apparent that our apartment was too small for three; therefore, a new house was purchased at 92 Scottswood Rd. We now had plenty of room—six bedrooms and 2 ½ bathrooms. The ½ bath was mine—adjacent to my bedroom. I especially enjoyed the toilet flush chain, which was different than anything I'd ever seen before. My closet had mirrors on one side of the doors that could be switched into regular doors. My father painted my walls a deep blue and built shelves to hold all of my precious dolls and toys.

New house in Riverside

5

We moved just in time for me to start kindergarten with Mrs. Melichar as my teacher. My first day, Mother walked me to school: down the street toward town, across the tracks, and finally across two more streets, those last two having crossing guards. I carried my orange juice in a juice bag which Mother had made. I entered class in my brand-new outfit, lovingly sewed by my devoted mother. This began a tradition which continued throughout my school years, even into high school—a new dress to begin each year. That first day was an unusual experience—there were many children my age with whom to play. My first lesson was learning to share, a totally new experience! I didn't have a lot of toys, but what I did have were mine and no one ever touched them, let alone moved them! This possession protectiveness was to carry on throughout my life with little exception.

Landmark Water Tower in Riverside

Thanksgiving was a very special time in kindergarten when we built a log cabin and dressed up like pilgrims and Indians. Coming home from school each day I would always enter my bedroom and check to make sure that nothing was out of place! Also, I believe that it was this first day of school when I decided that I really didn't like being an only child. Where was that baby brother? Why wasn't he adopted too? Do we only give away girls? Always in the back of my mind was the fear that if I did not behave or get good grades in school I would be given away again. I couldn't do anything about the fact that I wasn't a boy, but I surely could control my behavior. As the years passed, every decision in life was weighed on the scale of possible failure or potential rejection. Failure was defined by my parents as "getting a C." Fortunately this never happened until I reach college and received a C+ in second-year French because there were only five students in the class and the teacher decided to grade on the curve!

Kindergarten would also be an important year for my future. In the Riverside Public School system, IQ tests were given in kindergarten and repeated several times thereafter to make sure that each child was properly placed for success. It was then that my parents were informed that I would be going to college. Imagine—my school journey was just beginning and my future had already been decided! Since my primary goal ever since my adoption was to make sure that I was never again rejected, I determined that I would always know where I stood scholastically and accept my "fate." It was especially important to always please my parents. After all, if I failed to get good grades, they might give me away just like my original mother did, or so I thought. The truth was—all I ever really wanted to do was to get married and have kids.

I loved our new house, especially the park across the street where Daddy always enjoyed taking pictures of my friends and me. Mother spent much time on those curls!

After that first day of school and all the following days for the next eight years, I walked to school with Patsy and Johnny Nelson, new friends from just up the street. Patsy and I loved playing together. We looked forward to Saturdays when we would travel with our mothers to LaGrange on the trolley to spend our allowances at the dime store. Our town

**Carolyn with playmates
Nancy and Patsy Nelson**

did not have a dime store, movie theater, nor much of anything else for that matter. Riverside did not want to attract outsiders! Patsy and I always spent our allowances on paper dolls at the dime store. When we were not cutting those out, we were cutting out figures and furniture from an old Sears catalog. Johnny joined us periodically to play "wedding". I was always the bride, Johnny was the groom, and Patsy married us. Funny that later on I would be the one to become a minister! Our "weddings" always took place on the spacious lawn beside our house. It was a beautiful setting for any wedding what with cherry, pine, apple and weeping willow trees. Peonies and tulips added beauty. My parents spent lots of time keeping our spacious yard beautiful. Years later our yard was featured in the annual Riverside Garden Show. Life in Riverside was always quiet and safe. It was a wonderful place in which to grow up. It provided a means of security that helped in my journey toward acceptance.

Life for me became a pretty routine affair. Scheduling became the name of the game. Before leaving for school each day I practiced the piano for 20 minutes. My teachers at school had decided that I had musical talent. We purchased an old upright piano and lessons began. My teacher walked to the homes of all her pupils, and I used to watch for her expectantly at the window, that was, until later on when she introduced me to a new book of technique with lines and lines to fill in and special harmonies to learn. I hated theory! Therefore, I made a habit of losing my technique book. On the other hand, John Thompson's "Teaching Little Fingers to Play", my first performance book, was great fun and many years later when I became a piano teacher, I used that book for my students as well.

Practicing the piano three times a day, 20 minutes each time, was part of my daily routine. Dinner was always at 5:15 p.m., immediately after Daddy returned home from work. We had the same basic menu each night: meat (never a casserole), potatoes, vegetable, salad and dessert. Preparation for dinner included my helping with peeling potatoes (the only thing I was trusted to do) and setting the table. After dinner I always helped my mother dry dishes—that is, until we bought a dishwasher. I never learned to prepare any dish, much less a whole meal. This was not exactly good preparation for marriage, nor was dropping a lemon meringue pie on the floor between the kitchen and the dining room one night when we had special guests! That was an event that to this day I have never forgotten!

During those early years my parents made sure that I enjoyed experiences outside of the limitations of Riverside. Each spring we went to Lilacia Park in Lombard, a nearby suburb, to smell the lilacs and view the many varieties of tulips. This park was established by Colonel William Plum and his wife following a trip to visit lilac gardens in Nancy, France. Daddy made a movie of my stooping down to smell several of the tulips and of his lifting me up to smell the lilacs. Another delightful experience was being introduced to my first cat on a visit to friends of my parents who lived on a farm. Seeing cows for the first time taught me the new lesson that milk came from cows, not from the milkman! Those were the days when not only was milk delivered, but coal was as well. Coal came in through a large chute in our basement; later, we were fortunate enough to have a gas furnace. This was only possible because my father worked for the gas company and purchasing one was a special employee privilege. And then there was our garbage collection! Our garbage man scared me. He always came to the back door, collected our garbage can over his shoulder, and left to deposit the garbage in his truck, always coming back with the empty can. He never said a word. I always hid when he came. I was really frightened!

Not all my early experiences were positive, however. One summer we visited the cottage of one of my aunts and uncles. My uncle took me by the hand and led me down to the lake, supposedly to watch the boats go by. After a bit of "watching," his hand began to creep up my leg. I didn't fully understand what he was trying to do. All I did knew was that it made me feel uncomfortable, and I didn't like it. I immediately got up and ran back to the cottage. I didn't tell anyone of this experience at that time; however, later that evening as I lay in bed almost asleep, that same hand began to creep up my leg again! This time I jumped out of bed and ran downstairs to where my parents were playing cards. I screamed and told my parents what had happened. They believed me! It turned out that this had happened to other members of the family by the same uncle on previous occasions. We never visited there again.

Elementary school held many special memories. I was lonely being an only child. I spent many hours talking to my "imaginary friend". I would walk or roller skate around the block as I talked to my imaginary companion. Our "block" was not really a block—it was more like an island surrounded by parks. Fredrick Olmstead, who had designed Central Park in New York City, also designed Riverside in 1868. It was called "The Village in the Park." Today it is on the National Historic Registry. Frank Lloyd Wright built several homes in Riverside, the most famous of which was the Coonley House, built between 1908 and 1912, and located just down the street from our house. It is famous for its adjacent playhouse, with its "kinder-symphony" windows, conveying elements of a children's parade—balloons, flags and confetti. It was also the only house in the neighborhood that had a swimming pool, which I and other neighborhood children enjoyed.

As a child, I avoided getting into trouble; however, my parents never forgot the day I stole Beezy Jackson's beanie on the way home from school. My mother promptly escorted me to his house up the street to return the beanie and apologize. How awful! I hated Beezy!

Overshadowing all our fun times during these elementary days were the tragedies of World War II. My mom and I tried to offer a bit of assistance by walking to the town hall once a month to pick up yarn to knit scarves and mittens for the soldiers in the war. Because we lived in a suburb of Chicago, we had frequent "black-outs". These were practice air raids just in case Chicago was attacked. It was during these occasions that I learned to play bridge. My aunt Martha Lilly and cousin Bobby had come to live with us during this time because Uncle Bob was in the Army Air Corp flying over the "hump". Both my parents and Aunt Martha loved to play bridge, but they needed a fourth. I became that fourth! It was hard for me at first, but since I loved math, the game gradually became easy for me. I actually looked forward to those nights when the four of us would gather in the den, close off all the doors, shutter the windows, and play several rounds of bridge. After the war, Aunt Martha and Bobby again came to live with us, this time so that Bobby could go to Dr.

Carolyn and Bobby

Slaughter, a plastic surgeon, to have surgery on his ears, ears which stood out like a baby elephant's! It didn't help much! I still loved him dearly and wished he could stay forever!

It was shortly after the war that Kay and Hobart Peer came to live with us. Hobart was going to school in Chicago, studying to be a CPA, and they needed short-term housing. What was not short-term was our life-long relationship with them. When Hobart's schooling was completed, he and Kay moved to Champaign, Illinois where he set up his CPA practice and Kay joined the English department faculty at the University of Illinois. Each year until long after both my parents had died and I had a family of my own, I went down to the University at least once a year for a football game. Those Saturdays always began with the same sandwiches for lunch followed by a walk across campus to the football stadium. At the games during those early years, I sat between my dad and Hobart as they carefully explained each play. My favorite part was a student who portrayed Sioux Chief Illiniwek and performed his authentic Indian dance at halftime. It was a very sad day when that tradition was forced to end because of an NCAA ruling in 2007. After each game we enjoyed dinner in the Colonial Room at the Illini Union. These experiences instilled in me a life-long love for football. That love became a bit conflicted, however, when we moved to Michigan and I became a University of Michigan fan! I still went to the Illinois games, but sat on a different side of the field! My son Mark, who remains an Illinois fan, thinks I am a traitor!

Shortly after moving into our new home in Riverside, I began pressing my parents for a dog. My father was strongly opposed to this idea, but finally gave in and at least let me have a cat. I was delighted with "Boo Boo," my all-black kitten. Having a pet helped fill the void in my life as an only child. It still did not, however, solve the rejection problem. Somehow, in spite of all the great pluses in my life, fears of rejection still remained.

Of all my teachers during my elementary school years, Mrs. Pearl Dunbar was my favorite. We learned so much that third-grade year! As a field trip that year we visited a farm. Hardly any of the class had ever been to a farm! For me, the highlight of the day was finding a litter of baby kittens. Since Mrs. Dunbar traveled to Taxco, Mexico each summer, she sparkled our academic lives by telling us special stories of that city and its silver mines. I spent years hoping for the day that I could travel there. She even taught us some Spanish in preparation for a possible future trip. Years later when I did visit Taxco, it was just as I had expected—a small town with a large Catholic church in the center, surrounded by many small shops that sold silver jewelry.

Mrs. Dunbar decided that I had art talent and encouraged my parents to take me for lessons at the Art Institute of Chicago. My fondest memories, aside from the lessons, were riding the train from Riverside into the city, walking to the Art Institute, and having lunch at Marshall Field's. Today I am amazed that, once again, my mother really trusted me. After just one trip from outside the Institute to my classroom, she trusted me to find my own way to my classroom. These trips were especially fun during the Christmas season when we could view the animated windows at Marshall Field's, each one depicting a scene from a famous Christmas story. Every few years these windows would tell the story of "The Night Before Christmas". After viewing the windows, we would visit Candyland, see Santa Clause, and have lunch under the Christmas tree in the Walnut Room. We would, of course, do some Christmas shopping. I had one dollar to spend on each of my cousins. In that era there were many choices at that price. Today there would be few. I knew in advance what I would receive from Grandma Brainerd—mittens! Each year she knit a new set of mittens for each one of her grandchildren. At the time I was disappointed at her choice; later, when I became a grandma I felt differently. All my kids and grandkids now have mittens!

One special time in my third-grade class was learning how to turn cotton into fiber, and making soap. I'm seventh from the left in the back row.

Challenges in middle school included penmanship and grammar. Hours were spent with "push two three four, around two three four" in penmanship class. Next came the challenge of learning to diagram sentences in English class. I hated it at the time, but later was grateful as I launched into Spanish and French in high school and realized how important grammar was. In fact, later on I majored in Speech and English in college and taught Creative Writing at Grand Rapids Community College where I passed on to my students the importance of diagramming sentences! This particular task always began with my teaching my students that every sentence had to have both a subject and a verb! I knew that in fourth grade! Most of them didn't know that even by the time they reached college!

Each summer, or sometimes over Thanksgiving, we would visit my dad's parents in St. Paul, Minnesota. During those early years what I remember most was that the house was small and I had to use their outhouse, especially on chilly mornings, which was not fun at all! I shared a bed with Aunt Nellie. Each morning we all had to kneel around our chairs for long morning prayers led by grandpa. At the time I really didn't appreciate this tradition.

Middle School continued to present challenges. First there was Miss Allenby's sixth grade class, where I met Jim Danek, my first boyfriend. He invited me to go roller skating. My parents' response was absolutely "no"! This was not because it might be considered a "date", nor because I was too young, nor because roller skating was forbidden. Oh no! It was because he was Catholic! After all, we must be careful, even in 6th grade, just in case, God forbid, I might end up marrying a Catholic! So instead of going out with Jim to skate somewhere else, we ended up skating in my basement. It was fun, but not quite the same. Jim never invited me to anything after that! First boyfriend—lost!

It was about this same time that my mother decided we needed a cleaning lady. I'm not sure exactly where she found her but it certainly was not in Riverside! She came from Chicago on the train. She was a person of color and persons of color were not allowed to live in Riverside. In fact, although she was permitted to come to our home and clean, she had to leave Riverside on the 5:00 p.m. train! This became my introduction to race relations. Looking at her I innocently kept wondering, "Just what is the problem here?" She looked fine to me. She was always friendly and did a great job of cleaning. Was skin color that important, I wondered? Later I heard the story that one time, years before, a couple of color had tried to move into Riverside and they were immediately "discouraged" by the fire department!

My seventh-grade year was unique. My teacher was Mr. Nelson. He kept a fishpond in the middle of his classroom. It served as an incentive to behave. The consequence of misbehavior was a dunk in the pond. Although it worked then, it probably wouldn't be allowed today. Middle School orchestra began that year and I wanted to learn to play the violin. My parents made a deal with me: try out to play a piano concerto with the Women's Symphony of Chicago (an annual Spring competition when the Symphony played in our area) in exchange for violin lessons. Win or lose I would still get the lessons. This Symphony was a leading American orchestra that flourished in concert halls, on summer stages in Chicago, on tour and also hosted regular radio broadcasts from 1925 to 1952. It provided an opportunity for women musicians to perform since only men were allowed to join the Chicago Symphony Orchestra. This deal with my parent sounded "ok" with me, especially if I lost! However, that did not happen. I won and spent the next year learning the concerto picked out by my piano teacher. It was "Capriccioso Brilliant" by Mendelssohn. About that time another of my teacher's pupils inherited a Mason and Hamlin grand piano and had nowhere to place it since that pupil's family already had a grand piano. We needed two pianos so that my teacher could play the orchestra part on one piano while I did the solo work on the other. Borrowing this piano, not only for that year, but for many years to come, resulted in a great love for Mason and Hamlin pianos, a love which lives on with me to this day. No other piano that I have owned has ever measured up to that first piano; thus, it was a great personal loss when the owner reclaimed her piano ten years later. Oh yes! I did get those violin lessons, using my birth grandfather's violin, and managed to be first chair both in high school and college. This was not because I was so good—I was just better than the rest!

I have special memories of my vacations in Sharon, PA, especially those times when I was able to stay with Aunt Martha, Uncle Bob and Bobby. Bobby and I had great fun playing ping pong. He would keep telling me that if I let him win, he would be very mad at me. Eventually, as he grew older, he became much better at ping pong and beat me all the time! We also enjoyed his occasional visits to Riverside when he competed in waterskiing events in nearby communities. His father spent many long hours teaching him skiing tricks from their home on Conneaut Lake, Pennsylvania. Bobby was amazing! His trick skiing won him many medals. He even skied from on top of a ladder! In many ways he became the "little brother" I still dearly missed.

One thing for which I continued to be grateful was the commitment my parents had made to include my birth grandparents in all our holiday gatherings. They continued to be a vital part of my growing-up years. Grandma continued sharing with me stories of my birth family's heritage, retelling again and again the story behind the writing of the "Night Before Christmas."

My eighth-grade year included three special events: my playing with the Symphony, our first TV, and joining the church. Even though I was not too happy at first to be playing with the Symphony, I must admit that it turned out to be one of the most memorable experiences of my life. I even remember the conductor's name: Lillian Poenisch. It was a very challenging experience for me to play with these women, having had only one rehearsal on the day before the performance; however, it was actually fun traveling downtown with my mother to participate in this rehearsal. My performance at the concert went very well, except for a brief stumble which was quickly corrected; however, it was unfavorably noted by my teacher. The best lesson I learned from this experience, however, came from my school's music director who said, "The test of a great musician is the ability to pick up and go on after a mistake." That could be said for a lot of things in life.

Special event two was purchasing our first TV so that my father could watch football games. My mother feared that my grades would be ruined!

14

Having a TV was very important to me because by then I was a very serious football fan. Happily, watching TV never adversely affected my grades. To this day about all I ever watch on TV, except of course the news, are various sporting events, namely Michigan football and basketball and Tom Brady. Of course, now I have season tickets to the Michigan football games, the major highlight of my year!

Thirdly, I, along with several of my friends, were confirmed and became members of the Methodist Church. Even though we had gone through many weeks of classes, I am not sure any of us knew what it really meant to have a personal relationship with Christ. It was just the thing to do at the time.

More memorable for my mother than my joining the church was my refusing to wear a hat to church. She was horrified. What would her friends think? Fortunately, her friends all had daughters who were my age, and together we conspired not to wear hats ever—to anything! Our conspiracy worked through power in numbers! As my parents looked back years later, they would have been forced to agree that if not eating liver and not wearing a hat to church were the only problems with which they had to deal, they were very, very lucky. Actually, well into my adult years and beyond I still refused to wear a hat. Today the one exception is Michigan football games. My season ticket is facing the sun and late afternoon games can be blinding. Believe me, this is the only exception.

It was about this time that I began searching for a more personal relationship with God. I can remember building a simple altar in my room and spending time each day kneeling in prayer. I'm not sure why; I only know that this was an important time for me. I was obviously searching for something or Someone.

High school offered many new challenges. I was now in Riverside-Brookfield High School meaning that I was no longer only with Riverside classmates. Brookfield had been added and so had several new friends. Maryanne Sorensen, one of my closest friends from grade school, began dating Tom Layman of Brookfield and attending church with him. She enjoyed the Brookfield Baptist Church so much that she encouraged me to attend as well. She also introduced me to one of Tom's friends, Ken Panoch, and we became a faithful foursome. Neither Maryanne nor I had been very happy at our Methodist Church in Riverside. Both of us felt that, even though we had gone through confirmation class there, we really didn't know much about a personal relationship with Christ. I actually was bold enough to meet with the Methodist minister and inform him just how "wishy washy" I thought his church was. I told him that my friends who were Catholic and my friends who were Baptist all knew exactly what they believed, but I didn't have a clue. He invited me to teach Sunday School! I decided to stick with the Baptists! The preaching there was excellent as was the youth group, which the four of us regularly attended. Added to my already busy weekly schedule were High School Crusaders on Tuesday night, prayer group and Bible study on Wednesday night, Youth for Christ on Saturday night, and services both morning and evening at church on Sunday. We also had a Bible Quiz Team, which I joined. It was headed by Bill Gothard, a real wiz at memorizing Scripture. We always won. Bill invited some of us to join him in his home in LaGrange to participate in a Sunday afternoon radio program. This gave me another chance to play my violin. Neither Maryanne's nor my parents were very happy about this change in our church affiliation. They preferred that we remain at our former church where their friends worshipped. We both decided, however, to continue at BBC where I was baptized by immersion on my sixteenth birthday, an event which my parents attended. It would become a turning point in my spiritual walk with the Lord. I remember the pastor asking, "Carolyn, have you accepted Christ as your personal Savior?" Following my affirmative response, he announced that "on the basis of your confession, I now baptize you in the name of the Father, the Son, and the Holy Spirit." Later on, I remember reading that Martin Luther once said in a moment of spiritual doubt, "Remember you are baptized."

Our youth group especially enjoyed going once a year to the Village Church of Western Springs to hear Billy Graham preach and George Beverly Shea sing. These two marvelous Christian leaders would return at least yearly to this church where they both had formerly served. Saturday night Youth for Christ services were often held at Moody Memorial Church in downtown Chicago. Following these services our youth group would stop for ice cream at Charmet's Restaurant, near Water Tower Place. Although I was not aware of it then, all these spiritual experiences were steps on a journey that would eventually lead me into full-time Christian service.

The very first class of my freshman year in high school was Latin. This class lasted exactly one day for me! I hated Latin and quickly switched to Spanish which I loved from the very first day. It brought back memories of those special days in third grade when Mrs. Dunbar introduced us to Spanish and her travels to Taxco. After two years of Spanish, I switched to French and continued that language into my first year of college. I loved the opportunity to play the violin in the orchestra and percussion in the band. It was especially fun to play in the marching band at football games. I remember Sousa's "Washington Post March" where the cymbal had a solo. I also played the Grieg's "Piano Concerto in A Minor" with the orchestra—one year doing the first movement and the second year the second and third movements. During my sophomore year my father signed me up for driver's training which I promptly dropped! No driving for me! Actually, I was 22, married, had a child and a teaching position before I learned to drive!

Summers were spent both attending summer school and working at various jobs. I got fired from my first job at Petersen's Ice Cream Store in Riverside because I did not dish up ice cream fast enough. Working at a local bank later that summer proved to be a better fit for me. There I could daily practice my math skills! The last two summers before graduation I worked as a secretary at BBC. This was combined with babysitting Pastor Pettitt's three children while his wife gave birth to their fourth child. I remember how sad I felt leaving these precious children the day I left for college. They were very special to me. As I already mentioned, I had decided to spend part of each summer taking a class in summer school. This was primarily because I did not like history and social studies and summer school offered me the opportunity to get those classes out of the way as quickly as possible. As a result, by the time I finished my junior year in high school, I only needed one credit in order to graduate. Was there an alternative to spending my senior year in high school? With the encouragement of Pastor Pettitt, I enrolled at Bob Jones University in the fall of 1953 where I took a full load of college work and a second year of French in their Academy. Today I wonder just why I was in such a hurry? I missed all those special times as a senior in high school. Was I just anxious to exit the "program" that had been set up for me in kindergarten? Or was it because once I finished, I could get on with my chosen life—marriage and kids? Perhaps that was the same reason that I later chose to finish college early. I needed to complete the "program" as soon as possible.

One special event during my junior year in high school was our class trip to Washington D.C. and New York City, where our class enjoyed a special dinner together. Ken is on the left, toward the back. I am third from the right.

Bob Jones was a huge challenge for me. Being an only child, I had never shared a room. Nothing was ever out of place in my bedroom. At Bob Jones four roommates in one small room were way too many for me! The room had two bunk beds, one with three tiers. Guess who had to sleep on the top?

Jumping out of bed in the morning to a loud bell was not my style either. Nor was having someone else (the administration) decide when and what I would eat, how I would dress, how I would relate to boys, and many other rules, the penalty for infractions thereof being one or more demerits. I decided that I would beat the system. No one was ever going to give me a demerit no matter how much I hated the rules. I succeeded. I even received a letter of congratulations from Dr. Bob Jones Jr., the University president; however, I did not return. I must admit, though, that I did receive a great education there through many dedicated teachers.

I finished up at BJU that spring and returned to Riverside-Brookfield to graduate with my class and catch up with boyfriend, Ken, again. My yearbook photo carried the words, "Quiet, Poised and Self-Controlled". I have never forgotten those words. At the time I am sure the words clearly represented who I was; however, over the years, advice and circumstances changed that profile.

Before leaving BJU I had made the decision to transfer to Monmouth College, a small United Presbyterian Church liberal arts school in Monmouth, Illinois. Since I had completed one year of college while finishing high school, I entered Monmouth as a sophomore. Being a bit bored and not academically challenged, I spoke with the Dean of Women early on and shared with her my plan to graduate at the end of the following academic year. My plan included an extra load of classes each semester and attending Wheaton College for summer school in between my two years. She agreed to this plan, provided I remain on the honor roll. I succeeded in accomplishing this, as well as participating on the debate team, playing in the band and orchestra, taking piano lessons, directing a local church choir, acting in the drama club, and serving on the college evangelism team. Dating was not an issue since I was still committed to my high school boyfriend, Ken, who was attending Baylor University in Texas. At Monmouth I majored in Speech and Drama with a minor in English. I chose speech, I think, because I had had a crush on my speech teacher while at BJU. Little did I realize then how important a speech major would be in my future career as a minister! My parents had insisted that I also get a teaching certificate, sort of as an insurance policy, to make sure I could get a job upon graduation. Great advice! Happily, I not only graduated with honors, but was well prepared for my future as a teacher.

It was during my last year at Monmouth that I felt called to serve as a missionary teacher in Egypt. My mother had grown up in the United Presbyterian Church of North America and we often attended a church from that denomination during our visits to Sharon. On one special occasion that spring, a representative from the mission board of UPCNA came to Monmouth to share with us the opportunities for service in Egypt and elsewhere. I had felt strongly called to some form of ministry while in high school, although I knew that my church, and especially Bill Gothard, would not support my entering the ordained ministry as a pastor. Thus, it was on that special night at Monmouth I accepted God's call to serve in Egypt and quickly made plans to travel there the following August. The year was 1956 and Egypt was not the safest place in the world. Controversy over control of the Suez Canal dominated the news. My parents were very worried about my decision to teach there. Together we traveled to Pittsburgh to consult with my great Uncle George Long, who at that time was president of Pittsburgh Theological Seminary. Earlier I had shared with him my desire to enter the ordained ministry. Women in the ordained ministry was not a popular, nor even a very likely, possibility at that time. In fact, Uncle George was very firm about not having women enter the seminary as ministerial candidates. He did, however, strongly affirm my call as a missionary to Egypt, much to the disappointment of my parents who would have preferred my staying closer to home. To Uncle George, being a missionary, not a pastor, was an appropriate role for a woman! It is interesting to note, however, that my parents had always affirmed my talents and had taken the firm stand that I could pursue any career that I chose, regardless of the fact that I was a female. In some ways I was relieved by the decision to go to Egypt since that meant that I did not have to face rejection as a female ministerial student in a male-dominated profession.

That year, just before graduation, a picture fell out of a letter I received from Grandma Simmons. I picked up the picture. Grandma must have found an old picture of me, I thought to myself. Then I read the letter. "Now that you are graduating from college," she began, "I think you should know that you have a little sister. She is eleven years younger than you. Her name is Sharon. I'm sending you an old picture." A sister? I had a sister? Tears welled up in my eyes. Unbelievable! Why had no one told me before? She looked just like me! In fact, the picture was taken in front of our apartment building, just under that favorite window. Had she spent time looking out that window, too? Had she been given away also? And what about my brother? Where was he?

I carefully put away the picture. I had exams, papers, parties to attend before my June graduation. Why had Grandma picked this moment to tell me about my little sister? I had always wanted a little sister, dreamed of having a little sister, even pretended to my friends that I had a little sister. All those growing-up years, those lonesome, questioning years I'd waited for news about that baby boy. And now this—a sister. It would be many years before I would receive answers to these questions. In the meantime, I was able to enjoy graduation: cap and gown, recognition of my academic achievement—cum laude, which was amazing since I carried an academic load of 22 ½ hours my last semester and received all As at that!

One interesting event took place mid-summer. Although my family ties were Republican, my boyfriend, Ken, was an active Democrat. He was, therefore, excited when the 1956 Democratic National Convention was held in Chicago. He insisted that we attend. Getting from Riverside to Chicago was no problem as the Burlington railroad had almost hourly routes into the city. It was a short walk then to McCormick Place. Ken had hoped that we might have a chance to meet Adlai Stevenson, the projected Democratic nominee for president. Not very likely, I thought. However, as fate would have it, we did meet him—unexpectantly in an elevator! I will never forget the stunned expression on Ken's face. We were not prepared with pad and paper so no autograph was possible. Still, it was an unforgetable experience even for a Republican!

Since we were already downtown, Ken and I decided to pretend that we were an engaged couple looking for an apartment. We thought living on Lake Michigan would be a great experience. We took a bus north up Lake Drive. We found an apartment complex just south of North Avenue and, thanks to a friendly realtor, had a personal tour of one of the apartments. Of course we knew we would never be able to afford it, but just walking through one was lots of fun.

In August before leaving for Egypt to accept my position as an English teacher at the American College for Girls, a United Presbyterian Church mission school in Cairo, I attended the New Wilmington Missionary Conference in New Wilmington, PA on the campus of Westminster College. What a delightful experience that was! The best part was meeting Rev. Menes Abdul Noor, an Egyptian pastor who was serving a church in a small town in Upper Egypt. He taught me my first words in Arabic. I remember skipping up and down those campus hills shouting out new words in Arabic. These new words Menes carefully wrote down in my Bible, both in Arabic and in English. He also signed my Bible with a verse and encouraging words. Daily, Menes would laughingly skip along with me as we journeyed up and down those challenging hills, so typical of Western Pennsylvania. We spent every free moment together as my call to Egypt was confirmed and reconfirmed. I loved Egypt already! However, Menes and I behaved so badly that I received a letter of concern from the head of the mission board prior to my actual departure. Women in Egypt just didn't act like that! Little did I realize then just what a blessed friend Menes would be, not only during my stay in Egypt, but throughout my life. He had dedicated his life to reaching Moslems for Christ and spent years developing a program to support that mission. One year during a visit to their home in Cairo, I helped him translate this program into English. For many years his program was available to pastors throughout the Middle East, helping them share the Gospel with their Moslem friends. Menes travelled throughout the world with his message. Pretty soon the government got wind of what he was doing and tried to confiscate his notes. After that, I smuggled his notes out of Egypt and distributed them to several countries where he would be teaching. When Menes went home to be with the Lord many years later, his mission had been so successful that an article was written about him in Christianity Today with his picture on the cover. This was a special tribute to a wonderful servant of the Lord.

During the next few weeks prior to my leaving for Egypt, Mother and I shopped for whatever we thought I might need for the next three years.

Those train rides into Chicago brought back so many childhood memories, although without the Christmas decorations!

It was finally time to say goodbye. I'm sure that seeing their only child leave for the far-away land of Egypt must have been very difficult for my parents. Soon I was off to New York City by train to meet another teacher, Donna Lee Wagner, and board our ship, the U.S. Constitution, for our trip to Naples, Italy, which was the first leg of our journey to Egypt. I had met Donna Lee at the N.W.M.C. and was looking forward to our voyage together. Saying goodbye to my parents was very hard. They had done a wonderful job of parenting. They had made me feel accepted and helped me begin my journey "out of the rejection box." I would be eternally grateful to them for the wonderful life they had given me. I was especially grateful to my mother, who faithfully wrote to me at least once a week while I was in Egypt. Were it not for her writing and my saving her letters, much of this book would not have been possible. I am eternally grateful to a God who promised me, as He did Jeremiah (29:11), *"For I know the plans I have for you... plans for welfare and not for evil, to give you a future and a hope."*

Chapter Two:
The Egyptian Journey Begins

Our voyage across the Atlantic was a great opportunity to get to know Donna Lee better. She was an experienced teacher and traveler. I was not. This was my first venture out of the country and my first teaching position. Little did I realize then that many more trips throughout the world would follow this first, unique voyage.

As I mentioned before, my mother was wonderful about, not only writing regularly, but keeping the letters I sent them. These cheery letters began on September 4, 1956. They have become the basis of my writing this Chapter and the following Chapters concerning my time in Egypt.

I began my first letter home as follows:

"This trip on the US Constitution has been just delightful. It's like floating on a cloud where all the stars are just waiting to fall at your feet. Not only is the food delicious, but the service is magnificent. Our waiter has only two tables which include eight people each. All meals consist of about eight courses, but after the first day I decided against having them all. I wondered the first couple of days if I would become seasick, but I soon realized that I really didn't have time to fit being sick into my very busy schedule. We arise at 7:30, breakfast is at 8:00 and then a few rounds of ping-pong. At 10 we have two choices: exercise class or a movie. Following lunch most of us hop into our bathing suits for an afternoon on deck—swimming, shuffleboard or more ping-pong. After tea at 4 most of us just relax or see another movie, always first run shows. Supper is at 6 followed by an evening of entertainment, dancing, bingo, cards or just loafing. Donna Lee and I met two gentlemen from Sicily who enjoyed teaching us some Italian, useful at least for the next few days. They also found time to teach us some Italian songs and

dances. Instead of staying in Cabin Class for the evening we found that sneaking down to Tourist Class was much more fun and quite a bit livelier, especially the music.

"The weather has been great—warm enough to get a tan, but cool enough to relax, especially with the sea breeze and the air-conditioning.

"I'm really getting lots of linguistic practice! I speak Spanish to my bedroom steward, French to my deck steward, Arabic to practice with Donna Lee and Italian with John, my friend from Sicily. Italian is coming along nicely since in many ways it is similar to Spanish. In addition to playing lots of ping-pong I now play shuffleboard and miniature-golf. Dancing in the evening continues to be a fun (and new) experience. I seldom danced in high school and college, mainly because my church frowned on it.

"Between noon and four p.m. on Wednesday we passed the Azure Islands, owned by Portugal. In the evening we passed the U.S. Independence, sister ship of the Constitution. The next day we attended the captain's farewell dinner following our stop in Spain. About 100 of the 850 passengers disembarked there. Our dinner was spectacular: shrimp cocktail, scallops, filet-minion, vegetables, peach melba, cheese, fruit, figs, and dates. An Italian tenor was the star of the talent show, concluding the evening.

"Friday a young, short and fat Turkish male and I won the doubles ping-pong tournament. He was really good! The next day, playing ping-pong in my bare feet, I cut my toe; however, I was still able to compete in the shuffleboard tournament and win with the help, of course, of my Turkish companion. The surprise of the day was a fire drill, a bit late in the course of the trip if you ask me. The evening movie, "The Swan," with Grace Kelly was a real hit.

"Sunday, we had breakfast on deck so that we could watch the ship dock at Genoa. We were each given a five-hour pass, so we were able to take a tour of the city, a nice break from our sea-journey. After a rather quiet evening some of us decided to play ping-pong at 1:30 am. We looked a little bushed at 2:30 when we finally went to bed.

"On Monday, September 10, 1956 at 11:00 a.m. we docked in Naples; however, it was 2:30 p.m. before we were able to locate our luggage and our hotel. Donna Lee and I spent the rest of the afternoon and early evening just walking around town enjoying our first glimpse of Italy. Having a few days before we left for Alexandria, we decided on Tuesday to explore the island of Capri with friends. We climbed hills and looked back at stacked houses which looked like they were built on top of each other. In the evening we all strolled around Naples, enjoying the festive atmosphere and all the bright lights which formed a colorful chain along the two miles of the bay. We even went for a ride on the ferris wheel, bought hot roasted peanuts and finally ended up at a small restaurant along the sea for some of Italy's famous ice cream. Then on Wednesday Donna Lee and I took a tour to Pompeii. It took us three hours to walk through the city and we only saw about a third of it. The heat really got to us, making a swim later in the sea, off of Capri, very refreshing. Once in the water, we found ourselves surrounded by large moss-covered rocks which tended to be very slippery. Eating dinner in a local restaurant taught us a valuable lesson: spaghetti in Italy is just that—spaghetti with no tomato nor meat sauce. Bread is extra, but in large quantities. Seasonal fruit is always a delicious conclusion to any meal. Returning to the hotel for the evening we watched fireworks from our hotel balcony.

"Friday evening at 6:00 p.m. we boarded the Iskenderun, a Turkish ship, for our sail to Alexandria and began a nightmarish three days! Turks speak Turkish—that's it! The food was so terrible that you could actually see the dirt on the bread. The boat was small and rocked so much that some of our group spent the whole time in bed. Donna Lee and I managed to stay on deck most of the time since our cabins were small, hot, smelly and never cleaned. What a contrast from what we had become used to! As it turned out, these three days cost almost half as much as our wonderful 10 days on the passenger ship, the U.S. Constitution.

"We were a couple of hours late arriving in Alexandria. We were met by a man from the mission board, another man who assisted us through customs, a teacher from the school and one of the chauffeurs from the College. Customs went smoothly and soon we were on our way to Cairo. We arrived at the College at 9:30 p.m., just in time to enjoy a late

dinner at President Sarah Meloy's apartment. Best part—she has a grand piano! By the time dinner was over the servants had delivered our luggage to our rooms. Donna Lee and I have adjacent rooms on the third floor. My room is large and looks much like a college dorm room. There are eight of us living on this floor, each with her own room but sharing two bathrooms. The ceilings are very high to try to keep it cool during the warm summer months. We share two servants who make our beds, keep our rooms clean every day and do our laundry once a week. I soon learned that "pajamas" are "pajamas" in Arabic too! The meals are very good with lots of fresh fruits and vegetables.

"Our campus consists of two main classroom/dorm buildings, a library, home economics building, chapel, gardens, and tennis courts. When school begins, my daily schedule will be: 8:15 first class, 9:30 chapel, 10:30 tea, three periods before lunch, lunch, nap, classes 2-4, 4:30 tea, 5-6:30 study hall supervision and 7:30 dinner. A full day!

"I want you know," I continued, "that regardless of what you read in the US papers, the situation here remains quite calm. My daily schedule remains the same; however, not having traditional weekends (our days off are Friday and Sunday) is very different. Already my Fridays are being filled with invitations from students and special activities. I have yet to visit the Pyramids, having only seen them by moonlight from a distance as we traveled from Alex to Cairo the night we arrived."

This concluded my first letter home to my parents.

Seated at my desk some days later I hastily scanned the calendar before me. It read October 1st. In just one short week school would begin. A new era was unfolding before me and inwardly I felt a bit uneasy. This would mark the beginning of my teaching career. I somehow felt at an extreme disadvantage as I noted that not only was I the youngest member of the faculty, but also the only one who had had no previous teaching experience. I was so grateful for the promised Orientation session which was to begin later in the week. I had so much to learn about Egyptian life and culture.

In the meantime, I kept busy practicing the piano in preparation for lessons which would begin on the 12th with Professor Tiegerman at the Conservatoire de Musique. I found that I needed to also spend time working on my Arabic. Whereas the older students, whom I would be teaching, were fluent in English, the younger ones I sat with at meals did not know very much English. Beginning in kindergarten, the students studied English; however, it was not until they reached high school that most of their classes were in English. Each student took a class in the religion of her parents; therefore, since most of the girls were Moslem, an Imam was an adjunct member of our faculty.

One day before school began, Liza Yassa, one of our Egyptian teachers, and I made a fun trip to the Musky (bazaar) to purchase material to cover items in my room: a skirt for my washstand, a cover for my trunk, and additional fabric for curtains. I borrowed a sewing machine from the home economics department and in short order these new items were up and ready for inspection by my colleagues. Thank you, Mother, for those sewing lessons you insisted I take!

Our Orientation session, which was held on the front lawn of Dr. Willis McGill's spacious home, was a major help in my adjusting to life in Egypt. I listened intently as one speaker after another described the various aspects of Egyptian life. My notes included thoughts on Christianity, Islam and other phases of religious life in Egypt. I soon learned that my task as a teacher would be two-fold: to provide a factual knowledge of the subject matter I was teaching and to instill in my students the basic principles of Christianity by the life I lived before them. The returns on this latter task, I was told, were minimal. The number of converts among the Moslem students was very slim. Our task was to sow the seed and rely on God to bring forth the harvest.

It was the fourth speaker's message, though, that was to leave a lasting impression on my mind. Little did I realize then what a great affect her words would later have on my life. How happily I joined in the laughter which followed her staunch remarks on dating Egyptian men! The idea had never entered my mind. I had a very clear picture all my own of Egyptian men: short, fat, elderly, bald with three or four wives (with the exception, of course, of Menes)! The answer from her was: never date Egyptian men!

The dinner which followed the meeting was a most festive occasion. Brightly decorated lanterns adorned the garden, providing an enchanting background for our first get-acquainted party. Although the food was primarily American, the atmosphere was definitely oriental. Several "safroggies," clad in white, skillfully moved among the guests, catering to our every need. Their dark eyes sparkled from behind well-tanned faces and their every move spoke of grace and tradition.

Later that evening as I sat on my bed chatting with my new friend and colleague, Jeanne, our conversation just naturally turned to the events of the evening. Humorously I remarked, "I wonder if they really think we'd date Egyptians!"

Jeanne's face clouded. "Have you ever met an Egyptian man?"

"Yes, at the New Wilmington Missionary Conference and on the boat," I replied, remembering then that Menes was not fat and bald. He was, indeed, very handsome!

"I wish you could meet Mike," she continued.

"Mike?" I asked.

"Mike is one of the most wonderful men I have ever met. He's about everything any girl could want in a husband, except—I'm not in love with him."

"You have been dating an Egyptian?" I asked, remembering our earlier admonition.

"Yes, I have; however, the problem is that I have been dating Mike, but I really want to date his brother. That's where you come in."

"Me?"

"Yes, 'you.'" I would like you to go on a double date, supposedly with Mike's brother. Maybe if Mike got to know you, he would forget about me and I would be free to date his brother!"

The thought of dating an Egyptian somewhat fascinated me—intriguing, but dangerous? Why had we been advised against this?

Not waiting for my reply, Jeanne continued, "Mike is 26, a doctor, very handsome and I might add, very wealthy. They both belong to the Gezira Sporting Club and honestly you don't know what living is like until you've been there. I know you would have a great time and it would be just this once."

The whole idea seemed incredulous to me; however, with reluctance I finally agreed, making sure it was for "just this once". For someone who had made it a point to always obey rules, this for me was a first!

Lying in bed later, I suddenly felt a twinge of excitement stirring within me. It almost seemed like I was looking forward to this date. Whatever had induced me to say, "yes"? What exactly was I expecting, and why was I on the verge of being excited? Was disobeying the rules that much fun? Fretfully, I slept.

The sunshine was warm and comforting as it streamed into my room the next morning. It lay a gentle hand on my tired brow and coaxed me awake. I had been dreaming—of what, I could not remember. But with the dawn came a new day—a day to be lived, enjoyed and remembered for many years to come. It mattered little what the night had revealed; today was here at last and my heart was filled with anticipation.

As I walked downstairs to breakfast, my footsteps echoed the beatings of my heart. I want to live, live, live it kept repeating. With joy in my heart, I slipped quietly into my place at the breakfast table. Dr. Sarah Meloy's gracious smile added warmth to our little circle around the table. To my left sat fellow teachers Nadia, Nabila and Zizette and to my right boarding students Odette, Nazek and Elham. Although the school had not officially opened, many of our boarding students had already arrived and had joined us for breakfast. Now I was faced with learning new names to match the new faces. Some names, especially Armenian ones, were very difficult. The Armenians in Egypt have a long history, with their own language, churches, and social institutions. Fortunately, all the girls were very patient and understanding as I made additional attempts at their names.

As I looked around the table, I wondered about the homes from which each girl came. I knew from my orientation session that only girls from very wealthy families were able to afford private schools. The others either received no education at all, went to government schools or were married off to men of their parents' choosing. I noticed, too, that the girls were still wearing lovely cotton dresses, much like our girls in the States. As soon as school officially opened, the primary girls would wear blue uniforms and the secondary girls, light brown suits with white blouses.

A group of Elementary Students

"Miss Copeland," someone called, "Miss Roy wishes to see you in her office after devotions this morning if you are free."

I nodded my agreement and proceeded to wonder about this meeting. I had yet to receive my teaching schedule, but presumed I would be teaching English as previously arranged. However, I was in for quite a surprise a few minutes later as I entered Miss Martha Roy's office.

"Carolyn" she began, "I really have a problem. It seems that our math teacher will be unable to resume her teaching duties this year and after looking over your college transcript I see that you took math courses at Monmouth. I was wondering how you would feel about teaching algebra rather than English classes as we had originally planned."

I was stunned. Me? Teach algebra? With only two math classes in college? I had never studied algebra with the intent of ever teaching it. That being said, it had always been my easiest and favorite subject in both high school and college. Plus, I had always managed to skip all those "unnecessary" steps in order to get to the answer. Who needed those steps anyway? In spite of my initial reservation, I gave her my consent. "I'll do my very best," I promised. "Do you have any books which might offer me some help?" She handed me two books on teaching algebra along with the textbooks from each of the classes. I was assigned two classes each of 1st and 2nd year algebra and two classes of general math which were known as Irregular A and B. Students in these latter classes entered the College from other schools and needed a better background in English before taking regular math classes. Most of them, I later found out, spoke mainly French. Teaching math was enough of a challenge, but in French? What was I thinking of? I soon learned that skipping all those "unnecessary steps" in problem solving did not work with teaching math! Also, just because I had been a great math student did not necessarily make me a good math teacher. In fact, it proved to be just the opposite! It was a struggle!

The school itself was divided into three sections: the primary (grades 1-6), secondary (grades 7-12) and a two-year college division. Prior to entering the primary grades, the girls had finished two years of kindergarten. Most of the college students were studying home economics (in order to become good wives!). The students began their studies of English, French, and Arabic in I Primary; thus, by the time they reached the high school level they were quite proficient in all three languages. Through VI Primary the girls had all their non-language classes in Arabic; however as soon as they entered the Secondary division, all non-language classes were in English. Their total class load was usually nine.

Leaving Miss Roy's office with books in hand, I retired to my room to begin working on lesson plans. I had difficulty concentrating. My eyes kept wandering toward the clock as the minutes ticked off to 6:30 p.m.—my arranged date! I decided what I needed was a break. I made my way out onto the roof. There the heat of the noonday sun brightened my spirits somewhat and seemed to give my entire body a new lift. From my vantage point high above the campus I was able to observe blocks and blocks of varying activities. Directly below me the gardener was busily watering the spacious lawn, beautifully edged with flowers of all description. At the gate stood the bawab, the tall and dignified doorman in his long blue garb, silently awaiting the arrival of guests. Just outside the gate a military officer paced up and down, his eyes alert for any signs of disturbance. The traffic on Sharia Ramses, the busy street below, scurried by and little children playing near the roadside narrowly missed being hit. What a contrast I observed as I watched a lanky camel come to an abrupt halt at the traffic light on the corner. Where he once dominated the scene, now cars of every make ignored him as they raced by. Behind me in their rooftop dwellings, a crew of washerwomen were laboriously scrubbing away at the pile of clothes before them. Their scrub boards and wash basins were a far cry from the push-button existence we took for granted back home. Slowly they rubbed each piece, back and forth, back and forth, almost in rhythm. Even in a menial task such as this there was a profound sense of dedication. They were actually smiling!

Now it was "date preparation" time. What should I wear? I had put on a few pounds thanks to great Egyptian food and my clothes were beginning to show it! I hurriedly put together what I hoped would be an appropriate outfit and joined Jeanne at the gate to wait for our "dates" to arrive. Soon a new two-tone, blue and white Chevy pulled up to the curb and a young man in a white suit emerged.

"Hi!" he said casually.

"Hi!" replied Jeanne. "Yarvant, I'd like you to meet Carolyn. Carolyn, this is Mike's brother."

I took his extended hand and felt his eyes looking questioningly into mine. What was this all about? he probably wondered. My gaze shifted to the front seat of the car and there was Mike, Jeanne's date. We were quickly introduced and on our way.

The evening, though pleasant, had an air of uneasiness. Yarvant was polite, but obviously unimpressed with me. The feeling was mutual. In the theatre I found myself squeezed between Yarvant and Jeanne with Mike on

Jeanne's left. I had difficulty relaxing as I found myself guarding both my eyes and my words. Although nothing clicked with Yarvant, I experienced some positive vibes with Mike. He seemed more my type—quiet, unassuming, settled, and mature in contrast with his very outgoing, social brother. At least I learned one thing—all Egyptian men are not fat and forty! So much for a first date!

Saturday it was back to reality. I spent the morning assisting Miss Roy as she worked out schedules for teachers. My four classes of algebra and two classes of math would be in the morning, leaving my afternoons free for napping and giving piano lessons. All the "bug" stories I heard before coming to Egypt turned out not to be true. We have just as many bugs in the US as they have here: same number of flies, but more mosquitoes in the US.

As a reward for all our hard work that day, we had apple pie with cheese for dessert at our evening meal. Apples are very expensive in Egypt, so we don't have them very often. On the other hand, some items are very cheap—fresh dates and figs for instance. Eggplant is a new vegetable for me which I have come to enjoy. We either have it fried or cooked with meat and tomato sauce. Vegetables are fresh all year around and taste much better than those in the US. We have ice cream about three times a week, with mango sauce as a special treat.

On Sunday morning Dr. Meloy took four of us on a tour of five of the largest evangelical churches in Cairo. Although the services were all in Arabic, they provided us with a great introduction to Christian worship in Egypt. Only about ten percent of the population is Christian. Of that number the majority are Coptic Orthodox with a small number Coptic Evangelicals, a denomination formed by United Presbyterian Missionaries in the late 19th Century. As you can imagine, the worship services must have been shorter than an hour each for us to have visited five! Later that evening we attended the English worship service at the American Mission Church in Ezbekiah where many of our teachers sang in the choir.

Classes for our secondary students began the next day, but classes for the other students did not begin until the following week. I have 39 girls in my homeroom and an average of 35 in each of my classes. These girls are very different from American students. When I enter the classroom, they all stand up and say, "Good morning Miss Copeland". They remain standing until I direct them to be seated. As I called the roll, I made many errors in pronunciation just as I had feared; however, instead of laughing at me, each girl quietly and politely made the necessary correction. As I looked at their expressive faces I thought, "They really like me!" And they did! Each girl seemed to take a personal interest in my well-being. They were eager to assist me in every way possible. First on their "help" list was teaching me how to say, "sabahel keer," or "good morning" in Arabic. That was a challenge, but they patiently repeated it enough times until I finally mastered it.

All my apprehensions seemed to disappear as the hours slipped by. Each class added new warmth to my spirits and gave me inner confidence. By the end of that first day, I truly was experiencing real joy and gratitude that God had led me to this place of service. That "place" expanded a bit when two additional classes were added to my already full schedule: third year algebra for seniors in secondary school and an advanced math class for freshmen in our college division. In addition, one special treat was meeting Suzie Greiss who was to become my first piano student. She was an advanced pupil who over the next few months would be learning the First Movement of Schumann's A Minor Concerto, with my playing the accompaniment (orchestra part).

Several days later, my teaching routine took a brief interruption. As many new residents of Egypt often discover, "gippy tummy" as it is called, happens frequently. It happened to me and became a rather serious problem; thus, it was decided that I should travel to Tanta Hospital, run by our American mission, for some tests. Dr. Meloy accompanied me on the short journey. The ride there revealed a part of Egypt that the average tourist never sees. As we drove along, I caught glimpses of the countryside and was amazed at the striking contrasts. Much of the land was barren with only a few small, dark mud huts scattered here and there. Nearby, women sat sifting wheat, washing clothes in the Nile streams (by pounding their clothes against the rocks) or carrying huge bundles on their heads—bundles so large that you sometimes wondered how they could hold their heads up under such a heavy load. Tanta itself was very different from Cairo, where the dress is very modern. Here the men and women dressed mostly in typical village attire. The women wore long black dresses with black head coverings and veils. The men wore long flowing gowns which closely resembled American nightshirts: long sleeves with buttoned cuffs, neck open enough for about three buttons and a stiff shirt collar. Many of these gowns were striped. Other men wore what could best be described as typical American pjs.

The hospital looked much the same as other surrounding buildings: sandy-colored mud brick with large shutters and high ceilings, designed to keep the rooms cool in the summer and fairly warm in the winter. At the admittance desk Dr. Meloy and I parted company. She promised to look in on me before she returned to Cairo. A cordial Egyptian nurse took my bag and led the way down a narrow corridor to my room. I had the privilege of having the only room with a private bath. There were no windows in my room; however, the hall was lined with windows opposite my door, thus by leaving the door slightly ajar I had a lovely view of the hospital courtyard.

I changed into my pajamas and crawled into bed. Quickly I fell asleep, soon to be awakened by Dr. Meloy's promised visit.

"How do you feel?" she asked.

"My brief rest really helped. Could you reconsider and take me back with you?"

She smiled. "We'll miss you, but we want you to get a good rest and return to us completely well. Rev. and Mrs. Sims are coming here Sunday to conduct the evening worship service, so if you're feeling better by then, possibly you can return to Cairo with them."

She bent over and kissed me on the forehead before walking to the awaiting car. What a wonderful woman! She was of average height, fairly slim and perhaps in her late fifties, although she looked much younger. Her graying hair framed her face with soft curls and gave her a calmness quite in keeping with her lovely disposition. She was an inspiration to all who knew her and had the privilege of working with her.

What followed were a rather pleasant two days. Some of the nurses invited me to join them in the lounge to listen to records, sip Turkish coffee and eat peanuts! I also was able to go for a brief stroll in the gardens.

Sunday morning, one of the nurses took me on a tour the hospital, stopping long enough in the children's ward to play with some of the children, many of whom were suffering from malnutrition. The hospital's delivery room was immaculate, but far from modern. Since anesthetics are given only in rare cases, there was no equipment in sight for administering gas or ether. The room was equipped with a delivery table, a small crib for the baby, a makeshift incubator and a cabinet containing sterilized instruments. I wondered as I looked around just how the average American mother would feel about giving birth under these primitive conditions.

As we walked toward the medical wing, I noticed several visitors standing in the corridors. Glancing into one of the rooms I was astonished to see groups of men, women, and children sitting on the floor eating supper. I soon learned that when visitors come, they bring their lunch and stay the whole day, sometimes even overnight. Often, they have to bring food for the patient as well. If a mother requires hospitalization, she is often forced to bring her entire family with her! Others merely camp out all day, some into the night.

My thoughts were interrupted by a visit from my nurse.

"How about a walk in the park?" she suggested.

"Wonderful," I responded.

"The flowers are so lovely this time of year and it is very peaceful in the park."

As we sat on a small cement bench surrounded by palm trees and lovely shrubs, I couldn't help but agree with her. However, the air of tranquility soon took on an air of sadness as she shared with me her story.

"About five years ago," she began, "I met a young man right here in the park. We sat on this very bench and talked. Soon I discovered we had many of the same interests. Both of us loved to read and write poetry. We used to meet here every afternoon and read verses together. It didn't last long, though, for when my parents found out about it, they forbade me to ever see him again. I just couldn't face the possibility of having to marry someone else, someone my parents chose—someone I didn't even know which is our custom here, so I ran away."

"Where did you go?" I asked.

"I came to the mission here in Tanta and they let me work at the school to earn my room and board. That way I was able to finish school and enter nurses' training here at the hospital."

"Do you ever hear from your parents?"

"Mother writes now and then. My daddy died about a year ago, so my mother is all alone. She's sorry for what happened, but I'm afraid it is too late to do anything about it now."

"Why?" I asked.

"Because my wonderful friend never returned to the park after that and I know that I shall never see him again."

"But what will you do after graduation?" I asked.

"I'd like to go to the States with Miss Shirley our head nurse. Her term expires shortly after I graduate and she will be going home."

"Why do you want to go to the States?" I inquired. "Couldn't you be of more service here?"

"Eventually maybe I could, but right now the nursing profession is really looked down upon here in Egypt. There just isn't much opportunity for advancement. Besides I think I would enjoy meeting some American boys!"

How ironic, I thought! She, an Egyptian girl, was just dying to meet some nice American boy, and I, an American girl, have now been introduced to an intriguing Egyptian man! What did our futures hold?

The remainder of the afternoon was spent playing with the children of Drs. Clark and Paul. Both these doctors were career mission-doctors and had been in Egypt for quite some time. Dr. Paul paid me a visit later to give me my "marching orders": 10 glasses of water a day with two of them before breakfast, and more exercise. And here I thought that walking up and down three flights of stairs to my room at the College five times a day was enough exercise! Our flights are of the two-tier variety which makes two long sections for each floor. I eat on the first floor, teach on the second floor, and live on the third. That's a lot of walking! While at the hospital, my meals consisted of pigeon, rabbit, fish and chicken. I guess that diet must have worked because the doctor agreed that I was well enough to return to Cairo and resume my regular activities.

With the help of some fine medical treatment and a very rigid diet once back in Cairo, I was soon feeling much better. The rest had done me a world of good and I felt refreshed and ready to resume my teaching duties.

The following Wednesday was a very special day. A group of us went to the Bishop's tea and prayer meeting at the Coptic Orthodox Cathedral. On the first Wednesday of each month all the Christian groups represented in Cairo (American Mission, English Mission, Bible Society, Egyptian General Mission, and local Evangelical churches) meet for an afternoon prayer meeting preceded by a 5 p.m. tea at the bishop's residence overlooking the Nile. All these groups support each other's ministry regardless of minor differences in doctrine.

That evening I had a most unique experience. I was busily engaged in lesson plans when the soft beating of a distant drum caught my attention. In the hallway I met Liza who had just come from the rooftop quarters of the maids with an invitation for me to join them. "Ahlan, ahlan, ahlan"— ("welcome" in Arabic) they said in chorus as I entered the clean but barren room. On the floor seated in a circle were six of our kitchen staff clapping their hands to the rhythmic beating of a small drum. I soon found myself totally immersed in the music and in due time our hands and feet responded to the mysterious beats. Donna Lee, who had joined us, asked to play the drum. The request, having been successfully translated by Liza, was eagerly granted and the drum placed in Donna Lee's hands. Patiently the maids demonstrated the proper technique and soon Donna Lee was drumming away like a real pro. The maids encouraged us to stay a bit longer, but dinner time was approaching, and we needed to bid farewell and hurry downstairs to prepare for our evening meal.

On Thursday I had the opportunity to view my first Egyptian wedding in our chapel. Everyone brought gifts of flowers to the wedding. This time there were so many bouquets that fourteen of them had to remain outside the chapel. The bride and groom gave gifts of candy to all the guests. After the wedding some of the servants brought three bouquets to us, each containing lovely roses of various colors.

Friday saw us up early preparing to depart at 8:00 a.m. for a visit to our mission farm. It was located about a half mile from the pyramids and thus I had my first daylight glimpse of these three famous structures. The mission has one of the best and most modern farms in the area. They would not be considered "modern" in the US, as all the work is done by hand using only a few small implements. When it comes time to pick cotton, the whole family joins in and thus you see children spending the entire day picking cotton instead of going to school. In addition to cotton, rice, corn and cabbage are grown here. Milk is supplied by twelve hybrid cows. Rabbits and chickens are raised here as well, although they are so small that when one orders either rabbit or chicken at a restaurant one gets a whole one! The eggs are so small they resemble bird's eggs. Before we left, one woman invited us into her home which was a special treat for us. Her home consisted of three rooms, two of which were bedrooms and the third a general room. In this general room was a mud stove which was used not only for cooking but to heat their built-in mud beds—a rather unique idea.

On Saturday Donna Lee surprised me with a bag of peanuts which we shelled on the roof and let the wind brush away the skins. After the kitchen staff ground the peanuts into peanut butter, we made sandwiches complete with bananas! A great combination!

October 17th was Muled el Nabi, a Moslem holiday, celebrating the prophet Mohammed's birthday. For us it was not a day to sleep in. Instead, we were awakened at 5:00 am in order to depart for the pyramids by 5:30.

As I caught my first close-up glimpse of the Three Pyramids of Giza, I was in awe. My thoughts retraced history to the time when these three magnificent pyramids were built (between 2550 B.C. and 2490 B.C.) and I couldn't help feeling sad as I thought of the hundreds of men who died in order that these structures might be built. To me they were more of a tribute to the builders than to the pharaohs, after whom they were named: Khufu, Khafre and Menkaure.

We hardly got settled on the sand before the servants had finished preparing breakfast for us. "Come and get it!" Lois Finney, one of our teachers, called out. We all joined the group around the fire and after a moment of silent prayer, we eagerly filled our plates with bacon, eggs and toast. Next, we divided ourselves into two groups: one group to climb Khufu and the other to take a camel ride to the Sphinx. I elected to try the camel ride since a hike up the pyramid seemed a bit risky. It was not difficult to find an available camel. I also found an eager-beaver guide who was anxious to tell me everything he knew from ancient Egyptian history to my fortune, all for a mere piaster, about ten cents.

Up I went on my first camel ride. The guide instructed the camel to kneel down to help me get on. Riding a camel in Egypt is much like riding a horse in the States except that it sways in all four directions! I felt like an Arabian knight riding across the desert. The camel was definitely not in a hurry, but then, neither was I. I wondered if Donna Lee's group made it to the top of Khufu, a climb that had not interested me in the least! Too dangerous!

Leaving the area of the pyramids, we made our way down to the Great Sphinx. This unique structure has the head of a man, the face of a woman

and the body of a lion. Interpreted, this means that Egypt has the intelligence of a man, the beauty of a woman and the strength of a lion. I was not able to get a very close glimpse of the Sphinx because a large fence had been placed around it. Because of the international difficulties Egypt had been having with England, France and Israel, the rare treasures from the Egyptian Museum in Cairo had been buried around and under the Sphinx as a precautionary measure. This area was heavily guarded by Egyptian soldiers.

Returning from the Sphinx, I was surprised and delighted when my guide turned the reins over to me. He gave the camel, named Yankee Doodle, a gentle nudge and off we went! The ride was great fun and I was sorry to have it end.

By this time Donna Lee's group was halfway up Khufu and as I gazed in their direction one from the group waved.

"Hold on tight," I cautioned as I settled down on the soft sand. No sooner had I seated myself than I felt a gentle tap on my shoulder.

"Having fun?" Jeanne asked.

"Yes, I guess. I'm not exactly the outdoor type".

"You seemed to be deeply in thought when I came up. Would you mind telling me what you were thinking?" she inquired.

"Nothing really," I replied. This certainly was not the time nor place to bring up the subject of Mike.

"Well," she said, "if you won't tell me, I'll tell you. You were thinking about Mike and what a wonderful time you're going to have when you join us for dinner this evening."

"Oh...this is news to me!"

"Then you agree?"

"Agree to what?" I asked.

"Agree to a fabulous evening of soft music and exotic food at Omar Khayyam's."

"Omar Khayyam's? I have never heard of it," I said with some interest.

"It's magnificent! It used to be one of King Farouk's houseboats, but it has now been converted into an elegant restaurant. It commands a marvelous view of the Nile. I think you will really love it. Besides, Mike asked me to invite you."

"You are kidding!" I said with obvious surprise.

"No, I'm not. He really enjoyed our little foursome last week and has mentioned you several times since then."

"Is this another 'double date' affair?" I asked cautiously.

"Not exactly," she replied. "There will be the three of us this time plus Mike's friends, Dr. Anis Ragheb and his wife, Joy."

"Oh, I don't believe I remember your having mentioned them before."

"Possibly I didn't. Joy is from Chicago. She was head nurse at a hospital near Chicago when she met Anis. He was doing a residency at the same hospital. They dated for several months in the States and then he returned to Egypt. Joy followed soon after and they were married. She's expecting a baby any day now."

"This sounds very interesting, but isn't five a rather awkward number?"

"Not at all. In fact, it is rather common here. You see, most Egyptian girls are not allowed to date without a chaperone, even when they become engaged, so odd numbered groups are seen frequently."

"In that case, I'd love to join you. What time?"

"About eight. No one ever eats before 8:30 or 9:00 p.m."

The date and time were set. It sounded like fun! But why was I doing this? I should have known better. There was probably a good reason why we were cautioned not to date Egyptians. I just wasn't listening to rules, only to my heart.

Donna Lee's group had returned from their climb, tired and ready to return to the College.

It was shortly before eight that evening when Jeanne knocked on my door. "All set?" she inquired.

"Will be in a minute. Come on in."

"Wow, you really look nice!" she commented.

"Thank you. My mother made this dress; in fact, she still makes almost all my clothes."

Grabbing a white stole and taking one last glimpse in the mirror, I hurriedly followed Jeanne down the stairs.

As we walked through the gate, the bawab gave us a cordial greeting and escorted us to the curb. Mike arrived several minutes late—which seemed to be the rule rather than the exception in this country. Jeanne quickly introduced me to Anis and Joy, and we made our way down Sharia Ramses toward the Nile.

"So...you are from Chicago, Carolyn?" Anis asked.

"Riverside, to be exact," I replied.

"A very nice city, Chicago. I enjoyed my stay there very much."

"But you were glad to get back to Cairo, I bet!" exclaimed Jeanne.

"Yes and no. I really liked it in the States, and I wouldn't mind returning there someday.

"Carolyn, why don't you take him back with you? Joy wouldn't mind, would you?" Mike said jokingly.

"The way things are going in Egypt right now we'll probably all end up going back," Joy said seriously.

"Just how bad is the conflict with Israel?" I inquired.

"It's hard to know exactly," Mike began. "About all you can do is read the papers and listen to the reports over the radio. It doesn't sound too encouraging."

"Liza's brother is commanding a regiment near the Gaza Strip right now," Jeanne said. "From what I understand the situation is pretty grave."

"What about England and France?" I asked. "Do you think they will carry out their threats to bomb?"

"Much depends, I think, on the attitude of the United States. If they back up England and France, then I'm afraid we're in for trouble. Of course, England and France have been threatening us ever since we seized the Suez Canal last July," Anis added.

"Let's talk about something more pleasant," suggested Joy.

"A good idea," Mike said agreeably. "Well, Carolyn what do you think of Egypt?"

"I love it so far. The people have been just wonderful and I haven't even had a chance to be homesick." I noticed that we were turning onto the Nile road and glancing to my right I spotted a brightly-lit houseboat. "Oh, that must be Omar Khayyam's!"

"No," Jeanne replied. "This houseboat also belonged to Farouk, but it was bought by the Semiramis Hotel and is used as a tearoom. Omar Khayyam's is up the road just a way; in fact, you can see it now."

Sure enough, just ahead was the other boat, whose bright lights urged us on. We easily found a place to park and walked the short distance to the boat. The evening was a bit chilly and there was a soft breeze off the river. We traversed the narrow plank to board the boat and soon found ourselves inside of what appeared to be a "floating palace." Our host led us to a low, round table, surrounded by cushioned stools. The whole atmosphere was distinctly oriental. Maroons and greens dominated the scene. Richly embroidered drapes hung from the windows and exquisite Persian rugs covered the floor. Into our brass tray table was carved an intricate design of Arabic writing from the Koran and figures from ancient hieroglyphics. The small legs which held the tray were hand-carved from mahogany and were inset with mother-of-pearl and ivory.

"Their chicken is delicious," commented Jeanne."

"Sounds good to me," replied Anis. "How about you, Carolyn?"

"Fine," I replied

Our conversation continued pleasantly through our several-course dinner.

"I hear you went to the pyramids this morning. How did you like them?" Mike asked.

"They are really spectacular," I replied, trying not to return his lingering glance. Each time our eyes met, it seemed like he was looking straight through me, as if he were hunting for something and unable to find it.

"You must visit Mena House sometime. It is very nice there, really," he continued. "You should go there for tea some afternoon and play miniature golf."

"Miniature golf?" I exclaimed. "Here in Egypt? I thought that sport was only indulged in by Americans."

"Not at all," he replied. "It is very popular here."

After a few moments of silence, Joy exclaimed, "Look how late it is. Shouldn't we be going?"

"Time really flies when you are having fun," added Anis.

As we walked toward the car I couldn't help looking up into the starlit sky and watching the moon cast its silvery shadows on the beautiful Nile water. What a lovely evening!

I was still dreaming about my lovely evening as I returned to my room for the night. Glancing across the hall I noticed that Liza's light was still on. I gently tapped on her door.

"Come in," she said softly.

As I entered her room, I heard the faint voice of a news commentator speaking in Arabic. Liza was lying on her bed with her ear close to the radio.

"Is something wrong?" I asked.

Liza looked up gravely. "Sit down," she directed. I sat in silence until the voice faded away. Then Liza began.

"It looks pretty bad. The Israeli forces are attacking our troops in Gaza and it appears that several ships have been sunk. I wonder how long we can hold out."

"Liza," I asked gravely, "what effect will this have on us?"

"Right now, we are not in much danger. The Gaza Strip is quite far from Cairo. Anyway, don't worry about it. If and when the time comes, you will be told what to do."

"What about your brother?"

"I don't know. All word has been cut off. All we can do is pray."

"I'll do that I promise."

"Good night," she whispered.

"Good night," I replied and slipped quietly back to my room.

Despite what appeared to be a grave military situation, life at the College went on as usual. Gaza seemed an eternity away.

The following Friday a group of us went on a tour of one of King Farouk's former palaces. It was certainly different from touring the White House. Our guide gave us two hours of his time and described in detail each picture, each object and even showed us Queen Nariman's wedding dress. We were even allowed to wander around on our own. Best of all I got to play their grand piano!

Shortly after returning to the College, we all left in one of our buses for an evening on the Ibis, our mission's houseboat (not quite like Omar Khayyam!) on the Nile. It is located some distance from Cairo near the suburb of Maadi. We all brought knitting, sewing or reading material to enjoy as we relaxed on deck. The boat was originally used as a mission station and journeyed up and down the Nile, stopping at villages to share the Gospel. Now it was only used for parties such as ours. Dinner on the boat was delicious, and several of us pitched in to help the servants prepare it. To the amazement of the servants, some of us even offered to wash dishes following the meal.

On Saturday night, our teachers played host to about 200 guests, all of whom were Egyptian men and women who had studied in the US and had their degrees from American institutions. Among the guests were the Ministers of Interior Affairs, Education, and Communications. The speaker was United States Ambassador Hare. Following his speech, I was asked to play the piano for our guests. The only piece I knew by heart was the second movement of Beethoven's Pathetique Sonata. It was well received, and its conclusion provided a signal that our evening had come to an end.

The days which followed were grave ones indeed. We were constantly alert to the happenings around us and extra cautious in our conversations with each other. We heard very little; we read very little; few people seemed to know very much about what was going on; we asked questions, but seldom received answers. We all shared a sense of uneasiness which was difficult to hide.

The first real sign of trouble came rather unexpectedly on the afternoon of October 24th. I had just returned from choir practice at Ezbekieh

Church when I found a note in my mailbox which read: "Special meeting of American teachers in my office at 5:30. Please, be present," signed S.B.M.

A nervous chatter stirred among us as our group assembled in Dr. Meloy's office. I noticed that the bright smile which usually graced Dr. Meloy's face was missing. She appeared to be very tired and the lines on her face were drawn. The group fell silent as she rose from her chair and spoke.

"I have just returned from a meeting with Ambassador Hare and he has issued the following instructions: *'You are to be prepared at any time to be evacuated. You will be allowed only as much luggage as you can handle yourself. We suggest that you pack at least one small bag immediately to have on hand in case of an emergency. If an evacuation becomes necessary, the orders will be issued directly from my office.'*"

Dr Meloy paused before continuing. "I think you all understand the uncertainty of this situation. We hope the orders from Ambassador Hare will not be necessary, but we can't be sure. The situation at present is very grave. I want to tell you, too, that an American ship is docked in Alexandria at present and has room for any of you who feel you must leave now. I cannot ask any of you to stay. If you decide to leave, we will send you off with our blessing. If you choose to remain, we can promise you nothing. Either way, the decision will have to be yours."

Dr. Meloy then suggested that we each write a letter home with a message from Mr. "Rabbit" (Hare), noting certain passages of Scripture for our loved ones to look up for their "spiritual" edification: John 14:27, Luke 8:24, Ps. 27:14, II Sam. 24:9, Mark 15:42, Ps. 105:38, Phil. 1:23-24, Prov. 11:8, Romans 1:15, 1:10 and Prov. 3:5-6. This would hopefully give clues to our loved ones concerning our present situation and possibly our future whereabouts. This was to be the way we would be communicating in the future if necessary, because letters are censored.

I left the meeting absolutely stunned. Leave Egypt? I had just arrived! All of us knew that each one of us had to make her own decision: stay or go.

School remained open, but teaching was difficult. The weather was still quite warm and through our open windows came the constant sound of troops marching through the streets. All available men were being recruited to serve in the army, many without uniforms.

The girls said little about the war. Some had brothers fighting and were deeply troubled, while others seemed only faintly aware of what was going on. Most of those from wealthy families did not have family members serving in the military. I'm not quite sure how they managed to do this, but money speaks volumes.

Early Saturday morning I found tucked in my mailbox a small paper owl, inviting me to a Halloween party that night. It had been planned for some time and as it turned out it was just what we needed: a break from thoughts of war and destruction.

We began with a round of Truth or Consequences. The first consequence went to Mrs. Burns and Miss Bender. Being from the West, they were given what should have been an easy task for them—milking a cow. The "cow" consisted of chairs with two boards suspended across the tops. Hanging on the boards were two rubber gloves filled with water. Each lady was given a milk pail and stool. Then the fun began! The object was to see who could get the most "milk" through the gloves and into the pail. How fun! Neither lady got much "milk" into the pail, but they certainly got an abundance of laughs.

We next divided into two teams and began a series of relays. The object of the first was to pass the outside portion of a match box from "nose to nose" down the line and back again. Unfortunately, not everyone's nose was the same size and as a result passing match boxes proved to be very difficult, but hilariously funny!

As a final relay we selected two members from each team to engage in a candy-eating contest. In this contest there was only one piece of candy for each group of two women and it was safely suspended in the middle of a long piece of string. With each end of the string between their teeth, the two women started chewing toward the candy. The weight of the candy was quite heavy and invariably the string would slip from between their teeth and they would have to begin again. I marveled at their patience. After many unsuccessful attempts our team eventually won. As our reward we each received a lifesaver. The defeated team got to do cleanup!

We bobbed for apples, ate donuts and cider and spent the remainder of the evening chatting. It was so nice just to relax and forget for a moment the anxiety of the outside world.

As the evening drew to a close, several of the teachers had returned to their rooms. I was busily engaged in conversation with one of the remaining teachers when one of our house maids beckoned me to the door.

"You are wanted on the phone, Miss Copeland," she said.

"Thank you," I replied and hurried downstairs and into the office. I could not imagine who would be calling me at this hour of the night.

"Hello," I said uncertainly.

"Hi! This is Jeanne. Guess what? Joy just had her baby!"

"She did? How wonderful!" I exclaimed.

"She had a little boy about an hour ago. They named him Christian Anis."

"Is she allowed visitors?"

"That's why I called," continued Jeanne. "Mike thought you might like to go to the hospital with us tomorrow afternoon to see her. We'll only stay for a few minutes. Will 4:30 be ok?"

"That will be great. See you then," I replied and carefully replaced the phone. How nice of them to include me!

I walked slowly up the three flights of stairs to my room. The party had broken up and most of the teachers were preparing for bed. The "losers" were still cleaning up from the party and had declined my offer of assistance. Walking into my room and then looking out my window, I was aware of an unusual calmness which permeated the area. Shops which usually stayed open way into the night were already tightly barred and the "night prowlers" who customarily roamed the streets were nowhere to be seen. A bit of uneasiness swept over me and I quickly turned away. How would this mess end? Still feeling uneasy, I took refuge between the warm covers of my bed and fell into a troubled sleep.

The following afternoon as I prepared for my visit to see Joy, my eyes again gazed wistfully onto the street below. Calm still prevailed. Although the shops had opened as usual, there seemed to be fewer people on the streets. As I continued to observe the street activity, I noticed that no buses nor taxis had passed by. Why? I wondered.

I hurriedly left my room and met Jeanne on the way downstairs.

"Hurry up," she urged. "Mike is already here."

"I'm sorry. I didn't realize that I was late," I replied.

"You aren't really," she said as we moved briskly out the door. "Mike wanted to get an early start because of the strike."

"What strike?"

"You mean you hadn't noticed? There is a general transportation strike throughout Cairo and traffic is really jammed up."

"No kidding!" I said with obvious surprise. "I wondered why I didn't see any buses or taxis a few minutes ago. While I was dressing, I caught a glimpse of the street and noticed how quiet it seemed. Do you think it will last long?"

"Golly, I hope not," Jeanne replied as we walked through the gate.

Jeanne opened the car door and stood waiting for me to enter. To my surprise she beckoned me to take the front passenger seat beside Mike.

"Well, Carolyn, how *are* you?" Mike inquired.

"I'm fine. How is Joy?"

"I don't know, really. I haven't talked with Anis since late last night. I guess she had a pretty rough time," he said earnestly.

"Isn't that rather common here?" I inquired, remembering my observations in Tanta.

"Yes, it is. Most women prefer natural childbirth. It really is the best way, you know," this comment coming from the perspective of the Ob/Gyn that he was.

"No, I didn't," I teased, "but I will keep it in mind for future reference!"

I thought I caught a glimpse of laughter in his eyes as he digested my last comment. He turned and our eyes held for an instant. In that second, I somehow knew why I was sitting next to Mike instead of Jeanne. Had she told him how she felt? Or had he guessed and taken the initiative himself? Whatever it was, something had happened.

When we arrived at the hospital, Joy was sitting up in bed having her dinner. She was busily chatting with four other visitors between bites of food. When she saw us, she exclaimed: "I'm so sorry you didn't get here a couple of minutes ago. You could have seen the baby!"

"We would have loved to have seen him. Whom does he look like?" I asked.

"We're not sure. In fact, I don't think he looks like anyone. He does have my coloring though: blond hair and deep blue eyes."

"I bet Anis was glad it was a boy," Jeanne added.

"Yes, he was. In fact, his whole family was pleased. It is their first grandson after three granddaughters," Joy added.

We'd been there only a few minutes when Mike announced, "We'd better be going. Joy needs to get some rest."

"Nonsense," responded Joy. "I feel great!"

"Nevertheless, you still need your sleep," Mike said firmly.

Jeanne responded to his cue and, taking Joy's hand, bid her farewell.

"We'll see you just as soon as you're out of the hospital and all rested up," I promised as I followed Mike and Jeanne out of the room.

Little did I realize then that many months would elapse before I saw her again.

Writing home to my parents on Oct. 29th constituted one of the hardest tasks I have ever faced. As I sat there writing what I hoped would be a cherry, newsy, letter, beside me lay our evacuation notice and on the floor my packed bags ready to leave at a moment's notice. Yet when it came time this morning to make the final decision to stay or leave, something inside me just wouldn't let me go. All but two of us made the same decision. Our deep love for the people and the country overshadowed concern for the present danger. Of course, we were afraid—but so were my young students. Somehow when their little hands slipped confidently into mine, I just could not leave them. We'd all been through a lot and there would be more to come, but the Lord we served was greater than the enemies around us and He would take care of us I truly believed. He had promised in Psalm 91:3-4,11 *"He will deliver you from the snares of the fowler and from the deadly pestilence; he will cover you with his pinions and under his wings you will find refuge; his faithfulness is a shield and buckler...He will give his angels charge of you to guard you in all your ways".*

The day before, we had had four blackouts: one at 6 p.m., one at 7:30 p.m., one at midnight and one at 4:00 a.m. Each time we quickly and quietly gathered up our assigned boarders and herded them into the downstairs corridor and had them sit against the wall. Two of the four times were practice raids, but the other two times there was shooting. I believe an Israeli plane was shot down. We have had two blackouts so far today and are expecting another during the night. Just how long we will be here I really don't know. The US government has not actually ordered us out, but they have strongly advised us to leave. We have temporarily closed school, but do not plan to leave unless our lives are in great danger. We have an air raid shelter in the basement and beginning tonight we will use it. I conveyed all this in my letter to my parents. I tried to provide some basic information without unnecessarily alarming them.

Tuesday, October 30th was a very special day. Immediately after school, a large group of students and teachers gathered in the library building to celebrate Dr. Meloy's birthday. The tea was jointly sponsored by the library club and the alumni of the college. It was a special time for us to share our love and appreciation for Dr. Meloy. Dr.Meloy responded by saying, "I only hope that with God's help and guidance I can live up to this wonderful trust you have placed in me. I shall..." Her words came to an abrupt halt as the lights were instantly switched off. Dr. Meloy, realizing the seriousness of the situation, announced, "We are having a blackout. You are all to return to your homes as quickly as possible. There will be school buses waiting to take anyone home who does not have immediate transportation. Our teachers and boarders are to go directly to their rooms. You will be notified what to do in a few minutes. Now go!"

Another blackout! What did this mean? Taking my students, Odette and Nazek, by the hand, I led them down the stairs and out into the garden. The air raid sirens were blasting, and people were scurrying in every direction in order to find a place of safety.

We entered the main building, I took the girls to their room, and then went upstairs to mine. I lit a small candle and continued the letter I was writing to my parents. What was I to tell them? They, undoubtedly, knew more about the situation than I did. Our paper in Cairo had very little to say and one could only guess at its validity. By in large it left its readers completely in the dark as to what was really happening.

I was still deeply in thought when the all-clear signal came. A few minutes later Lois Finney came into my room.

"Carolyn," she began. "We expect to have several more air raids before the night is over. As you know, you are responsible for the boarders in Room 2B. When the next siren rings, go to your group immediately. Double check to make sure every girl is there, and take them to the classroom corridor on the first floor. Have them sit quietly with their backs to the wall until the all-clear whistle blows." She paused. "Dr. Meloy will give us instructions for the night raids later."

She was barely out of the room when the sirens resumed their blasting. I walked quickly from my room and down the stairs to 2B. The girls were some of my second-year math students and mature enough to know how to conduct themselves. Some of the younger ones, however, were frightened and needed reassurance.

When we were all assembled in the dark corridor, Diane, in the temporary absence of Lois, took charge. One of the girls suggested that we sing Christmas carols. When Lois and Dr. Meloy returned from their final room check, we were all seated as instructed, singing "O Little Town of Bethlehem." Dr. Meloy updated us on the fact that this had only been a practice drill, but that the next one, if it came, would be real. No one knew where the enemy would strike. If and when that happened, we were to gather up our boarders and take refuge in our air raid shelter, which had been constructed prior to World War II underneath the basement of the adjacent classroom building. It was equipped with mattresses, lights, heaters and bathroom facilities.

It was almost dinner time before the practice raid ended. The electricity throughout Cairo had been cut off. This had been done as a precautionary measure in case there was a sudden attack.

It was a solemn group that gathered around our supper table that night. As we ate our meal, I watched the flickering candles cast weird shadows against the wall. I could feel the tension mounting and knew that all of us were close to tears. What could we do? None of us wanted to leave. We had fought the idea since it had been first presented to us. What would happen if we stayed? I looked to Dr. Meloy for the answer as she rose to speak.

"We just received a report from Ambassador Hare. England and France are preparing to carry through with their threats to bomb Cairo despite pleas from President Eisenhower. He is begging them to agree to some peaceful settlement concerning the Suez Canal, but they seem determined to use force. Israel is still waging war over the Gaza Strip and threatening to come closer at any moment. Should an attack come during the night remember to take a blanket and a flashlight, go directly to your assigned girls, and proceed to the air raid shelter. Please make sure before your girls go to bed this evening that they have their robe, slippers and an extra blanket at the foot of their beds. Mattresses and pillows are in the shelter." She hesitated and looked compassionately over our little group. "If there are no questions, please return to your rooms and get some sleep if you can."

I returned to my room and began earnestly to finish my letter to my parents. I knew so little. What could I say? Would my letter even reach them? Regardless, I had to write to them as I knew they were already very worried. I chose Psalm 91 as a basis for my letter. It had been such a comfort to me, and I hoped it would be to them as well.

That night we had two very brief air raids. Though brief, they were none the less warnings that trouble lay ahead—very serious trouble.

The following day dawned bright and sunny as usual. Since school had been closed temporarily, we had very little to do. This would have been the perfect day to take a long walk to a nearby park; however, due to the prevailing conditions we were advised not to leave the school grounds. Instead of a walk, Dottie Cushman, another American teacher, and I engaged in a game of table tennis on the roof. For a while it appeared that everyone had forgotten the happenings of the previous night. People meandered freely in the streets below as if nothing unusual had happened. It wasn't until later that afternoon that I really became worried. I was having tea with Jeanne in the Home Economics Building when out of the stillness of the late afternoon there came once again the sound of anti-aircraft units firing in the distance. So great was the impact that the doors and windows shook as if being hit by an earthquake. Immediately Lois entered the room

"They are only practicing," she said reassuringly. "I seriously doubt if there will be any real raids this afternoon."

"What about tonight?" Jeanne asked.

"Your guess is as good as mine. All we can do is sit tight and wait."

"But surely England and France will not go against the wishes of the U.S.?" I volunteered. "I thought they were our allies."

"They are," replied Lois, "but they are also very determined to regain control of the Suez Canal."

"Even at the risk of severing connections with the U.S.?" Jeanne asked.

"I don't think it will come to that, regardless of what happens," continued Lois. "President Eisenhower has not as yet stated what he intends to do if England and France do carry out their threats."

"So, where does that leave us?" I inquired

"Right in the middle of what is liable to be a pretty big mess!" volunteered Jeanne. "I wish I would have left with the others."

"No, you don't," I began. "You just think that now when things seem so uncertain. You know as well as I do that it would take more than a few air raids to induce you to leave. You love it here as much as I do."

"That's what you think! Everything is new to you now, but after you've been here a while it won't seem quite so glamorous," Jeanne stated boldly.

"It may be true that some of the 'glamor' as you put it may wear off in time, but the love I have in my heart for this country and its people goes deeper than the outward crust of glamor and no amount of time will ever change that."

After dinner we all retired to the solitude of our rooms and I worked on finishing the letter to my parents. I had written only two short paragraphs when the sirens went off.

As I raced down the stairs, I glanced at the hall clock—8:30 p.m. Some of the younger girls were already in bed. Others were undressing while still others were painstakingly trying to write by candlelight, since we still had no electricity. I quickly gathered up my girls and we made our way down to the shelter in the dark. Some of the girls were able to sleep on the mattresses while others just lay there and stared into space, too frightened to sleep.

About 1:30 a.m. the all-clear signal was given. The girls returned to their rooms. On the way back to my room I met Dr. Meloy.

"You will have to leave," she explained to us. "I just don't see any other way. England and France have already carried out their threats. They just bombed the airport. The night is not over yet. No one knows how much more damage may be done. Our plans for an air evacuation will have to be canceled. Instead, a car convoy will assemble in front of the American Embassy at seven this morning and you will be driven to Alex where the 6th Fleet is waiting for you. I'm not sure just where they plan to take you, but I do know that you must leave. Miss Roy and I will have to stay to take care of the boarders"

I was stunned. No, no! I cried to myself. I don't what to leave. The tears flowed as I stumbled up the stairs to my room. Lord, why? Still troubled, I crawled into bed and tried to get some sleep.

Shortly before dawn the sirens rang again and we descended the stairs, gathered the girls, and made our way back to the shelter. We waited and listened. Actually, we heard very little. Occasionally the distant sound of anti-aircraft could be heard. Then about 5:30 a.m. it was all over. I walked out on the roof and looked up into the star-studded sky. How easy it must have been for the enemy to spot us even in the dark! The stars which illuminated the sky set a clear path of light along the Nile and served as a powerful beacon to anyone approaching Cairo from the sea. How useless the blackouts seemed now! God's light was so much more powerful than ours that even at a time like this it could not be dimmed. This thought brought momentary peace as I felt God's presence not just with me, but with all of us. Even if we had to leave now, we knew that God in His own time and way would bring us back to this land we had come to love so much. With this love deeply implanted in my heart, my faith and courage renewed, I made the final preparations to leave. It was so hard to know what to take or what to leave behind. It seemed logical to assume that we would be taken to some place in Europe; thus, I chose a varying assortment of warm clothes for the trip. As I placed the rest of my things in my trunks and secured the locks, I wondered if I would ever see my things again. Feeling a surge of guilt, I immediately dismissed the thought from my mind. Of course, I will return! Now was not the time to lose faith.

About seven, our little group gathered in the courtyard to bid farewell to those we were leaving behind. Dr. Meloy and Miss Roy would be staying behind at the College to see that all the boarders were safely delivered to their homes and Evelyn McFarland, who was supposed to leave with us, simply disappeared and did not return until after we had made our departure. A child of missionary parents, Miss McFarland had been born in Egypt, had spent her entire life there, and was determined to die there if necessary. She was not leaving.

Saying good-bye to our boarders was very difficult. One by one they flocked around us, tears streaming down their cheeks. I wondered if they realized how very difficult it was for us to have to leave. We had come to love them dearly, even in such a short time.

Dr. Meloy accompanied us to the embassy. The College had donated all their school buses to aid in the evacuation. Three hundred cars were lined up for blocks. Those individuals without transportation piled into the school buses.

Jeanne had said very little during our brief ride to the embassy. Now I watched as she briefly left the group and walked to a nearby phone booth. I wondered whom she might be calling. I didn't have to wait long for an answer. Within a few minutes the familiar blue and white Chevy pulled up in front of the Embassy and there was Mike! He spoke briefly with Jeanne and then motioned to me to join them.

"Mike is going to drive us to Alex. Please come with us," Jeanne coaxed.

"I wonder if I should," I replied. "I thought we were supposed to stay together."

"I don't think it really matters," Jeanne countered. "Just getting there is what is important, and Mike's car is much more comfortable than the bus!"

As we were chatting, Mike was busy contacting an older couple who appeared to be lacking transportation and offered them a ride. Somewhat reluctantly I agreed to join them. Before departing I bid a final farewell to Dr. Meloy. The lawn of the embassy was almost empty now as most of the evacuees were already loaded into their assigned vehicles and were waiting patiently for the convoy to get started. I gave Dr. Meloy a hug and promised once again that we would be back soon. Even with that hope in my heart and voice, there were still tears in my eyes. I wondered. Did she notice that we were riding with Mike? What must she be thinking? Our "sins" were about to find us out!

It was 11:30 before the convoy finally got under way. What a time to travel across the desert! The trip was bad enough in the late afternoon or early morning let alone during the heat of the noon-day sun. Even with the car windows open, it was stifling. As far as I could see ahead or behind, there was a steady stream of cars. Overhead we saw French and English planes watching our every move, making sure that we had included their citizens in our convoy. Along the side of the road Egyptian tankers hunkered down, prepared to return fire should the French and English decide to bomb.

Instead of focusing on the potential threats around us, I decided to turn my attention to our new friends in the back seat.

Turning slightly, I asked, "Have you been in Cairo long?"

"Just since last night!" Mrs. Baker, our guest, replied.

"You mean you arrived in Cairo right in the middle of all this trouble?"

"We sure did! Why they ever let us in I'll never know," Mr. Baker commented. "When we arrived at our hotel late yesterday afternoon, they informed us we couldn't leave the premises, so we've spent $500 getting here, seen nothing, and now we are leaving."

"Were you with a tour group?" I asked.

"We were while we were in Europe, but we decided to come here as a side trip on our own. I've always been interested in archeology and I was especially anxious to visit the Egyptian Museum."

"I hear it is fascinating, although I've never been there myself," I added. "Where were you staying?"

"At Mena House," replied Mrs. Baker.

"Oh, then you did get to see the pyramids at least," I said consolingly.

I peered out of the window and caught fleeting glimpses of other vehicles as they passed our slow-moving convoy. Many Egyptians were leaving for vacation homes in Alex or to their farmland a safe distance from Cairo.

As we continued our journey, Mrs. Baker inquired concerning a statue she had noticed in front of the Cairo University. I explained to her that this statue, called "The Awakening of Egypt", depicts a woman lifting her veil, representing the awakening of Egyptian women. Its erection was a big step forward for all Egyptian women.

"I haven't noticed many women wearing veils. Have they disappeared?" she asked.

"Not entirely," I replied. "Some of the farm women still wear the traditional black garbs with matching black veils, but few still cover their faces. In some remote sections of the countryside, unmarried girls continue to be veiled, but this is gradually disappearing. Now that women have the right to vote, they are becoming more and more active in civic affairs."

"But isn't the illiteracy rate still quite high?" inquired Mr. Baker.

"Yes, it is. But a new program of 'Each-One-Teach-One' is making great strides toward addressing this problem."

"How does this program operate?" Mr. Baker asked with obvious interest.

"The project was begun by our mission a number of years ago. Small groups of villagers were formed with a missionary in charge of each group. These groups were given lessons in written and spoken Arabic, using the Bible as their textbook. When the members of these groups had completed the course, they, in turn, formed other groups, followed the same process, and so the chain began. Several thousand farm families have learned to read and write through this program."

"I imagine this is one of the primary tasks of the mission," concluded Mrs. Baker.

"Yes, it is. It is through this program that many of the underprivileged are reached with the Gospel."

While I was engrossed in conversation with the Bakers, Jeanne had fallen asleep. Mike had been listening intently but had said nothing. Finally, he asked, "I suppose you won't be coming back for a while, Carolyn."

"I don't know, Mike," I replied. "I surely hope we will. I wish we didn't have to leave. In just the few weeks I've been here I've come to love Egypt and her people very much. It truly breaks my heart to have to leave so soon and under these tense conditions."

"I hope you will come back to us," he said earnestly. "We shall miss you."

"What will you be doing after you leave us?" I asked anxiously.

"I don't know yet. I imagine I will have to give assistance wherever it is needed. It is difficult to know just where the enemy will strike."

"Will you be in danger?"

"I don't know. It's one of those things you accept when you become a doctor. The welfare of my people is my primary responsibility, not my personal safety."

"Do you ever worry about dying?"

"I did once, but I don't anymore."

"What caused you to change your mind?"

"A number of things." His lips tightened and his eyes stared straight ahead. I knew it was time to change the subject, yet I wondered why my question had disturbed him so much. Was he so secure in his faith that death no longer worried him? Had something effected his life to such an extent that he no longer cared whether he lived or died? I knew one thing for sure—he did not care to discuss it. I was to later learn that he had been married before and his wife and young child had been killed in an auto accident.

As I glanced out the window, I noticed that the cars ahead were slowing down and soon the entire convoy came to a stop. I nudged Jeanne, still sleeping soundly, and opened the door.

"Let's get out and stretch," I suggested.

"Why are we stopping?" she asked.

"I don't know. Isn't that the Halfway House up ahead?"

"Yes, it is. I think I'll see if I can get us something to drink," Mike replied.

"Hey, wait!" I called. "A man is coming with some cokes!"

Mike turned and gave us a warm smile. "It looks like they have everything well organized. They are passing out lunches, too."

Lunches? For the 1,800 evacuees from all over Egypt? Incredible!

Soon my lunch bag arrived and opening it I found two sandwiches, an apple and three cookies, along with a coke. Embassy personnel must have worked all night to make 3,600 sandwiches!

We returned to our cars and continued our journey. Armed Egyptian guards were still patrolling our route. Their presence helped us feel at least some measure of security in the midst of a very volatile situation.

"Just how dangerous is our position at the moment?" I asked Mike.

"You can never be sure" he responded with concern. "England and France promised not to bomb our convoy as long as their citizens were among us. If you look directly ahead you can see several cars bearing French and English flags on their hoods. This is our signal to these countries that we are keeping our part of the bargain."

"Surely, they wouldn't bomb their own people?" Jeanne questioned.

"I doubt it, but you never know," Mike replied.

Trustingly, I laid back, closed my eyes, and peacefully fell asleep.

About 6:30 p.m. we finally reached Alex. As we moved slowly along the coast of the Mediterranean Sea, we were suddenly brought to an abrupt halt. Darkness hovered around us as one by one the car lights were switched off. Another blackout! This time I was truly scared. We seemed to be in a very vulnerable position. From somewhere in the darkness a flashlight appeared. Through the open window Mike murmured softly to the stranger beside our car. Up ahead the cars were beginning to move. We proceeded slowly, uncertainly, without our lights. At the next corner we were directed to turn left and proceed about two blocks inland. As soon as we reached a reasonably safe distance from the sea we stopped. I glanced nervously at the Bakers, huddled in the back seat but said nothing. Mike changed seats with Jeanne and placed himself between us. He put his arms around both of us and drew us close to him. The awareness of his presence was reassuring, and I felt my body relax a bit.

We sat in silence for what seemed like hours. Mike glanced into the rearview mirror from time to time but saw nothing. We waited anxiously for the all-clear sign, but it never came. Sometime later a young man approached our car and handed Mike a piece of paper. Mike lit a match and hurriedly scanned the note. It read, "Windsor Palace Hotel, RC 19747, Apartment No. 95."

"Do you know where it is?" the stranger inquired.

"Yes, I know, but is it safe to go now?"

"It is comparatively quiet right now. If you leave immediately you have a good chance of reaching the hotel before we have another attack. Move cautiously and dim your lights," he replied and disappeared.

The hotel was not difficult to find; in fact, it was only three blocks away. Mike had returned to the driver's seat, continued along the designated road and dropped us off at the front door of the hotel while he searched for a place to park.

The lobby was crowded, but orderly. One by one the rooms were assigned, and the keys distributed. Number 95 turned out to be on the ninth floor! Fortunately, they had an elevator!

Jeanne and I left our bags in our room and returned to the lobby. Soon Mike joined us.

"I can't stay but a minute. I have to get back," he said gravely.

"Get back where?" Jeanne cried out.

"To Cairo. I must get back. I will be needed in Cairo tomorrow morning at the very latest."

"But why?" Jeanne protested.

"I am being called into the army and I have to report for duty first thing in the morning," he answered solemnly.

"Mike, you can't be serious!" I said in bewilderment.

"I'm afraid I am serious. A general state of emergency has been called and all available doctors are being inducted. I have to leave immediately. Both of you...please write me when you can and let me know where you are and that you have arrived safely. Good-bye for now," he said and turning away, departed.

I was moved by his actions. What a great price one had to pay to be a doctor in this country!

Jeanne and I left the lobby and were directed to the adjacent dining room where we enjoyed a delicious seven-course meal. Jeanne was clearly frightened. "What are we supposed to do if we have an attack during the night?"

"Go to the lobby, I imagine. It seems a bit safer than the ninth floor," I replied.

"You'd better sleep with a flashlight under your pillow then, that is, if you intend to sleep."

"I'm going to try. We have a long day ahead of us tomorrow. They are picking us up at 6:30 in the morning. I told the boy at the desk to ring us at 5:45."

We returned to our rooms and prepared for bed. I blew out the candle beside my bed and slid under the covers. Lying there in the darkness I thought of my parents back in Riverside. As I closed my eyes, I said a silent prayer that God would give them peace and that He would keep our group safe in the days ahead.

During the night there was another air raid, but I was too sleepy to notice. The next thing I knew it was morning.

"How did you manage to sleep through that air raid?" Jeanne exclaimed. "I'd barely gotten my eyes closed before those guns began again. Sometimes they sounded as if they were perched on our roof."

I walked across the room and opened the drapes. The bright Egyptian sunshine lifted my spirits. I closed my eyes and breathed in the fresh morning air. It was hard for me to believe that less than twelve hours ago this same air had been filled with the murk of gun smoke. I thought of Mike and wondered where he was and if he were safe. I waited expectantly for Jeanne to mention his name, but she did not. Didn't she care? Had she already abandoned him in favor of his brother? And why was I so worried? What about my feelings?

I hurriedly dressed, gathered up my belongings, and made my way down to the dining room, leaving Jeanne to put the finishing touches on her hair and make-up.

Once in the lobby I found myself momentarily alone. I'd been left alone many times in my life, but never had I felt such an overwhelming sense of emptiness as if I were being drained of all my innermost feelings. For days I had wanted to cry and couldn't. After all, in the eyes of my students I was a fully-mature, courageous adult. To my colleagues I was the baby of the family—the twenty-year-old fresh out of college. Yet I no longer felt like an inexperienced child. I had suddenly grown up, turning from a life of sheltered innocence to a life of responsible independence. I was prepared for whatever lay ahead. I had fought to remain in Egypt and lost. I was determined I would not lose in my fight to return. My task was surely not complete. It had only just begun. I realized then that one is never completely alone—God is always there. He had guided us through perilous days, and He would surely guide us in the days ahead. I vowed to fill each day with the memory of my few wonderful weeks in Cairo and keep forever burning the hope of my eventual return.

As I entered the dining room, I spotted the Bakers.

"Good morning," Mr. Baker said cheerfully.

"Good morning," I replied. "I trust you were able to get at least a few short winks last night."

"We did at that," Mrs. Baker confirmed. "Only once or twice did the shooting really disturb us. I guess we were both so sleepy we were oblivious to what was happening around us."

"Do you know yet where we are going?" I asked Mr. Baker.

"I believe to Naples, but I'm not sure. There has been much speculation, but no one really knows for sure."

Mr. Baker glanced at his watch and rose from his chair. "It's after 6:30 now. We'd better be going."

I took a final sip of coffee, gathered up my belongings, and left the dining room.

Outside people were boarding buses. Jeanne and I approached the first one and scrambled aboard. Seats were not to be found; standing room only. I glanced around to try to discover who these other people were—Embassy personnel? Oil company representatives? American University teachers? None of them appeared to be as sad to leave Egypt as we were. I wondered where the rest of our mission family were.

Before our bus pulled away, a young army officer and a representative from the Embassy boarded the bus. Their instructions were brief and concise. We were to have our passports ready when we arrived at the customs office. Our baggage would not be checked individually, but rather, each bus would be checked through as a unit. We were to keep our cameras out of sight. The Egyptian army had been instructed to shoot on the spot anyone attempting to take pictures.

We received further instructions at the Custom's House and again at the docks. I shall never forget the parting words of the custom's officer as he handed me my exit visa.

"We hope you'll be back soon" he said with a smile.

"I hope so too," I replied, blinking back tears.

As we drove the short distance to the docks his words kept ringing in my ears. They wanted us to come back. Regardless of their feelings toward our country and its allies, they had accepted us as individuals, as good-will ambassadors who loved their country and who desperately wanted to stay. They had given us protection when we needed it and had aided us in every way possible with only one hope in mind—that we would return.

We were taken from the docks in large landing crafts. Three American tankers waited for us in the harbor. Our craft moved alongside one of them, clearly marked U.S. CHILTON, our destination.

I noticed that many Americans had already boarded the ship and were peering intently at our little group as we prepared to join them on deck. Our luggage at this point was separated from us to facilitate our climbing up the narrow ladder which led from sea level to the deck. I had no sooner reached the safety of the deck when a young naval officer directed me to a large table nearby, filled to the brim with slices of cake and steaming cups of coffee. Above it flew a banner of welcome: "We knew You Were Comin' So We Baked a Cake" the title of a popular song. My hand shook as I grasped the small paper cup and drops of coffee spilled on the deck. I was suddenly overcome with emotion. The trials of the past few days were over, and we were safe at last! Tears of relief, mixed with sadness, flooded my eyes. I looked once again at the banner and the U.S. flag above me. My heart reached back to the people I had left behind and I was filled with compassion and sadness. I had come to give them something and yet, they had given me so much more than I could possibly ever repay. They had given me their trust, their understanding, and most of all their love. My gaze shifted once again to the flag and I silently thanked God for my country and for the high ideals for which she stood. When I looked back, the shoreline had disappeared.

Our two nights and one day aboard the Chilton were an unforgettable experience. We were so crowded that people were sharing berths in the trooping quarters. There were over 1,200 persons on our ship, including the marines who had come with the navy in case rescue efforts were needed. Including the naval personnel, this was almost double its normal capacity. Since it wasn't constructed for passengers, there were, of course, no lounges, not even spots to sit down. I slept in a room with 289 others on a bunk five up! All five beds were suspended by chains and of course moved with the flow of all the occupants. As unpleasant and uncomfortable were our sleeping quarters, I have never eaten more delicious food! We feed our navy well! The spirit of the crew was unforgettable. The captain told us that as soon as the crew received orders to come and rescue us that the morale of the crew rose 100%. Suddenly, training in guns and ammunition ceased and training in diapers and formula began. The nursery they set up of boxes and pillows was unique. I've never seen happier sailors and marines as when they carried babies and small children up and down the spiral staircases. The crew made all of us feel very special. Years later I was to read on their Wikipedia site that this was considered the most memorable experience of their vessel's long history.

We arrived on the island of Crete about 9:30 a.m. on November 4th and began transferring passengers and luggage from the Chilton to the U.S. General Patch. The two other evacuation vessels were also unloading passengers. The total number of evacuees consisted of our American mission personnel, U.N. representatives, American Embassy workers, industrial personnel, American University teachers, French and English personnel and a few tourists. The number of children was large and daily increasing. Two new babies had been added to our number already and two more were expected before reaching Naples. We were still traveling "berth" class, but had regular cabins and used the mess hall; in addition, this transport carrier came equipped with lounges, ping-pong rooms and a movie theatre. We had religious services every morning.

I think one of the hardest things about leaving was deciding what to take with me and what to leave. I was only able to take two suitcases and my overnight bag. I tried to pack with the idea that I might never be able to retrieve the things I left. I managed to squeeze in most of my winter clothes (yes, it does get chilly in Egypt), my camera, my knitting and three pairs of shoes. My phonograph, typewriter and most of my records and jewelry had to be left behind. It was very difficult to pack with bombs falling outside and only a dim flashlight to see by. This whole experience seemed unbelievable—as if I were seeing it in a movie. But at the same time, we were very grateful, both to the U.S. Navy and especially to the Lord for keeping us safe.

Chapter Three:
The Journey Sojourns in Europe

*W*e were not sure, but we imagined that some of us from the mission would go to Frutigen, Switzerland, at least until we knew whether or when we could return to Egypt. The small town of Frutigen was familiar to several of our missionaries who had spent time there during their summer holidays. We spent time there during their summer holidays. We will need to arise at 5:00 a.m. tomorrow morning to disembark at Naples. As I look back over these last few days, I am amazed at now calm I have remained through it all. Somehow, I know in my heart that the Lord will take care of us. You never believe you can be calm in such a situation until you experience it, and it is amazing the peace that God gives you to deal with whatever lies ahead.

On November 6th we arrived in Naples, Italy. While waiting to disembark, cameramen from the Associated Press, International News Service and several local papers took pictures of our group. After going through a very orderly procedure of customs, we were all driven to the hotels to which we had been assigned by the Consulate. Our mission group of 63 was divided up and sent to different hotels. Three of us from the college were at the Terminus Hotel, which was first class! No sleeping in swinging berths, suspended by chains! The first thing I did upon landing was buy a warm coat! It was chilly in Naples!

The morning of November 7th, we had a mission meeting at the Oriente Hotel. At this meeting it was decided that nineteen of us would go to Frutigen, Switzerland and remain there indefinitely, or at least until the situation was such that we could return to Egypt. Thus, the following afternoon we left for Frutigen by train. We changed trains in Rome but had no time to see anything except their gorgeous station where you had to buy tickets to use the restrooms! And they were co-ed at that!

The train ride through the mountains to Frutigen was beautiful beyond words! I know now as never before why everyone raves about Switzerland.

Frutigen, we learned, is a municipality in the Bernese Oberland in the canton of Bern. Its elevation is 2,625'. It is surrounded by mountains and lots of snow!

The Village of Frutigen

We were met at the station and taken to the Sieber-Mueller Pension. Our bedrooms were located on the second floor: all unheated but each equipped with fluffy featherbeds. The Board of Missions paid the pension $3.00 per day room and board for each of us. Sleeping and eating were great—I even learned to eat sauerkraut!

By November 16th, we had had a week to get used to living in that beautiful village. The villagers spoke only German and most of us spoke only English and French. That made for interesting shopping! First on my shopping list was the purchase of a hat and mittens. These were essential for our daily hikes around the village and up into the hills. Side trips to Adelboden, at an elevation of 4,429', to watch a ski jumping event, and to Thun for a visit to an abandoned castle, occupied the first couple of days. On Sunday we attended church, which, of course, was in German. The minister mentioned our presence and announced the arrival of a new baby to one of our missionary couples. During the service he baptized eight of their own new babies. Most evenings were spent gathered around the pot-belly stove, located in the lounge, singing sogs, playing games and keeping warm.

After two weeks of viewing majestic mountains and enjoying snowy walks, I decided to set off on my own for what I called my "European Adventure". I had no maps and no definite plans. What amazing trust for a twenty-year old tourist! My parents sent me my savings of $200 which I added to my $3.00 daily allowance from the mission and set off. First, I purchased a Eurail Pass for several weeks of unlimited train travel. On my day of departure, unfortunately, a heavy fog had settled high in the mountains and I was unable to see much of the scenery.

Arriving at my first stop, Bern, the capital of Switzerland, I immediately searched for a place to eat. Two ham sandwiches later I decided to take a brief sight-seeing tour of the city. The first stop was to see the famous bears of Bern. This stop proved to be disastrous! I leaned over a bit too far to get a better view of the bears, only to have the lid of my camera case fall into the hands of one of the bears! I now have a marvelous picture of the bear holding up my case! Diverting the bear's attention with a handful of peanuts, the zookeeper went in and retrieved my camera case. It had just a few bite marks but was still useable.

My next stop was the famous musical clock tower. I managed to get there just as the clock struck one. A large gold man appeared and struck the gong once with the hammer and then animals paraded around the clock.

At 1:45 p.m. I caught a train for Geneva, arriving there about 4:10 p.m. (Trains in Switzerland are always on time!). By taxi I soon arrived at my hotel, Pension Tourelle, centrally located in the heart of the city.

The next day I had fun just sightseeing on my own and, of course, shopping. In one shop I found a clerk who could speak English; however, it wasn't long before I found myself switching to French and she followed suit. We both laughed. Geneva is in the French-speaking region of Switzerland. Italian and German are spoken in the other two regions. While I was in the shop the time came for us to observe three minutes of silence to mourn for Hungary. On November 4 Soviet forces had invaded Budapest and other parts of the country. The Hungarian resistance continued until November 10th with over 2,500 Hungarian deaths. This moment of silence was observed throughout Switzerland. In addition to concerns about Hungary, Switzerland was also concerned about the continuing conflict in the Middle East. Because of a shortage of gasoline throughout Switzerland, all private vehicles, as well as taxis and buses, did not operate on Sundays.

I arrived in Paris on November 22nd after an eight-hour train ride and went directly to the Hotel Egypte. Trains in Europe are built with compartments for eight persons with an aisle on the left side. I was fortunate enough to have half of a compartment to myself. The station in Paris was just a short distance from my hotel. I was also fortunate that my hotel room was large and heated! I was delighted to discover that my room overlooked one of the busiest streets in Paris and was only three blocks from the American Express and the Opera.

As soon as I got settled, I walked to the American Express and purchased tickets for three tours. While I waited for my tours to begin, I wandered through several department stores. I was especially interested in their toy departments where I noted that their boys' section featured cowboys, Indians, and Davy Crockett merchandise. The girls' section had the usual: dolls, doll furniture and special miniature tea sets which included wine glasses—typical of French meals. My next stop was at a small grocery store where, miracles of miracles, I found peanut butter! It was imported from Mexico since Europeans in general don't eat peanut butter. This along with a purchase of bread and some apples provided me with lunches for the rest of the week. I had also pilfered some jam from breakfast. As the days went on, I developed the habit of saving a role from breakfast to make fresh sandwiches after my initial purchase of bread had been consumed.

Following lunch, I scurried off to join my first tour: a trip to Versailles. It was rather chilly out, but the sun was shining brightly as we drove the twelve miles to Versailles. We spent about two and a half hours touring the palace and grounds which, of course, are lovelier in the summer when all the flowers are in bloom. The famous Hall of Mirrors was disappointing in that the mirrors were so old that they hardly provided much in the way of reflection.

After a visit to the enchanting cottage of Marie Antoinette, we returned to the American Express. It was now close to 6:30 p.m., giving me just enough time to freshen up before departing with Lion, my new friend whom I had met on the bus, to see an American movie, "Bambino Caballero" with Robert Mitchum. Lion was a ski instructor from northern Switzerland.

On November 23rd, I hurried through breakfast and took my usual three-minute walk in the crisp air to the American Express where a bus was waiting to whisk our group off for a trip through Paris. One of the places I enjoyed the most was the Sacre Coeur Church, located in the Montmartre section of the city. We were fortunate to arrive there at noon when the chimes were playing, and it was enchanting. I had the pleasure of being with twenty young people from India who had been in the U.S. under the International Farm Youth Exchange and were now on their way home. Among the group were three Americans who were teaching at an army base in Berlin.

In the afternoon we toured historic Paris on the left bank of the Seine River, highlighted by our stop at Notre Dame Cathedral. This cathedral is considered one of the finest examples of French Gothic architecture. Its enormous and colorful rose window and the abundance of its sculptural decorations, set it apart from earlier Romanesque styled buildings. It has one of the world's largest organs, combined with immense church bells.

Our next stop was at the law court where we saw lawyers in their long black robes and white ties. Our final stop was at the Sorbonne University, built in 1283, a huge, drab building two blocks long and five stories high—not very impressive from the outside. In the evening Lion and I went to Paris' loveliest theatre and saw a French movie, "La Terreur des Dames", a comedy most of which I understood without much difficulty. The stage show was marvelous. It lasted over an hour but was well worth the time. After the show we took a bus tour of the city on our own, just to see Paris at night. Everything was amazingly safe and I never experienced any hesitation nor fear. God is good— all the time!

Early the next morning I went to mass at Notre Dame in hopes of hearing their famous boys' choir. Unfortunately, I learned that they had sung at an earlier mass. The magnificent organ music, however, almost made up for our disappointment and set the stage for a marvelous spiritual experience. Later in the day I once again boarded the train and left for Brussels, Belgium.

After a four-hour ride, I arrived in the heart of the city and quickly found my hotel, the Home des Infirmities, a residence for nurses. For $1.75 a day I enjoyed a warm room and breakfast.

Despite the gloomy weather the next day, I hopped on a bus and proceeded to search for the American Express. I didn't have the faintest idea where it was, so I just kept asking policemen. Eventually I got there and found a city tour about to depart. I met a charming girl on the bus, a secretary for our armed forces in Italy, with whom I spent the remainder of the day. We had lots of fun shopping in their large department stores, paying special attention to their lace and glass works for which Belgium is famous. We both bought dolls for friends and lace for ourselves.

A new day dawned with bright sunshine and all the trimmings. I walked for an hour before returning to the hotel to retrieve my luggage and proceed to the train station. My next stop would be Amsterdam. The 3 ½ hour trip by train was very interesting. My compartment companion, this time, was a young Jewish teacher from Israel. We had such an enjoyable time chatting together that we decided to stay at the same hotel, but of course not together, and explore Amsterdam. We found a very nice hotel in the center of town with reasonable prices. After a delicious meal of pork chops (me), potatoes, peas and coffee for 60 cents, we went to an American movie, a musical, "Viva Los Vegas", which was very good.

66

The morning of Wednesday, November 28th it rained and looked dark and dismal when I arose about 7:30 a.m. My spirits were lifted, however, when I was told that it usually rains every morning in the Netherlands but is mostly sunny by ten or eleven. With that in mind I proceeded to the local American Express and purchased tickets for an afternoon tour of the islands of Volendam and Marken. We left at 2:00 p.m., traveling by bus and then by boat to our first island, Marken. There we were invited into a typical Dutch home, where we inspected their kitchen (spotless of course) and their bedrooms, equipped with cupboards set in the wall. The Dutch mother of the house showed us her children's apparel—typical Dutch clothing, which is still being worn on this island. After a quick look in a gift shop, where I purchased more Christmas gifts for friends, we hopped on the boat once again to travel to the second Island, Volendam. There we visited a typical farm and saw how they make cheese. We were each given a sample to encourage us to buy more. The highlight of the day, however, turned out to be meeting my seatmate on the bus. He was a U.S. diplomatic representative who was on his way to the Suez Conference in Cairo. He had previously lived in Cairo, so he was familiar with the current situation. I, of course, was very interested in knowing if he thought there might be a possibility of our returning to Egypt soon. His response was discouraging as he did not feel that our returning would be possible for at least several months. Currently he was the only American citizen who the U.S. government was permitting to return to Egypt. In fact, all passports were being stamped "not valid for travel in Egypt"; thus, instead of talking about the political situation, we chatted about Egyptian foods we did or didn't like, the places of interest we'd visited, and the restaurants we liked. I also met a delightful woman on the bus who, coincidentally, was born in Riverside, Illinois! One of the nicest things about traveling is meeting new, fascinating people.

I was up early the next day, looking forward to a morning tour of Amsterdam. Before departing I consumed a delicious breakfast of two fried eggs with toast and jam for 25 cents!

My seatmate on my morning tour was an ex-GI who had been stationed in Europe and was taking a brief tour of the continent before returning to the States. He had a master's degree in architecture and was very interested when I told him I was from Riverside. The Coonley House in Riverside was the only Frank Lloyd Wright masterpiece which he had not seen and therefore he was most interested in learning more about it from me, since my family's home was right down the street!

Our tour took us first to a diamond factory where we learned how diamonds are cut, shaped and polished. After a general tour of the city, we stopped at the Rijksmuseum where we were able to view the paintings of various Dutch masters, especially Rembrandt. His famous work "The Night Watch" was there, along with many other equally famous works. The afternoon was spent window shopping and enjoying the somewhat milder weather.

As I looked at the calendar the next morning, I realized that I had missed Thanksgiving! Here it was November 30th, and I had forgotten to celebrate our American holiday! Perhaps I could find a turkey substitute for my peanut butter sandwich for one day! No such luck! Back at the hotel, I hurriedly prepared to make the 7:32 a.m. train for Koln, Germany. Despite the early hour my breakfast was waiting for me when I entered the small dining room of the hotel. The Dutch were so gracious. It seemed that they couldn't do enough for you, especially at the small hotels where there were only five or six guests. They prepared enough food for twice that number!

I arrived in Koln at 11:45 a.m. and proceeded immediately to the Dom Hotel which was only a block away and right across the street from the famous Koln Cathedral. The church's twin spires reach 515 feet. Construction began between 1248-1473 and finished sometime between 1842-1880. Restoration after WWII's damage began in 1950 and continues into the present.

After a restful night I arose early to travel by train through snow-covered mountains toward the old city of Trier, known for its well-preserved medieval buildings, including the ruins of three Roman baths. I had decided that I really did not want to travel during the Christmas holidays. My parents reminded me that my cousin, Joanne Kline and her husband, Jim, lived in Birkenfeld, Germany, where Jim was stationed with an air force squadron. My plan was to stay there through Christmas and then, hopefully, return to Egypt. Upon arriving in Trier, it was good to see Jim's smiling face as he greeted me at the train station. From there we traveled by car to Birkenfeld, where my cousin was waiting to welcome me.

Birkenfeld is a town of about 7,000, the district seat of the Birkenfeld area in southwest Rhineland-Palatinate, founded in AD 500 by Frankish-German farmers. If the American Air Force population were to be included it would, of course, be larger. Very few of the townspeople spoke English. There were no supermarkets. Groceries were available at the base or in various shops in the village. Young men on bicycles delivered fresh, warm bread to homes each morning.

The day after my arrival was Sunday. That day I had the pleasure of teaching a Sunday School class of 7-9-year-olds. I was subbing for their regular teacher, Carl Reid, who was out of town visiting his brother, Harold, in Traben-Trarbach, a small village nearby. After services at the base chapel, we all went to the snack bar for lunch and then home for a restful afternoon. We gathered later that day to make popcorn to sell at the local movie theatre, one of Jim's projects. Even the dog helped out by eating the scraps we accidentally dropped.

Monday evening Joanne introduced me to Carl. He and I soon realized that both of us were very involved in music. Excitedly, he took me over to the chapel to show me the organ. He was a gifted organist. There was also a piano nearby which gave us an opportunity to play impromptu duets. Carl was an Airman 2nd Class, tall, light complexed, and wore glasses. He was from Niles, Michigan. I realized that we would be seeing a lot of each other before I returned to Egypt as the two of us were now on a committee to plan the base Christmas program. I helped him with

We will probably be seeing a lot of each other before I return to Egypt as the two of us are now on a committee to plan the base Christmas program. I am helping him with Junior Church by reading Bible stories to the class 3-5-year-olds. I also have the opportunity to lead a short discussion at their Wednesday night service concerning our Mission in Egypt and more specifically our evacuation.

A lot happened in the week that followed. Carl and I spent most of his free time together. Unexpectantly, we found ourselves falling in love after only a week. We became engaged one sunny day atop a hill overlooking the town. As a result, I sat down at the end of that week and wrote the following letter home to my parents:

"Dear Mom and Dad,

This is one of those letters that a girl writes home to two special people, her parents, once in a lifetime to try to describe to them on paper the most wonderful experience of her life. It's hard to put into words just how you know when you've met the one person whom God had picked out all along just for you. I always knew down deep in my heart that the minute he came into my life I'd know him—that it wouldn't take years, months or even weeks to discover what it took God only one short week to bring to pass. Carl and I are engaged. Two days ago, he took me up on a high hill overlooking Birkenfeld beside an abandoned castle and proposed. I was not even surprised. I think I knew from the moment Joanne introduced us that this person was the individual I had waited all my life to meet. We did fall in love suddenly, but I think others knew before we did what was happening. As Joanne said, we were like one person from the moment we met. We don't have just one or two common interests, but in almost everything our lives blend beautifully together. What can I tell you about him? Nothing except what Joanne keeps repeating, 'Your parents will just love him.' It is truly amazing how a couple can go together for one week and surprise no one at the end of that week when they become engaged. Actually, we haven't officially told anyone. People just see us and sort of glow all over because they're so happy for us.

"Now I suppose you'd like to hear more about Carl and our plans. Carl joined the air force after high school and has completed 2 ½ years. He will receive his discharge in May of 1958 and plans to go to Bob Jones University to prepare for the mission field or possibly home mission work. Just when we'll be married is uncertain. If I go back to Cairo, we shall be married in June; if not, we've set February 14th as our tentative date. Carl has a five-day pass beginning Friday, during which time we shall be searching for an apartment. With his $50-a-week and my $90-a-week salaries and with apartment rent at only $25 a month, we should make out ok. In addition to the above we have a food allotment, PX and Commissary privileges, and free medical and dental care.

"We traveled to Idar-Oberstein yesterday and picked out our rings and are getting them tomorrow. They are matching gold bands which we will wear in the traditional European tradition on our right hands until we're married. Carl has a ½ carat diamond which he'll have set in white gold for me as soon as we buy a piano and a few other things we need. The air force will begin investigating me in about a week, a process which takes about a month. Even if we wait until June to get married, we still want to get this process completed now. A letter from the Board this week informed us that the Board wants all of us to remain here in Europe for the winter at least until something definite happens. They also gave us the option of going home and breaking our contracts. I shall not break mine; however, should we receive instructions to return to Egypt, I shall write them immediately to inform them of my approaching marriage just in case they should not want to bear the expense of sending me back to Cairo for such a short *period of time. I have put on the back of this sheet approximately what I'd like published in the paper. Please don't mention our wedding plans as they are, of course, very indefinite. I know, Mother, how much you'll miss not being right here to help me plan my wedding, but you can be sure that letters will fly fast and furiously for there are so many, many ways you can help Joanne and me with these plans. There is one very special wish I have that only you can fulfill...that is, for a wedding dress made by the same wonderful person who has been sewing all my other lovely things for the last fifteen years—you Mother! Joanne is getting me some bridal books and very soon I shall cut out some pictures of approximately what I'd like and then you can pick the pattern which comes the closest to what I want. Joanne and I will order the invitations for our friends here and for any at home who should receive them; however, I feel that in most cases an announcement will be sufficient. To try to tell you all the plans we are making as I write at 3:00 a.m. would be impossible in one letter. Joanne will be my Matron of Honor, Donna Lee my bridesmaid, and Jerri (her daughter) and Willie (her son) will be my flower girl and ring bearer. If we don't know far enough in advance or if for some reason you can't come, I guess Jim will have to give me away; but it surely won't be the same without Daddy. We are being married in the Evangelische Kirche in Birkenfeld with a small reception at Joanne's afterwards. We are going to keep expenses at the minimum and having Joanne make dresses for the three girls and having just cake, open-faced sandwiches, coffee and tea at the reception should help too.*

"I really had a busy day today. Early this morning I went out to the base to practice the organ as I am playing for a wedding in the afternoon. After a coffee-break with Carl I hunted all over town for a copy of the wedding march with no luck so we used a phonograph and a record which sounded much better than I could ever have done with only one day to practice. After a quick snack with Carl, I walked back to Joanne's, changed my clothes, and returned to the base to play Christmas music on the organ for twenty minutes before the wedding service began. Carl and I discussed wedding plans with the Chaplain over coffee later that afternoon. We now have a book, <u>Harmony in Marriage</u>, which we are reading together. After a delicious dinner at Berkoff's downtown, we picked up our rings in Idar-Oberstein and spent the rest of the evening with friends.

"You'll probably be getting letters by the score as I haven't begun to tell you all the little details. Oh yes, Carl has an acre of land near Niles, Michigan in a wooded section near a three-mile-long lake. Sound nice? We are taking a roll of snapshots of our life here to send to you and to Carl's parents as soon as we get them developed.

Much, much love, Carolyn"

Looking back now, sixty-four years later, I am wondering how my parents reacted to such a letter! Now, not only as a mother, grandmother and great-grandmother, I can't even imagine receiving such a letter! Were my parents as hurt then as I would be now? I was their only child. At least I have four children, but only one daughter. I never saved their letters as they did mine. I would love to be able to read their responses. Did they support my decision to marry Carl after such a brief courtship? Could they affirm with me that this was truly God's will for my life? More importantly, did I really believe this or was I only caught up in the moment—a moment I had never experienced before?

My next letter to them indicated that Carl and I would be meeting again with the chaplain to continue planning our wedding. Since we had no idea if or when I would be returning to Egypt, we could not set a definite date for our wedding. Also on the agenda for this week was a continuation of our search for an apartment. Although rent was minimal, so were the available apartments. We finally found one we liked on a road called Wittelsbacherweg. It had one all-purpose room (kitchen, dining, living room) with a pot-belly stove in the center for heat, one bedroom and one bath, shared by four apartments. Washing clothes and taking showers could only be done on a designated day when the landlord provided hot water. We couldn't make a firm decision at that time, but the house seemed to be the best possibility.

It was December 16th and Christmas was rapidly approaching.. After a lovely dinner at the Club, Carl and I went to a Christmas musical at the chapel. Three German choirs from Trier sang under the direction of the parish priest of Birkenfeld. Our choir sang *The Christmas Story* and I was asked to sing the solo part. The choirs from Trier joined us in singing *Silent Night*, of course in German, to conclude the program.

After a free dinner at the Club the night of December 23rd, we set off for an evening of caroling with a group of Germans from Birkenfeld. We caroled at the various hospitals and in the housing areas of the American military personnel. Afterwards we all gathered in the chapel lounge for coffee and cookies.

Christmas Eve morning finally dawned. At ten we had the children's Christmas party at the Club. Jerri was in the ballet group to begin the program. I played the piano while Chaplain Lawson led in the singing of Christmas carols. Santa arrived and distributed gifts to the children, followed by refreshments for all. The adult choir sang the *Christmas Story* again while the junior choir pantomimed the action. After the service, Carl and I exchanged gifts. I gave him a leather billfold and he gave me a necklace and earring set to match my new Christmas dress which my mother had sent. Later that night Carl and I along with several couples attended the Christmas Eve service in Baumholder (the nearby Army military base). We didn't arrive home until after 1:00 a.m., just in time to enjoy the festivities at Jim and Joanne's Christmas Eve party. We danced 'till almost 4:00 a.m. and then set up their children's toys and filled their stockings.

Christmas for us began about 9 a.m., as we enjoyed a pancake breakfast with friends with Carl making the pancakes. He was a great cook! We had dinner at 9:30 that night: turkey and all the trimmings as well as pecan pie, peach pie, and spice cake for dessert.

On one of Carl's days off we had fun touring the countryside, especially along the Nahe and Moselle rivers. We loved all the picturesque castles we saw along the river banks. We especially loved Idar-Oberstein where we had purchased our rings.

The day after Christmas I received a notice that I was to return to Egypt. Although saddened by the thought of a separation, both Carl and I felt that I had not only an obligation, but that it was God's will for me to return and finish the task which I had so recently begun. The next few days were filled with last minute wedding preparations before leaving for Egypt.

On December 30th I received a confirmation letter with instructions for my return to Egypt. My departure was set for January 3rd. I was to travel by train through Bern to Zurich where I would meet the rest of the group and later depart by air for Egypt. Of course, Carl and I were saddened to be apart for a time, but we both knew God would provide just as the Apostle Paul had promised in Romans 8:28 that *"all things (would) work together for good to those who love God, to those who are called according to His purpose."*

Chapter Four:

The Journey Returns to Egypt

Nee Year's Day 1957! Was it possible? Were we really going back? The suddenness of our long-awaited news left all of us in a state of disbelief; but there before me on the desk lay the freshly opened telegram bearing the wonderful news. I wondered if anyone really knew the two-fold happiness I felt in my heart—a happiness warm with the prospect of my return to Egypt and ultimately with the future trip back to Germany to the man I loved.

So much had happened these passed eight weeks: the evacuation, our memorable cruise aboard the Chilton, our arrival ten days later at Naples, our brief sojourn in Frutigen, Switzerland, my solo journey through Europe, and finally my very special time in Birkenfeld, Germany. What wonderful memories I had of that time, especially those days spent in Frutigen: hiking along the rugged countryside and into the mountains, the hospitality of the villagers. These villagers graciously took us in and made every minute of our stay enjoyable. We learned to get to know them and appreciate their way of life. As we lived with them, spoke with them, worshipped with them, we came to understand more and more the true meaning of I Corinthians 13, that great love Chapter.

Not all my time away, however, had been spent in Frutigen. I had spent several weeks traveling through Europe and a month visiting my cousin's family in Berkenfeld, Germany. I had met Carl and become engaged. Now I was going back to Egypt and to Mike. I still had not sorted out my mixed feeling concerning Carl and Mike. If I were so deeply in love with Carl, why did I find my thoughts turning so frequently to Mike? The more I read in the papers the more anxious I had become over his well-being. Had he been sent to Port Said after it had been so cruelly and needlessly bombed? Sometimes I even wondered if he were still alive. Knowing Mike and his dedication to his work, I knew he would be among the first to respond to the urgent call at Port Said. I hoped deep in my heart that he was still alive. Since Jeanne had returned to the States and had not planned on returning to Egypt, I knew that she was out of the picture. There would be no more double-dating. What, I wondered, had kept the memory of that final night in Alex alive in my heart? Why had saying goodbye to Mike been so difficult?

It took less than three days to make the necessary arrangements for my return. One short trip to Bern provided me with my re-entrance visa and a brief phone call to Zurich confirmed my plane reservation. With these matters finished, I proceeded by train to Zurich to meet up with the rest of the group. The train trip through the mountains to Zurich was enchanting. Never had I seen such gorgeous scenery. Tiny villages nestled high in the Alps were completely locked in by deep drifts of snow. It all resembled a fairyland. How quaint were the homes with their pointed roofs and their colorful facades. Many homes had family inscriptions painted across the front or over doors and windows. The homes, like the people, had a clean, well-scrubbed look. As we passed village after village, I couldn't help but notice the striking resemblance of each one to the other: a tall, steepled church in the center, surrounded by small homes, stretching for miles into the mountainside.

I arrived in Zurich shortly before dinner and proceeded immediately to the Swiss Air office to deposit my luggage and reconfirm my reservation. Our flight was to leave at 11:00 p.m. We would be taken by bus to the airport. Only nine of our mission group had been granted re-entry visas; the rest had to remain in Frutigen, at least for the time being. Only full-time teachers were permitted to return; the career missionaries who were not teachers were forced to remain behind.

Our little group set out to find a place to eat, with prices consistent with our slim budget. Much to our amazement we found a very reasonable restaurant and gorged ourselves on wiener schnitzel and all the trimmings. We even had enough money left over to enjoy a movie!

We boarded the plane and as usual left on time. I glanced briefly at my ticket and noted with humor that I was "Mr. Copeland" not "Miss Copeland." That should entitle me to extra special treatment, I mused whimsically. I glanced down at my seat belt which was securely fastened and began to relax. It was almost midnight and I was beginning to get sleepy. Yet I was also very excited. We were actually going back—a dream come true. With that happy thought in mind, I peacefully dozed off.

About 5:30 a.m. we stopped at Athens, Greece where we enjoyed a brief snack before re-boarding the plane. As we flew over Athens and out toward the sea, I caught a faint glimpse of the Acropolis perched high above the city. I dozed off again for a bit, that is, until my breakfast arrived at 6:30 a.m.

It was close to 10:00 a.m. before the faint shoreline of Alex came into view. As we moved up the Nile toward Cairo, I pressed my nose to the window and made a game of trying to pick out villages and other familiar landmarks. Then at last I caught sight of the pyramids. The pyramids meant home—home at last!

Entering the College campus, I was struck by the fact that everything looked the same—just as if we had never left. Climbing up the stairs to my room and opening the door, I found everything just as I had left it—dust and all. I laid my suitcase carefully on the bed and walked across the room to my closet. Peeking in I noted that everything was still there: my trunks, typewriter and phonograph. I opened one of the trunks and peered inside, trying to decide which wrinkled dress to wear to the staff Christmas party. I decided on a bright red taffeta dress that, of course, Mother had made. It was perfect!

The night of the party dawned clear and crisp. I arrived as usual right on time. I'm not quite sure how long it was before Dr. Meloy spotted me. Right away she commented on my dress.

"How nice you look, my dear," she began, gazing from top to toe.

Dinner was a festive occasion as usual. People like to party in Egypt. Each of us shared our excitement at the prospect of reopening school soon; but by far the happiest notes were those shared by the group that was now reunited after several months of separation. The teachers who had remained were overjoyed to see us once more and hear about our various journeys. The meal, as always, was delicious: tomato soup, shrimp casserole, roast turkey and suet pudding. Dr. Meloy's house servants served us, and for a change it was nice not to have to do cleanup. While at my cousins in Birkenfeld, everyone pitched in.

The best time came when we had our gift exchange. Like everyone else I was wondering who had my name. To my surprise it turned out to be Dr. Meloy.

"Oh, how lovely," I exclaimed as I dipped into the small cotton-lined box and discovered my carefully wrapped gift—a silver fork and spoon set. How thoughtful and she didn't even know I was engaged!

I glanced across the room and saw Donna Lee opening her package from me. It had been such fun picking out a special gift for her. She smiled with delight as she opened the silver broach I had selected. Inscribed on it were the words in Arabic, "Alhamdulillah" (praise to God). Next came more gifts for me from the other head teachers: an Egyptian calendar with Eastern Christmas clearly circled for January 7th, a turquoise imitation scarab, a pyramid paper weight, and a string of beads made from hippopotamus teeth.

Things began settling down after New Year's and within a short time almost all of our students had returned. Although most of them were not great students, they were, however, motivated to stay in school in order to postpone the inevitable: an early, arranged marriage, often to a much older man. Marriage itself loomed as a vast unknown before the eyes of these innocent girls. The prospect was often frightening. If, however, they were able to finish high school and perhaps a year or two of college they would be in a better position to become an active part of the husband "selection" process. This process was extremely limited and always initiated by the parents. Dating was very different than in the States. Couples did not go out alone. They were always accompanied by a carefully selected chaperone who could be a brother, a sister or another relative. Usually, the first meeting with a prospective husband and his parents would be a formal introductory tea, followed by a series of family outings and dinners which would help the couple become better acquainted. When sufficient time had elapsed, a proposal would be made by the man's parents to the girl's parents, which in some cases the girl could accept or reject; however, in many cases the decision was left entirely up to the parents. It could be said with certainty that the goal of every Egyptian mother was to find her daughter a suitable husband—one who came from a respectable family, was wealthy and had the earmarks of being a good husband. Age would not make a difference; thus, many Egyptian girls were married off to men twice their age. Often the couples were first-cousins. Sometimes there were medical consequences, resulting in some form or other of birth defect. At the school we had a special education classroom to minister to those students who had special needs, many of whom were children of first-cousin parents. One might ask, were these arranged marriages happy? Happiness is a relative thing. Yet, could you even imagine being happy with a spouse that you barely knew? Would love come later? How could you choose a life-mate with so few, if any, from which to choose? This process would not appeal to American women! They are used to having a choice, being independent, pursuing careers. This is not usually the case in Egypt, at least it wasn't back in 1956 when I lived there! During the day most women were at home. There were tasks to do: meals to plan, servants to direct, husbands to care for, and daily visitors to host, especially relatives living close by.

Therefore, most of my students tried to do their best to stay in school as long as possible. They also had a strong desire to "help each other." In class, for instance, their attitude was, "how could one rightly refuse to share an answer with a friend when that friend had requested help?" To call it cheating was to bring immediate rebuke from the class. She was not cheating. She was helping her friend. She had no malicious intent. She would have given you or anyone else her most precious treasure were you to ask. To even admire an item brought an immediate "itfadelli"—"take it; it is yours". Here was a problem I struggled to solve, and it became even more complex as time went on, especially during exam week. This was a cultural conflict that was difficult to understand and to handle.

Being so rigid with rules brought guilt to my mind. I certainly had not been rigid concerning the rule about dating Egyptian men! For as much as Egypt and her people and culture had come to mean to me, I was still a young American woman who had wanted to be part of Egyptian social life, regardless of the rules. I had followed the rules all my life. Now it was time to have fun!

Now that I was back in Egypt and school had resumed, it seemed as if I had never left. The only difference was my changed status. I was engaged and in Egypt that is cause for quite a celebration. Because in Egypt there is nothing worse than spinsterhood, instead of offering me their "Best Wishes", my students "Congratulated" me because I had been "selected" by a young man to be his wife. It was at our school's Christmas party that the girls first noticed my ring. Their excitement really embarrassed me. Even my fellow staff members seemed pleased.

When school opened on January 5th, almost all my students knew about my engagement and rushed up to me with "mabruke" (congratulations in Arabic). When I went to my first hour class they had written on the board "Congratulations Miss Copeland" and my fourth period class wrote the same plus "Best Wishes for a happy life". The first thing they all wanted was a physical description of Carl. They had a hard time imagining a man with blond hair and blue eyes. In the afternoon my II Secondary A class greeted me by singing the Arabic wedding march and engagement songs, clapping out the time with their hands. We all laughed, had fun, and didn't do much algebra!

I was busily preparing lessons in my room the morning of January 14, when one of the servants came by to tell me that I had a phone call in the office downstairs. Who could it be, I wondered? It was Mike. He had just learned of my return to Egypt and was most anxious to catch up on news.

He inquired about Jeanne. I could tell him very little—only that she had returned to the States and would not be coming back. After a moment of silence Mike asked, "Will you have tea with me after class on Wednesday?" Conflicting thoughts passed through my mind as I pondered my answer. Perhaps right then I should have said "no". Had I realized then what the next few months would hold, I'm sure my answer would have been "no." However, I was young and full of adventure and deeply intrigued by the fact that we had been advised not to date Egyptian men. It reminded me of my days at Bob Jones University when any personal male-female contact was forbidden. I guess you know what my answer was, for had it been otherwise, there would have been no dating story to follow.

As I waited by the gate, I tried to picture Mike—to remember him as he had been that last night in Alex. So many months and events had happened since then. It seemed strange waiting alone without Jeanne. I questioned her loyalty to Egypt, to her students, and to Mike. How was she able to not feel compassion toward Egypt and those she had come to love here? So eager had she been to return to the States that she had remained only three days in Naples before flying home. How could I convey this to Mike without hurting him? And more importantly, how exactly did I feel about Mike and he about me? Was Mike's invitation only to learn about Jeanne or was he wanting to connect with me as well?

Mike's familiar Chevy pulled up to the curb and I slipped in.

"Well, Carolyn, how are you?" he asked.

"I'm fine. How are you?" I asked in perfect Arabic.

"Pretty good," he replied. "I've missed you. I have thought about you a lot, but I didn't know you were back until a few days ago when my cousin, Miss Iskander, informed me."

"Miss Iskander is our college receptionist. I remember meeting her early last fall, but I never had an opportunity to get to know her. It's hard, you know. We have 72 teachers and of that number only 16 are Americans. The rest are here only during school hours and I rarely see them, much less really get to know them."

"My cousin is very nice. It was through her that I met Jeanne."

"Oh?"

"She invited me to a picnic at the college and Jeanne was there. Somehow we managed to get introduced and a few weeks later I began taking her out."

"Have you heard from Jeanne recently?" I asked cautiously.

"She sent a postcard from Naples saying that you all had arrived safely."

"You mean she hasn't written to you since?"

"Not a word."

"I'm sorry, Mike," I said sympathetically. "I wish I could give you some explanation, but I'm afraid I can't. She hasn't written to me either."

"Don't worry about it," he said without smiling.

We drove in silence for a long while, both of us deep in thought. As we crossed the Nile and headed south in the direction of the pyramids, I turned to Mike and asked,

"Where are we going?"

"To Mena House. Have you ever been there?"

"No" I replied. "What is it like?"

"Right now, it is being used as a luxury hotel. It is the ideal place for honeymooners to go: quiet, secluded and very romantic."

"It seems that I have heard of it before, although I can't quite remember where."

"You may have heard it mentioned in connection with the Cairo Conference which was held there in 1943," he replied.

Yes, now I did remember reading about this historic site. Built in 1869 as a hunting lodge, Mena House played host to some world-famous names including Winston Churchill, Richard Nixon and King George V. It was named after the founding father of the first Egyptian dynasty, King Menes. It later became the site of the World War II Cairo Conference of November 22-26, 1943 attended by President Roosevelt, Prime Minister Winston Churchill and Generalissimo Chiang Kai-shek. The result of this conference was a Declaration stating the Allies' intentions to continue deploying military force until Japan's unconditional surrender. Later, Mena House not only became famous because of this historic conference, but also because of its scrumptious food and its picturesque location.

"Oh, now I remember," I continued. "Were you living in Cairo at the time?"

"Yes, I was attending the English Mission College. I don't remember much about the conference, though. I was only 13 at the time."

Again, we lapsed into silence. The sun was slowly drifting into the horizon, casting multiple colors across the sky. All about us silence reigned supreme as the shades of the afternoon sunlight disappeared in the West and the stars peeked through the twilight. With the windows open and the cool air flowing in, one couldn't help but feel refreshed, despite a rather tiresome day of teaching. I was glad it was Thursday because tomorrow would be a holiday—a day to catch up on some much-needed sleep.

As we approached Mena House, I was suddenly aware of the exquisite beauty of the pyramids at sunset. I remembered that first night after our arrival in Egypt when I saw them for the first time silhouetted against the moonlit sky. Somehow today they meant so much more to me—they had become a symbol of a country and a people whose memory would live eternally in my heart.

Seated on the patio of this historic mansion, I gazed intently on the beauty surrounding us. The hotel itself had four levels, each one a small progression above the one before. From every window, graceful balconies provided a wonderful view of the pyramids. To the right of the hotel lay a series of tennis courts and to the left a miniature golf course.

"I had no idea they played miniature golf here," I remarked with surprise.

"It is one of our favorite pastimes. Have you ever tried it?"

"Not recently. I played occasionally while I was in high school and enjoyed it very much."

"Tell me, Carolyn, how did you pass the time while you were away from us?"

"Oh, I traveled a bit—did the usual things. Nothing spectacular, but I did have fun. It was quite an experience, really. I enjoyed meeting new people and trying my hand at speaking French. You know, even after studying French for three years I still had trouble making myself understood, especially in Paris. I guess if you don't speak Parisian French, you are not understood!"

"What part of Europe did you like best?" he asked.

"Switzerland, I think. Of course, I spent the most time there which could have been the reason why I came to like it so much. The scenery was spectacular. Those little Swiss villages look as if they came straight out of a fairy tale. The only problem was that I spoke only French and English and everyone in Frutigen where we stayed spoke only German."

"I love Switzerland too. I have been there many times."

Just then the waiter emerged from the hotel and walked briskly in our direction.

"What would you like to order?" Mike asked me.

"I know it isn't proper at this time of day, but I'd love some ice cream."

Mike laughed and gave our order to the waiter.

"Now it's your turn to tell me what you've been doing," I began cautiously. "You know you really had us worried that last night in Alex. I wondered so many times afterwards if you'd arrived back in Cairo safely. Then, as I read about the happenings at Port Said, I really became anxious. How did things turn out?" I asked with obvious concern.

"Not very well I'm afraid," Mike answered. "You know, of course, that there was massive destruction. The horrible part of it was that it was all so unnecessary. Port Said wasn't a military base, in fact, there weren't even troops there. Almost 30,000 people were killed and all of them innocent civilians. If you could have been there and seen what was happening it would have broken your heart. When I arrived in Port Said there were three hospitals. Within hours after I got there two of them had been completely demolished and the one where I was working was severely damaged. My best friend was killed instantly as he was performing an emergency operation in the same hospital where I was. Honestly, Carolyn, I shall never forget this as long as I live. It was a nightmare."

"But why, Mike, would the French and English do such a terrible thing?"

"I just don't know." He paused. "I lived in England for so many years while attending med school, yet I never really came to understand the English people. I certainly can't understand this. What did they gain by all this destruction? We still have the canal and you know, for the first time in my life I really didn't care if I lived or died. At least the dead were rid of their suffering. The most pitiful sight were the cries of the injured. There toward the end we were having to amputate without morphine. There just wasn't any to be had."

"That seems inhuman!"

"Unfortunately, the English and the French weren't thinking much about humanity when they bombed Port Said. They had only their own selfish interests at heart."

"I sometimes wonder if that were not true also of our government when they withdrew their offer of aid for the new Aswan Dam. I have a strong feeling that much of this could have been avoided had the U.S. not gone back on her promise," I remarked.

"Perhaps the U.S. had her reasons, but it put us in a rather desperate position. If the U.S. wouldn't give us the money we needed, the only other alternative was for us to seize control of the Suez Canal," Mike responded.

"And as a result, I almost didn't get to come here!" I remarked with emphasis.

"That would have been a pity!" Mike responded with equal emphasis.

"Don't tease," I replied earnestly. "If you only knew all the red tape I had to go through to get here!"

"I can imagine," he mused. "Well, now that you're here we'll have to make sure that every minute of your free time is spent enjoying yourself. May I see you again sometime soon?"

"I'd like that very much" I replied without thinking about the possible implications. Why had I neglected to tell him I was engaged?

"I'll talk to Joy and Anis. I know they will be anxious to see you again."

"Wonderful. I'm so anxious to see little Chrissy. I bet he's grown a lot since I last saw him."

"He's really cute. I'm sure he's the first blond Egyptian in history!" he remarked jokingly.

I looked at my watch and realized it was time to get back to the College. Before I had time to rise from my chair the waiter was behind me, easing it out from under me. Mike gave him a tip and taking my arm led me back toward the car. I took one last look at the pyramids before entering the car. The sunset was gone now and only the stars could be seen as they dotted the still-blue sky. Would I always feel this happy and secure? I felt I really belonged here, but what about Carl? Where did he fit into God's call for me to come to Egypt and most of all, what about Mike? As if in answer Mike's hand touched mine as we drove into the twilight.

As the days passed, my students became more and more demanding of my time, not only in class, but during my free time as well. The invitations to tea, to the cinema and to parties of all sorts flooded in. I did my best to discourage them, mainly because I just didn't have time to accept all their invitations. I had a full teaching schedule plus I was having to spend many hours putting the finishing touches on my wedding plans. I asked myself repeatedly, "Why do I continue to see Mike? Are we just good friends or does he have something else on his mind?" I was troubled.

My students persisted. Now they formed groups of three or four and together planned a party. I obliged, even though my time was so very limited. I did, however, find these parties lots of fun and the students were thrilled. Their families went out of their way to make me feel welcome. When my students were not hosting parties in their homes, they were taking me out to dinner, to the cinema, to the opera and to special exhibitions or events.

Friday, January 25th arrived—my 21st birthday. I wondered if anyone remembered that it was my birthday. Promptly at nine a.m. a somewhat outdated Chevy pulled up in front of the school and Mary and Jeannette jumped out. These were two of my Armenian students from III Secondary B. Jeannette's father owned a textile factory in Heliopolis and the family was quite wealthy. Her brother, Yarvant, had met Donna Lee on one or two previous occasions and had expressed an interest in continuing their friendship. Donna Lee, however, having already met Egyptian men during her summer at Agami Work Camp years ago, was somewhat hesitant to become involved, yet could not hide her joy at seeing him again.

As Yarvant emerged from the car, one could not help but notice his deep-set dark eyes following us as we moved toward his waiting car.

"Good morning. Is this early enough for you?" he asked jokingly.

"Early?" replied Donna Lee. "For a Friday morning this is still Thursday night. Don't you know we always sleep in on Fridays?"

"So, for you two this outing was a real sacrifice."

"Yes, indeed," I replied. "It will take us weeks to recover!"

"You better recover fast as we will soon be taking a horseback ride across the desert to our family's tent," Jeannette added.

"A horseback ride across the desert?" I questioned.

"Yes," Jeannette replied. "Have you ever ridden a horse?"

"Oh, yes, a long time ago, but never across the desert!" With that I neglected to mention that my "horseback riding" had been childhood pony rides at an amusement park! This ride looked different, but still looked like lots of fun. And it was!

Desert Party with Students

Since you will later learn that I became a strong University of Michigan fan, I need to note here that the M stood for Monmouth, not Michigan!

Enjoying the Party

When we arrived in the tent area, I was surprised to discover that ten young people were already there and had lunch prepared. Not only that, but as I arrived, they all began singing "Happy Birthday"! As it turned out they did not know that today was actually my birthday; only that it was sometime during the month of January. So, they were surprised too! After lunch all of us jumped into a jeep and started back across the desert. About two miles from the tent, we ran out of gas! The choice was either push the jeep or hike the rest of the way. We hiked! Fortunately, it was January and not very hot!

Since the teachers thought my birthday was the 26th, I had another party the next day, the highlight of which was a cake, almost as delicious as my mother's "Never Fail Cake." I received several gifts, among them a dozen roses from one of my students.

Reading over my letters that Mother had saved, I realized once again how very busy I was, participating in so many social events: dinners in student's homes, dinners at the Oberge, dinners everywhere! I soon realized that if I were to keep eating at this rate, I would probably not fit into the wedding dress that my mother was making for me. Mother and I exchanged notes and details about the upcoming wedding in each letter and with each one excitement grew. Yet how could I continue planning this wedding with Carl when I was still seeing Mike? Could I still keep on claiming that our get-togethers were not really dates? What was I thinking? More importantly what was Mike thinking? Where was God in all this? Was I even asking Him? Probably not.

There were still very few Americans in Cairo. Because of this we were often invited to events at the American Embassy. In turn we entertained Ambassador Hare frequently at our place. At one particular event I was again asked to play the piano and did a short rendition of Tchaikovsky's Piano Concerto in B flat Minor, the only piece I knew by heart. Hopefully my repertoire would increase once my piano lessons begin with my new teacher, Madam Fenninger de Rogatus.

My first lesson was a bit upsetting. Madam Fenninger said that I played Beethoven like Tchaikovsky and she happened to prefer Beethoven! I am working on Beethoven's Pathetique Sonata, Movement Two. I love it—*my* way—but will concede and play it *her* way!

One of my most unforgettable trips during this time was a visit to Mohammed Ali's Palace. Our trip through the gardens was especially lovely. One of the most fascinating sights was a huge tree called a Weeping Tree which spreads its branches to the ground. The branches take root again and thus another tree is formed. This one tree now extended almost the length of the garden and formed arches over the walk which led to a lovely flower garden. Another large, delicious meal at the home of yet another one of my students followed this trip.

The "heart" of every February is Valentine's Day. We had quite a party at Dr. Meloy's flat. After a delicious dinner of creamed chicken on hot biscuits, ice cream and cake, our group of twenty "old maids" played "heart" games! The first game was a love story made up of twenty-five questions, the answers to which were the names of flowers. The second game was a love-letter where the blanks were to be filled in with names of fruits and vegetables. The last game was the most fun. On the table were a series of twenty-five old pictures, each one representing a member of our staff. It was up to each of us to guess who the person was just from the hints on the picture. For instance, for Miss McFarland they had an advertisement from some travel agency urging people to travel to "Far Lands." For me they had a picture of Little Red Riding Hood which read, "Fairy Tales came true for her in Germany."

The following day a group from our staff went on a guided tour through five of Cairo's mosques. At each one we had to put canvas slippers on over our own shoes—slippers so big that we looked like circus clowns. The largest mosque was the Mohammed Ali Mosque situated atop the Citadel.

While there we were invited to form a circle, sit on the floor, and listen to a brief summary of Islamic theology, followed by a extensive description of the interior of this magnificent mosque. Learning more about the Islamic faith helped me better understand the religious background of most of my students. Knowing that Islam emphasized good works as a basis for salvation, also helped me realize why it was so hard to distinguish Moslem students

from Christian students. Both were loving, giving, and anxious to do acts of kindness toward us. For the Christians it was *because* of their saving faith in Christ; for the Moslem it was, not only from a deep love and respect for us as teachers, but *for* their hope of salvation. At death their good works would be weighed against their bad deeds and hopefully the good would outweigh the bad. How grateful we should be as Christians, knowing that our salvation is by grace alone, and not on the basis of good works!

I arrived back at school just in time for Donna Lee and me to leave with Odette, one of our boarding students, for a visit to her uncle's home to celebrate her birthday. Her uncle is a Catholic priest, living just outside of Cairo. He is trying to begin a Boys' Town of Egypt, just like the one begun by Father Flanagan in Nebraska. At present he has only 27 boys, but is hoping to increase the facilities in the future in order to accommodate more boys. That evening several of us went to the Russian Exhibition of Folk Dances at the Opera House. It was superb! The music was Russian of course and included pieces by Tchaikovsky. The costumes and dancing were exceptional. The program which began at 9:30 p.m. lasted until after midnight, but it was well worth it. This is the usual timing for events in Cairo. I guess everyone can sleep in the next morning!

Trips to the Musky (a smaller part of the larger bazaar) were always fun. One particular day my piano student and friend, Suzie Greiss and her parents took me on an extensive "buying" trip! Mrs. Greiss was full of ideas of what my trousseau should contain, but unfortunately my purse didn't quite meet the challenge! Suzie picked out a lovely bracelet and ring set which her father bought for her. To my surprise he bought me a pair of silver earrings. He and Mrs. Greiss helped me pick out some silver and pink galabia material to be made into an elegant robe. Our next stop was the copper shop where I picked up a Turkish coffee service. The plate was very unique—copper with inlaid silver in a typical Egyptian design with Carl and my names in the center in Arabic. This stop was followed by a visit to the gold market. Mr. Greiss has a friend who deals in gold and through him I was able to purchase two solid gold bracelets. I had noticed that many women in Egypt wore several narrow gold bracelets on their wrists, representing their dowry, or bride price. The bracelets I purchased will remain on my wrists for life. Right now, the price of gold in Egypt is only $30 an ounce. Needless to say, it is much more expensive in the States.

Our day trip concluded with lunch at the Greiss' home, a thirteen-room mansion on Ramses street. Following lunch, Suzie and I performed a mini-concert for the family in the French Room. This reminded me of the first time I came to Suzie's house. The doorman told me that she was waiting for me in the Green Room, wherever that was! I later learned that every room had a name.

Many Sundays were spent, first with services at Ezbekieh Church where I sang in the choir, followed by trips to sporting clubs or students' homes for lunch. Lunches were usually so long that they ran into tea-time, but of course at a different venue. Other outings included concerts like one particular piano recital I remember at the Opera House. Sitting in a box and peering down at the pianist through opera glasses was a new experience for me. Later, I was delighted to learn from Suzie that this box had been reserved by their family for the entire opera/concert season. This concert was a very special one, given by George Themeli, a blind, Greek classical pianist. It was given as a benefit for the people of Port Said. He was outstanding. It was amazing how a person with such a handicap could be such a marvelous pianist. He played works by Beethoven, Mozart, Schubert, Schumann and Chopin and was called back many times for encores.

Special trips extended into March. The weather was delightful; however, the flies were in abundance! Picnics were few and far between. We did, however, have one. One Friday, one of our students and her whole family picked up Donna Lee and me for a trip to Fayoum, a city 100 kilometers southwest of Cairo, located on Lac Karon. It was Donna Lee's birthday and I was the only one who was aware of that. The funny part was that the last time we were with this group it had been my birthday. You can imagine their utter astonishment when right after lunch I pulled a large birthday cake out of a basket and began to sing happy birthday to Donna Lee! After quickly gobbling up the delicious cake, we all went for a sail on the lake. Egyptian "feluccas" are similar to our sail boats, but not equipped to navigate without adequate wind.

Thus, we found ourselves paddling back to shore! Fishermen nearby waved and gave us knowing smiles.

A sad event for Mike and me was the departure of Joy and Anis who were leaving for the States. It took less than twenty-four hours for them to receive government permission to leave and then actually depart. We waved good-bye to them at the airport and Mike and I began our sad journey back to Maadi without them. The air was cool as we drove along the Nile. There amid the trees, dark shadows were creeping up and in the stillness of the twilight I thought back to the happy hours we had spent with Joy and Anis. Already I had begun to sense their absence. I felt a bit uneasy. Where did we go from here? Mike and I were now alone. I glanced across the seat at Mike. He smiled back reassuringly.

"We're going to miss them," he remarked sadly.

"I just can't believe they've left. After having to wait so many weeks for a visa, I had begun to wonder if they would ever get permission to leave."

"It's sometimes very difficult. Lots of red tape involved," Mike replied.

"Such as...?" I asked.

"Such as knowing the right people for one thing. And then, a little bit of ready cash here and there. With Moslems it isn't too difficult, but with Christians it's an entirely different story. Sometimes the government does their utmost to keep Christians from leaving."

"But it seemed as if everything went so fast there toward the end," I remarked.

"True, but it was just the result of many months of serious effort on the part of many individuals."

"Have you thought seriously about your plans for next year?" I asked.

"Anis mentioned to me just before he left about the possibility of his obtaining a contract for me to join him at Little Company of Mary Hospital in Evergreen Park, Illinois, south of Chicago, where he will be working. If he can arrange it, I will be leaving here by the first part of next year."

"How did he happen to choose Little Company of Mary?"

"It's right near Joy's folks who live near 95th Street and Western Avenue. Is that close to Riverside?"

"It is a little more than ten miles away. Riverside is a suburb on the west side of Chicago and Evergreen Park is on the south side."

"Would you mind if I lived only a short distance from your home?" Mike cautiously asked.

"Mind? Of course not!"

"I just thought that under the circumstances it might be a bit awkward."

"Under what circumstances?"

"Well, you'd be married by then and I..." He paused as if lost for words.

How had he found out that I was engaged?

"And you what?" I cautiously asked.

"Carolyn, maybe I shouldn't say this, but I think you know already how I feel about you. If you weren't already engaged to someone else, I would ask you to marry me."

I was stunned. For a moment I could say nothing. For all these many weeks during which I had felt myself being drawn closer and closer to Mike, I had failed to consider whether or not Mike shared my feelings or that he might have even deeper feelings toward me than I toward him. How was I to respond?

Tenderly he drew me into his arms and kissed me. Feelings that I never knew I had, or denied having, surfaced and with it a serious change in our relationship. No longer could we continue our relationship on a mere friendship basis. Joy and Anis were gone and now we were alone. Was this the beginning or the end? I sighed deeply and shut my eyes, enjoying at least for the moment the comforting feeling of just being loved.

We drove in silence for a long while. I glanced at the clock. It was past eleven.

"Why don't we stop for a few minutes and just sit and talk?" I suggested.

"We can't," Mike replied uneasily.

"Oh? Why not?"

"Well, to begin with it wouldn't be safe to park here along the corniche and even if it were, the police wouldn't allow it."

"What do you mean 'wouldn't allow it'?"

"It's against the law to park anywhere in Egypt when there is just one couple—unless, of course, you can prove that you are married. Even then they frown upon that as they feel it doesn't set a very good example."

"Oh, great! Where, then, does a couple go to talk without a lot of confusion and red tape?"

"There just isn't any place. You see here in Egypt couples seldom go out alone which is why we were usually with Joy and Anis. Couples are either accompanied by a chaperone or another couple."

"In other words, when you go somewhere to 'talk' they make sure that is all you do!"

"That's not necessarily 'all' you do but it's all you do in public."

"I'll remember that," I said jokingly.

Another kiss followed. I wondered how Mike could drive and kiss at the same time. Must take practice! I personally had no experience driving, little experience kissing and certainly no experience doing both at the same time!

Mike looked at me with a questioning expression. "You are engaged, aren't you?"

"Yes, but I am at this moment very unsure of my feelings. I was so very sure when Carl and I became engaged that this was 'it', but now I'm not so sure."

"What made you change your mind?"

"Meeting you, going out with you, and now this. It's made me feel rather confused inside."

"You don't have to make any decisions right now. After all, you have several more months before school ends. We can continue to go out together, that is, if you want to."

"You know I do. It's just that it doesn't seem quite fair. If Carl were here it would be different. I could date you both and then make a decision."

"I'm glad he's not here. I'm just selfish enough to want you all to myself."

"You flatter me."

"No, I really mean it. I'd like to spend every possible moment with you."

"Well, you know that I *do* have a job! It involves so much more than just teaching. I'm constantly besieged with invitations from students to go to the cinema, to lunch at Groppi's and to so many teas that I wonder sometimes how I manage to not gain weight. It must be those three flights of stairs to my room!"

"The girls really love the American teachers. They are very special to all of us."

"It is actually more than that. The Egyptian teachers have family obligations and do not have time to socialize with their students as much as we Americans do. But I agree, our spending time with our girls means a lot to them and to us."

"It means a lot to me, too. After all, you are entitled to have some free time."

"That's what I keep telling myself, but as the days go by, I seem to have less and less. It is very difficult to accept all the many invitations I receive."

"I have the perfect solution. Just spend all your free time with me!" We both laughed.

Within a few short moments we were pulling up in front of the College. Even before we had a chance to say "goodbye", Hassan, the bawab, was opening the car door. Hurriedly Mike pressed my fingers to his lips and whispered a tender goodnight before relinquishing me to Hassan. I watched his car disappear in the distance and a shiver crept across my shoulders. What had I gotten myself into? Hassan, alert to my every movement, was quick to remark, "Are you cold, Miss?"

Startled for a moment, I quickly regained my composure and turning toward the gate remarked quietly, "It's nothing, Hassan. Shall we go in now?"

The days that followed left me little time to think of Mike, or even Carl for that matter. Lesson plans were due, exams needed to be written, and in the midst of all the schoolwork, Donna Lee decided that I needed a cooking lesson! Her target was Mr. Miller, one of our missionaries who was living alone at the moment in Maadi, his wife still in Switzerland with some of the other missionaries who had yet to return to Egypt. Donna Lee bought and prepared most of the meal. Some lesson! I got to peel the potatoes, slice the tomatoes and take the tips off the strawberries. Just like at home! No wonder I did not know how to prepare a full meal! Poor Carl!

It is now April 1st, April Fool's Day in the States. I looked out my window at all the sunshine and thought about all the snow that probably was still on the ground both in the States and in Germany. Having everyday here in Egypt filled with sunshine has been a unique experience for me. The people, too, bring sunshine into my life as they enjoy, along with me, the plans for my wedding. Many wish they could come to Germany this summer and attend my wedding in person. In the meantime, I am sharing with them my wardrobe plans. I wish I could sew at least one dress for my honeymoon, but unfortunately, I do not have either a sewing machine nor the time. There is, however one American teacher who has a machine and is an excellent seamstress. I am sure that, if I asked, she would agree to help me. We can always take a trip to the Musky and purchase wonderful cotton, an Egyptian specialty. Besides, trips to the Musky are great fun; that is, unless you get lost in its winding aisles and persistent merchants. It is a challenge to bargain with them. It helps to always be accompanied by an Egyptian who can bargain for you in Arabic and get the very best prices.

Right now, my Moslem students are fasting during Ramadan (from sunup till sunset); therefore, by order of the government, we must dismiss school each day at 2 p.m. In order to accommodate this early dismissal time, we have shortened each class period by five minutes, with chapel lasting for thirty minutes and recess for twenty. After class each day I plan to work with the Christian students on a play for Easter. This will be more fun than work!

This week I experienced my first sandstorm. Unfortunately, it happened at night. I was up most of the night opening and closing windows. It really didn't matter. The sand came in with windows closed or opened and either way the windows and doors rattled. Sleep was impossible. The next day one of my classes was scheduled to enjoy a trip to the pyramids; however, the gusts of sand were so invasive that we could not even leave our bus! We turned around and visited the Fish Gardens of Zamalek instead. Zamalek is a small community on the island of Gezira, located in Cairo, between the two branches of the Nile. The fish aquariums are inside giant rock formations and are surrounded by picturesque flower gardens. We were having such a great time that it was hard to convince my students that it was time to return to the college.

That afternoon I had an audition with three Italian music professors at the home of Madame Fenniger de Rogatis. She had asked them to hear me play my sonata before I performed it for the Cairo Musical Society on Saturday night. I was very nervous at the audition—actually more nervous than I was later on when I played it the following night for the Society. In the middle of that performance, the piano began to shake, and I realized it was not my nervous imagination but rather an earthquake! Those around me tapped me on the shoulder, interrupted my playing, and ushered me down the stairs and out of the building to safety! I never did return to finish my piece!

One particular Saturday during recess, we had the annual staff-student basketball game. The student team consisted of the IV Secondary B championship team. You can obviously guess which team won! The consolation was that our staff team only lost by four points: 13-9, yours truly making the nine points for the staff.

One very unique experience I enjoyed was making peanut butter. Having been raised on peanut butter and jelly sandwiches for lunch every day as I was growing up, I really missed not having peanut butter readily available in Egypt. So once again I was up to the roof to shell the peanuts and watch as the wind carried the shells and skins away. As before I took my completed project downstairs where I watched one of the cooks grind away as I dropped in the peanuts. More peanut butter, homemade, but rather dry!

A new trip for me came a few days later when students from III Secondary B invited me for a day of relaxation in Zefta, a small town located some 60 kilometers from Cairo. We were entertained there in the home of a relative of one of the students whose mansion overlooked the Nile. Later in the day we walked out to the barrages (dams built across the Nile to control the water flow) and had our lunch in a beautiful garden overlooking the river. I became officially "engaged" in a mock ceremony which the girls did in my honor according to an ancient custom. They did their traditional dances and sang their ceremonial songs. It was great fun!

I am eagerly looking forward to a trip to Luxor over Easter vacation. I will be chaperoning a group of my students on a five-day excursion to not only Luxor but Aswan as well. The trip will cost $33 and will include everything: transportation, hotel, food and sightseeing. I can hardly wait!

As the month of April progressed, so did my relationship with Mike. We managed to spend many evenings together, dining at the Oberge, dancing on the rooftop restaurant of the Semiramis Hotel, and watching sunsets at Mena House. I was troubled. I knew I was engaged, but there were times I just chose to forget. I was young and having too much fun with Mike. But was this fair to Mike? Was I giving him a mixed message? Why was I continuing in this relationship when I knew how he felt about me? Our conversations were becoming serious.

"Have you thought at all about my wanting to marry you?" he cautiously asked one evening.

"Yes, of course," I replied. "I am just so confused."

"Why?"

"I thought that Carl was the one that God had picked out for me and everything seemed perfect."

"And then what happened?"

"I met you."

"And?"

"Now I'm just not sure. Other American women who are married to Egyptians have shared with me that blending lives and cultures has been difficult."

"In what way?"

"Well, for one thing American women often work outside the home, perhaps until they begin having a family. After that they usually stay at home, at least for a while. It appears to be different here. Wives don't work and are kept very busy at home. They have servants to manage and nannies to supervise. I understand that the usual practice is that each child has his or her own nanny. I'm not sure I would like that."

"Why not?"

"Because I would like to raise my own children, spend significant time with them, be a full-time mom."

"But how could you do that and take care of your husband, entertain your friends, enjoy socializing at the Sporting Clubs?"

"And have sex three times a day?" I joked.

"Party-pooper!"

"No, I'm serious. That is exactly what these women claim."

"Well, I guess I would have to adjust my schedule so I could come home for lunch every day!" Mike countered.

We laughed and dropped the subject. We were treading in dangerous water. My confusion and uneasiness were growing. Fortunately, we were not able to spend much time alone. Mike had introduced me to a couple, a Naval attache and his wife, who were only too happy to socialize with us, often on a weekly basis. A great bonus for me in this relationship was free peanut butter from the U.S Military Commissary, shipped in from Wheelus Air Base in Libya. It was way better than the dry stuff I helped make.

At the same time these events were occurring, I was busily planning my wedding. I was very excited about the sketches my mother was sending me of my wedding dress. Suzie delivered my finished bathrobe yesterday and it was gorgeous. Can you imagine yards and yards of light blue brocade sparkling with pink and silver threads and lined with pink satin? I am counting on the fact that both my wedding dress and the rest of my wedding wardrobe will fit come August. I managed to lose four pounds last week. Five more to go and I will be back to my normal weight. It is so easy to gain weight here as the food is not only delicious, but also fattening! Yes, I truly love life here in Egypt, but I continually ask myself, is Mike a significant part of that? I so enjoy planning my wedding, but am I sure who the groom should be? I am very troubled. How can I decide? Lord help me!

Weekly trips to various sites continued. Especially memorable was a visit to the ruins of ancient Memphis and Sakkara. These ruins date back to the 3rd Dynasty (2780 to 2719 B.C.). The Step Pyramid of Djoser, a huge statue of Ramses II, and an alabaster sphinx are probably the most important sites there; however, we were privileged to also visit the Serapeum, which is an underground gallery hewn out of solid rock with tomb chambers opening on each side, each one containing the coffin of a sacred bull. There are twenty-four in all. Near the Step Pyramid we visited the tombs of King Ti and Ptahhotep, the walls of which were covered with ancient Egyptian paintings. It was a very hot day and all of us returned with sunburns. It was only 96 degrees, which, after yesterday's high of 108 degrees, should have seemed cool!

Palm Sunday was a special day here in Cairo. After a sunrise service at the College, I attended a worship service at a nearby Coptic Orthodox Church with one of my students. Small children carried palm branches to begin the service, much like here in the States. After a delicious dinner at the home of one of my students, Zizette Farid, we spent the afternoon making crosses and donkeys out of palm branches. When they dry, they will be kept as special reminders of this day.

A week later it was time to perform the Easter play that my students and I had been diligently preparing. This was such an exceptional group of girls. They put their hearts and souls into making this play a blessing to those who heard it. I saw several people with tears in their eyes. The play was the story of a girl, who, because of a broken leg, had been unable to attend the Easter church service. Instead, the choir girls came to visit her and as they sat around her, singing some of their Easter music, the girl with the broken leg began to tell the Easter story. Another girl who had the leading role in the play, not only had an effective speaking voice, but also a very lovely singing voice. Her rendition of *"The Stranger of Galilee"* was very moving. I was so very proud of all my girls.

As the month of April came to an end, so did Ramadan. Every Moslem student was now in a very festive mood, preparing to celebrate the feast of Eid al-Fitr, signaling that Ramadan was over. Since it was a holiday, I had the day off and spent it with my American friend, Lorraine, who is helping me sew my going-away dress. I am so delighted to have the opportunity to make my own dress! I still will have a dressmaker do my coat. I am excitedly counting the days till my August 2 wedding! I am at least momentarily excited—probably until the next time I see Mike! I am not only feeling confused, but also very guilty. Is it too late to make a choice? And if not, which one will I choose? They are both so very different. Carl is much like me in many ways, especially with regard to music. We both love to travel and enjoy learning new languages. He literally swept me off my feet in the short period of time I was in Birkenfeld. Mike, on the other hand, is calm, elegant, professionally secure, and a solid presence through each and every situation we encounter. He puts no pressure on me to make a decision, although I know that he truly loves me and hopes that I will change my mind and at least stay in Egypt for a while. Leaving Egypt will be hard, not only because of Mike, but because of my great love for the country and its people. I have continued to feel, despite the circumstances, God's firm call on my life here. Will that change? I wish I knew. What about Ken in the United States? He is expecting me to return. Must I make a choice now? Most importantly, what about God's call on my life? Could I still be involved in significant ministry if I were to marry Mike and remain in Egypt? Could I even continue to teach? Not having a future ministry was unthinkable and probably would become the deciding point when faced to make a choice. How could I abandon God's plan for my life?

The following week was spent accompanying my secondary school seniors on our long-anticipated trip to Upper Egypt. We left Cairo on the night train, arriving in Aswan the next morning at noon. Although our tickets were not first class, at least they were not with the animals!

After lunch at the hotel, we left for our first excursion by a felucca to Elephantine Island, named that because the island's rock formations resemble elephants. Our next stop was Kitchener's Island, named after England's Lord Kitchener. This island is less than one kilometer long and just ½ a kilometer wide. The beautiful Aswan Botanical Garden is located there. It is reported that any vegetable, except broccoli, can be grown there. Sailing back to the mainland we enjoyed one of those marvelous Nile sunsets. It reminded me of the popular saying that "He who drinks of the waters of the Nile will surely return to drink again," if only to view the sunsets. Hopefully, no one takes the part about "drinking the waters of the Nile" seriously!!

Our next stop was to the alabaster granite quarry, where we were able to purchase vases whose sides are translucent, allowing light to shine through. These pink vases reminded me of the Apostle Paul's words in II Corinthians 4:7, *"We have this treasure in jars of clay, to show that the surpassing power belongs to God and not to ourselves."* Just like light shining through the small cracks in these vases, so also does God's light shine through the cracks and weaknesses of our lives as we witness for Him.

Our final stop for the day was at the Aswan Dam. Pictures were not allowed as this is considered a strategic military site.

Following our visit to Aswan we made our way down the Nile to the ancient city of Luxor. Early the next morning we crossed the Nile by felucca and proceeded by car to Thebes, the city of the dead. The ancient tombs and temples of the pharaohs were the greatest attraction in the Valley of the Kings. We were taken into several of the tombs and were awestruck at the task the early excavators must have had as they explored these ancient relics. We especially enjoyed seeing the tomb of King Tut; however, most of the valuable relics from that tomb were housed in the Egyptian Museum in Cairo.

Sunday was Eastern Easter, a week later than Western Easter. We had the privilege of attending a Coptic Evangelical Church in Luxor and although the service was in Arabic, Edna Morrison, one of our career missionaries, sat beside me and explained much of the service. After the service we left by horse and carriage to visit the Temple of Karnak, located just outside Luxor, across the Nile. It is very difficult to adequately describe all the historical relics enclosed within these temple walls. According to my notes, this temple dates from around 2055 B.C. to around 100 A.D. and is dedicated to gods Amun, Mut and Khonsu. It is the largest religious building ever constructed, covering about 200 acres and was a place of pilgrimage for nearly 2000 years. Karnak was known as a very sacred place. The great temple at the heart of Karnak is so big that St. Peter's, Milan, and Notre Dame Cathedrals could all fit within its walls. The Hypostyle hall is 54,000 square feet, features 134 columns, and is still the largest room of any religious building in the world. Our next stop was at Luxor Temple, begun by Amenhotep II around 1392 BC and continued by Tutankhamun (1336-27 BC) and Horemheb (1323-1295 BC) and finally added on to by Rameses II (1279-13 BC). It is close to the Nile and laid out parallel to the riverbank. This temple originally contained several statues of Rameses, the largest of which now stands in front of the railroad station in Cairo. All this information I gleaned from a knowledgeable guide and carefully written notes.

We left Luxor later that day, again by train, and arrived back in Cairo Monday about noon. It had been a delightful, but exhausting trip.

May brought visitors from Beyruth, Germany. Mike offered, along with me, to escort the group for visits to the Citadel, Mohammed Ali's Palace, a lunch at Groppi's, and a shopping trip to the Musky, my favorite place to take visitors! In the evening we shared a traditional Egyptian meal at a local restaurant followed by a visit to the opera house to see an Arabic operetta, featuring the life and customs of the fellaheen (peasants). The next day Mike took us to the Gezira Sporting Club for lunch. This club consists of three swimming pools, a racetrack, stables, an 18-hole golf course, a miniature golf course, a cricket course, volleyball, croquet, badminton and thirty tennis courts.

Membership is very limited and expensive! A visit to the Barrages' Tea Gardens completed our afternoon. That evening Mike took us to the Semiramis Hotel for the usual roof-top dining and dancing. At the time this hotel was built in 1906, it was considered the most luxurious hotel in all of Egypt. It faces the Nile and is located in the Kasr al-Dubara district of Cairo, only a couple of blocks from the Kasr al-Dubara Coptic Evangelical Church where my dear friend, Rev. Menes, years later became senior pastor. That church provided instant translation for the worship services which made it the perfect place to bring visitors. Incidentally, the word for "pastor" in Arabic is "Assis". After I became ordained, Rev. Menes began calling me "Assisa". Ministers in Egypt are viewed with great respect and are never called by their first names, even in private. My special relationship with him has lasted for many years.

Menes and I

As the days passed, my relationship with Mike kept surfacing. Problems kept mounting. What was I going to do? I should have said "no" to his first invitation. I was now much too involved, emotionally and socially. I continued to be very troubled. Did I truly love him or only the fun that we had together? I continued to be very confused and unable to make a decision.

While juggling my schedule to include my teaching, piano and social life, I continued to make wedding plans. The date, August 2, was finally set and the site for the reception confirmed. Detailed plans had been shared with my parents who, of course, had no idea about my growing relationship with Mike. I'm sure they would not have approved. Neither would the Mission. Continual tips to the boab kept him silent!

In spite of this troubling situation, I continued to work on my "going-away" dress. I bought lovely brocade material at the Bazaar and my friend, Lorraine, helped me complete the outfit. I was able to get away for an overnight and relax at her house. We even splurged and had a late dinner on Friday evening at the Abdeen Palace, one of the former residences of King Farouk, now used mainly as a place for government business. It also housed an upscale restaurant, famous for their outstanding food. Lorraine also continued to share with me about her life, married to an Egyptian Moslem. She was very unhappy. She also did not know about Mike. This only added to my confusion, except of course, for the fact that Mike was a Christian, not a Moslem. Yet, an Egyptian male is still a male! Could I ever adjust to life as a wife in Egypt? Not if I listened to Lorraine!

Once a week I had "boarders' duty" when I helped the students with homework for an hour and then supervised bedtime. One evening, I was relieved of my boarders' duty at 9:15. Mike picked me up and we enjoyed dinner at the home of our friends from the Embassy. Dinner in Egypt is always much later than in the States. Since our friends got all their meat, as well as peanut butter, directly from the commissary in Libya, we had good old American fried chicken with apple pie and ice cream! Although they lived in Maadi, where there was an outdoor market, they found that it was not very appealing to search for meat there. Meat is hung in plain view, sometimes with cattle and sheep heads included! It needs to be purchased daily or it obviously spoils.

I was privileged one Sunday morning to attend Catholic mass with Odette, one of our boarding students. It was the First Communion for eight little girls, and I was really amazed at how much of the French-speaking service I understood. In Egypt, we did not have Protestant-Catholic issues. Most of our Christian students at the school were Roman Catholic, Greek Orthodox, Armenian Orthodox, or Coptic Orthodox, with a small minority being Coptic Evangelical, a break-off from the Coptic Orthodox Church. This denomination was begun in 1854 by the United Presbyterian Church of North American. The American College for Girls was part of that denomination. Originally called the Synod of the Nile, it became officially independent of the Presbyterian Church USA in 1958.

Later that day, I enjoyed a noon meal with Mike at the Heliopolis Sporting Club, a club similar to the one in Gezira. Here again, only the very wealthy were members. Mike had membership in both. This was followed by a visit to the Zamalek Shooting Club for an afternoon of pigeon shooting. We were only observing, of course, but it was still fun. Most of the men were placing small bets on the contestants just for fun, as gambling is forbidden in Egypt.

Dinners with Mike and our Embassy friends continued on a regular basis. One special evening was spent in a restaurant located in a large tent in Sahara City. Sitting on camel saddles and eating on small, round tables was a new experience for me. I later purchased a similar table at the bazaar, consisting of a round brass tray perched on mahogany legs, inlaid with ivory and pearl. After dinner Mike drove me to Maadi where I stayed overnight at our friends' home. It is so quiet in Maadi that it is often hard to fall asleep. I am so used to sleeping in Cairo where noise goes on all night!

Early one morning, two of our fellow missionaries, Ken Bailey and Ken Nowlan, picked me up and we drove to the American University of Cairo where they were singing a duet for a Christian fellowship group and I was playing the piano. It was the first accompanying that I had done since coming to Egypt. Following this, we hopped on a bus and rode out to Maadi where our Christian Endeavor group was having their outing on the Ibis, the Mission's houseboat. We rode English bikes in the afternoon, something I had not done in a long time. Later we stopped to attend a bazaar, held at the College, to raise money for the children living in the garbage dump. Over 100 lbs. (about $300) were raised. Most of Cairo's population live well below the poverty level. CEOSS (the Coptic Evangelical Organization for Social Services) has an extensive ministry among the Zabbaleen, the garbage collectors of Cairo, who live among the garbage they collect and recycle. This ministry dates back to the early 1940s.

Later that same evening Mike and I, along with our friends, had dinner at the Oberge and this time had our picture taken. Both of us looked very serious.

Was I truly happy? More importantly, where was God in all this? I had felt His strong call on my life coming to Egypt in the first place. It was supposed to be for three years. Why was I cutting it short? Had God's original call changed, or had I allowed personal circumstances to alter that call? These were all puzzling and disturbing questions. What answers would immerge? Would I make the right choice? Did I really have to choose? Why not just stay in Egypt, complete my three years and then decide? What were our thoughts as we enjoyed yet another dinner at the Oberge? It was easy to get lost in the moment. The entertainment that night was superb—four Spanish dancers who gave a series of dances, native to their country. This, as always at the Club, was followed by a traditional Egyptian belly dancer. It was quite a lengthy program, making my return to the College very late, or rather, very early the next morning!

Dates with Mike continued, especially at the Semiramis Hotel. Dancing under the stars was a unique experience for me since I had not danced in many years and, in fact, was not supposed to be doing so while in Egypt. As I already stated, I was not supposed to be dating Egyptian men period! I was spreading my wings! No, actually, I was being disobedient!

As the school year drew to a close, one event was very special for me: two of my students would be performing in our spring piano recital. Suzie would be playing the first movement of Schumann's A minor concerto; the other student whose name I can't remember, Capriccio Brilliant by Mendelssohn.

I would be playing the second piano part for both. The concert was a great success. Both students did an excellent job and received many compliments.

Relaxing in the suburb of Maadi and enjoying some American-made apple pie had become a routine pastime. Maadi is so very different from Cairo. It is an international community with an American School and a community church. Many of the women there take Arabic classes to try to keep up with the local culture, especially when going to the market. I think if I were to live permanently in the Cairo area I would not choose to live there. I would prefer to live near my Egyptian friends. Mike has a house in Maadi, but also an apartment in the suburb of Zamalek. I can only visit there when others are present-never alone.

The temperature right now is between 105-110 degrees. This is considered cool for this time of year. One doesn't really feel the heat here as much as in the States because it is so dry. Also, school is usually over by this time of the year, but had to be extended because of the evacuation. Afternoon naps are essential. They became a habit for me, one which lasted long after I returned to the States.

It is June and the hot weather continues! A quick trip to Alex and the Mediterranean Sea was a great way to escape very hot Cairo. Swimming in the cool Sea is always lots of fun. In addition, we rode surfboards out to a small island where we did some diving and scampering among the underwater rock formations. Our hostess for the day, the sister of one of my students, later cooked us a dinner of mostly Syrian dishes.

It is now exam time for my students. Government exams are extremely important, especially for those girls who wish to go on to the university. Post-secondary education is free, but entrance is by examination only. Those who fail the exams can attend the American University in Cairo, but tuition there is too expensive for many families. The weather is horribly hot, the flies are awful, and the noise outside my classroom is deafening.

Following exam week comes graduation. Suzie's parents are having a formal graduation party for her at their very large home on Sharia Ramses. This will be followed by a visit to Ismailia, a small village 100 miles away, where their large plantation is located, eventually returning to Cairo for Suzie's graduation.

As my date to leave Egypt draws near, I feel a certain measure of sadness in leaving Egypt, mingled with happiness at the thought of returning to Germany and Carl. I don't think I ever fully realized just how homesick I was for the States until last Friday at the College commencement when I was asked to play the Star-Spangled Banner before an audience of 200 as our

U.S. Ambassador led us in tributes to our government and to Egypt. Tears freely flowed. For many of us it takes a trip away from the United States and from the liberty we enjoy there to fully appreciate just how great we have it back home. Suzie was selected to read the Arabic essay she wrote, which was a great honor for her. An additional event on this week-end's schedule was a reception at Suzie's, honoring ten women from the farms of the U.S. who were on their way to a conference in Ceylon. I wonder how impressed they were with the farms or the elegance of Egyptian society!

Later in the week, a party was held for those who were graduating from our two-year college-level program and preparing to finish their education elsewhere. Suzie will be attending Chatham College in Pittsburgh. Also honored on this occasion were all the brides-to-be, including me. This special ceremony included traditional bridal songs and dances in Arabic. I spent the night at Suzie's where we practiced the piano for two hours in preparation for performing at the evening reception the Greisses were giving to honor a number of Cairo's most noteworthy musicians.

The time came for me to make a decision: Carl or Mike. Which would it be? I'm not sure I knew at the time, nor certainly did not know later, why I chose Carl. Perhaps it was in deference to my parents and the sacrifice it would be to them to lose their only child to a permanent life in Egypt. It certainly was not lack of love for life in Egypt on my part.

As I prepared to leave Egypt and embark on a whole new life married to Carl, I also thought of Ken, my former boyfriend, who was still finishing his education at Baylor University. I think the secret of what Ken and I felt for each other lay in his mother's statement that you never realize how much someone means to you until you lose that person. There were times when I felt I loved Ken very much, but at those times he never seemed to need nor want my love. I guess maybe that's why it was so easy to turn to Carl because in him I found a person who would accept the love I so badly had wanted to give to Ken. It probably would not have been possible to have just been pals for life. It's funny though. We used to plan weddings, homes and families together, always "when we get married" meaning to someone else on the outside, but down deep inside possibly thinking of each other. We both knew this even before I left, but we were both young and had many tasks to complete before thinking of marriage and yet up until the day I left for Egypt I had hoped Ken would break down and tell me how he really felt about me. I don't think he knew, really, until I left and fell in love with someone else. He still had to finish his education. Perhaps someday I will be able to talk to him and make him understand how very special our relationship was even though it did not end in marriage.

Carl and I took as our life verse Romans 8:28, *"We know that in every-thing God works for good with those who love him, who are called according to his purpose."* I'm sure God had a purpose in bringing Ken into my life, especially since it was through his influence that I made my initial commitment to Christ. I'm equally sure that He now has reasons for bringing Carl into my life as the person with whom He wants me to share the rest of my life. But why did Mike come into my life? What purpose did that serve? What important lessons did I learn from that experience?

Saying goodbye to Mike was very difficult. How could I adequately explain to Mike just why I had made the decision to marry Carl? I'm not sure I even knew. Did I not love both of them? Yes, in some ways I did. Perhaps I should not have married either one of them at that time. And, of course, there was also Ken. At that time, I felt that God had a big part in helping me come to the decision to honor my engagement and marry Carl. I remembered all those things I had previously written concerning God's leading in my relationship with Carl and acted accordingly. It was still difficult and painful for Mike to accept. He insisted on having a farewell party for me at Farouk's former palace in Alex before I left. Many of his friends attended, including actor Omar Sharif. At that time Omar Sharif's wife was the popular movie star, not he. Later on, I was to learn of Omar's popularity in the States and enjoy his many films.

The producer seated beside me at dinner that night had studied at the Pasadena Playhouse in California and had just returned from a business trip to the States. He was hoping that as a result of this trip, several Egyptian films could be translated into English and shown in the States. Between chats with several of the guests, I gazed around at the lovely palace. You really needed be here to fully appreciate its grandeur. King Farouk had his own seaport here as well as his own airport. The palace grounds covered several acres, some of which were densely wooded. He liked to hunt. Since Farouk was no longer in Egypt, his various palaces were now used exclusively for private gatherings or hotels. My farewell festivities were held under a cloud of sadness as the realization of my departure loomed overhead. Was I making the right decision? Only time would tell.

Sadly, as Mike drove me to the dock, I was not even able to have a moment alone with him, much less kiss him goodbye. I took one last look into his eyes and realized the sadness he was experiencing. I was sad, also, not just because I was leaving Mike, but especially since I was leaving Egypt.

I wrote a letter to my parents from the deck of the "Achilleus", the ship that would take me back to Europe and Carl. The ship was quite nice and very comfortable. Our cabin for four was small but at least I had a bed and not a chain hammock like on my first trip across the Mediterranean! The ship was "open port" which meant that you were free to meander through all the classes and facilities, except of course, the sleeping and dining quarters. My three cabinmates, all German teachers from Cairo, spoke only German—a good opportunity for me to begin to learn German! My tablemates all spoke French which meant I at least could converse at meals.

Having these experiences this year helped me really understand the true meaning of happiness. Happiness is not what you have, but rather what you are. It is a certain feeling inside which makes life worth living. To many Egyptians, money is very important, especially when considering marriage. To many of them, love is secondary and hopefully will follow, not necessarily precede, marriage. Children, as I mentioned earlier, are often raised by nannies. Wealthy homes have many servants: gardeners, cooks, housekeepers, drivers, etc. Just grocery shopping is a full day's job since Egypt has no supermarkets. The refrigerators are so small that daily trips to the market must be made for perishable items. Life is thus very different in Egypt from what my life had been like in the States, yet in many ways it was a welcome change. I learned to love their more relaxed life style and the strong affirmation I always felt from my students and friends. Would I ever return? What had God planned for my future? Would it be continued ministry, if not in Egypt, in Germany? In the States? I would soon learn to live with unanswered questions.

Chapter Five:
A Journey through Marriage

The days following my return to Birkenfeld, Germany were filled with preparations for both our wedding and the move into our new apartment. Fortunately, our apartment was at least partially furnished which made our move a bit easier. My wedding dress, which my mother had so lovingly made, arrived even before I did. I was amazed at all the delicate mixture of pearls, lace, and sequins which adorned the dress. It must have taken hundreds of hours to complete. I only wish mom and dad could have been there to see me walk down the aisle in that gorgeous dress!

Donna Lee arrived a few days before the wedding and moved into the apartment with me. We talked well into the early morning hours, as we had much catching up to do. I knew I would really miss her!

August 1st was our first "marriage". Carl and I went to the courthouse and were legally married by the Justice of the Peace, a requirement throughout Germany. He, of course, did not move in with me that night, as we did not consider ourselves married in the eyes of God. That night we held our rehearsal at the church, followed by a dinner at the Club.

The day of our wedding dawned bright and clear. It was also unusually hot! The church looked lovely with a background of candles and flowers. Willy and Jerri were adorable as they led the procession down the aisle. Joanne and Donna Lee followed. Then came the big moment when I entered on the arm of Cousin Jim. Carl was waiting at the altar, all smiles. It was truly a very special moment, that is, until Willy began playing with the fringe on the altar cloth! The candelabra slowing began to move toward the edge of the altar! Fortunately, Joanne (his mom), was right there to gently "discourage" him and the service went on as planned. I was told later that I said, "I thee bed" instead of "I thee wed"!

About 100 guests gathered at the Oderberger Hotel for a reception "feast" of small sandwiches, cake and beverages. At the appropriate time, I threw my bouquet, directing it at Donna Lee! She had not yet met her "forever beloved", but I was sure that one day some lucky guy would claim her.

Our honeymoon was spent in Bavaria, probably the loveliest part of Germany. Our trip began in Heidelberg, followed by Rothenberg, Dinkelsbuhl, Garmish, (with its Linderhof Castle), Neuschwanstein Castle, Herrenchiemsee Castle, Berchtesgaden, and Salzburg, Austria. Since Carl was such a history buff and spoke German we had a very smooth transition through these lovely spots. He had spent a lot of time researching this area and kept on reading as our honeymoon progressed. He especially loved Ludwig II.

Settling into our apartment took a bit of adjusting! It was very small, and the kitchen was just a corner of the living room—not much room to fix a meal. That really didn't make much difference, though, since my first meal of meat loaf, scalloped potatoes and green beans was a total flop! Carl liked none of those!

It wasn't very long until I received an urgent phone call, inquiring as to the possibility of my teaching a fifth-grade class at our American Military Dependent's School in nearby Baumholder. That was an exciting idea! The only drawback was a very bumpy bus ride through the mountains from Birkenfeld to Baumholder each day. That, however, turned out not to be the only drawback. The other was the fifth graders! You have heard of Army brats; well, these were prime examples! What a challenge after having taught very polite, Egyptian girls! I somehow did manage to meet these challenges for at least a few weeks; that is, until the day I found out I was pregnant! The bumpy ride plus morning sickness did me in! Medication did not seem to help; thus, it was decided that I would return to the States at least for a brief period until I was feeling better. Leaving was very difficult, but it seemed like the only choice given the circumstances.

My parents were at the airport that December day, eagerly awaiting my arrival. It had been over a year since they had last seen their only child and they were very excited. Knowing that they would soon have their first grand-child was the icing on the cake so to speak.

The first few months at home passed quickly and soon Carl returned from Germany and we were together again. My parents graciously wel-comed him into the family. The original thought had been that Carl and I would move to Greenville, South Carolina after the baby was born and Carl would enroll at Bob Jones University; however, Carl decided that the Lord was leading him in a different direction and he reenlisted in the air force. He did not have to report to his new post in Greenville, Mississippi until after our baby was born which was good news for me. I did not want to travel during those last months of pregnancy.

Mark Copeland Reid was born on June 4, 1958 at LaGrange Community Memorial General Hospital in nearby LaGrange, Illinois. He was 22" long, weighed 6'6 oz. and looked like a chicken that had just fallen out of the nest! Carl's parents arrived shortly thereafter to view their new grandson. These were joyous times! One very special occasion was the visit of Grandma Simmons to view her new great-grandson.

Carl left for Greenville a couple of weeks later and Mark and I followed in August. Mrs. Strickland, a widow, rented the upstairs of her house to us along with kitchen privileges. Soon after our arrival, the principal of the high school called and asked if I might be available to teach Speech and English. Mrs. Strickland agreed to babysit with Mark which made my decision to accept the appointment much easier. There was, however, one problem. The high school was on the other side of town and I did not know how to drive! I had repeatedly refused to learn! While in high school my father had signed me up for driver's training and I had "unsigned" myself many times! I did not want to learn to drive! I had lived most of my life in Riverside where I could walk wherever I needed to go or simply take the train. This time, however, I had no choice. I had to learn to drive, like it or not. Finally, one day as we were driving through the city of Greenville, Carl said, "Today is the day." He stopped, got out of the car, and said, "I am walking home. See you there" and left! In the midst of traffic, all I could do was move over to the driver's seat and take the wheel. I did make it home without a scratch, but not very happy. I know, however, that Carl's move had been the only way. Otherwise, I still would not be driving!

A few months later Mark and I moved in with friends from our church, as Carl and I needed to experience a brief separation. While there I learned a valuable lesson. Jessie, a person of color, came to babysit with Mark while

I taught. Since the schools in Greenville were segregated, I had not had opportunities to interact with persons of color. The situation in the south, I learned, was very different than what I had experienced in Riverside. My friends took caring for Jessie very seriously. I remember one time when she was ill, they took meals to her and provided medical care for several days. Mark and I came to love Jessie very much, but I still did not quite understand what life was like for her outside of her relationship with this family. Obviously, segregation was still very evident throughout the south and Greenville was no exception. This was further apparent when I went to apply for my driver's license. The written exam included extensive essay questions, targeted at persons of color who would possibly have difficulty with the answers.

Teaching in a southern high school was a real challenge. I soon learned the importance of football, especially when it involved players receiving college scholarships. One star on Greenville's team had offers of football scholarships from several schools. He was also below flunking English! Basically, he did nothing in my class. When he received an F at the end of the first quarter, I was called into the principal's office. An F was not acceptable. Billy would lose his scholarship offers. I had to change his grade. This I refused to do. I am not sure how this Chapter of his life ended, but I do know how that Chapter ended for me. I resigned from my position after the first semester. I also realized that I was pregnant again, the result of Carl and my repeated attempts to mend our troubled marriage. Having few alternatives, Mark and I returned to Riverside to live with my parents and Carl remained in Greenville. My relationship with Carl continued to deteriorate. He revealed to me one night while we were still in Germany that, at the age of thirteen, he had been raped by a visiting male child evangelist. He had hoped that marriage would rid him of this memory and that we would be able to have a normal, healthy relationship. He had, however, been so deeply affected by that incident that he had over the years developed homosexual relationships. Having lived a very sheltered life I knew very little about homosexuality. What I did know was that I was very hurt because of his infidelity. On the other hand, I truly believed that he never meant to hurt me and I sincerely felt that eventually things would change, but they didn't. We tried, especially during the months of my second pregnancy, to seek counselling, but all our efforts failed. Counselors felt that the situation was not reconcilable. Carl was with me, however, when our second little boy, Ronald Brainerd Reid, was born September 6, 1959 at LaGrange Community Memorial General Hospital. He weighed in at 7'1 oz., not much bigger than Mark.

Following the birth of Ronald, Carl and I separated and ultimately divorced. It was devastating to me. How could I face yet another rejection? Carl preferred guys; I was a gal. Several questions haunted me: Should I have stayed in Egypt and married Mike? Would I still be able to serve the Lord as a divorced female? Lord, where are You in this situation?

The only alternative for the boys and me now was to remain in Riverside and live with my parents. Three weeks after Ronald was born my mother died of cancer. Her funeral was in Riverside, but she was buried in Pittsburgh's Allegheny Cemetery. Great Uncle George conducted the service in Pittsburgh which afforded me the opportunity to once again meet the gentleman who had so greatly influenced my spiritual journey, especially my going to Egypt. Losing my mother at such a young age (she was only 57) was devastating for me. She, along with my dad, had always been such a huge support for me throughout my life. Life without my mom presented a very dreary future for all of us, especially my dad. Upon our return to Riverside following the burial, my dad hired a full-time housekeeper to help with household chores and my little boys. Anna was a wonderful addition to our family and dearly loved by all.

One afternoon Dad and I were sitting in the living room chatting when the doorbell rang. Dad went to the door and a perfect stranger entered. A young man walked to the center of the living room, looked me straight in the eye and asked: "Are you Gayle"? I was stunned! However, I realized instantly who this was. It was my baby brother! Although my name had been changed to Carolyn Jean shortly before my adoption was finalized, I never forgot my birth name, nor the fact that I disliked it! David quickly informed me that our grandmother had told him where he could find me. But why? I had been the one who all these years had never forgotten that little baby boy! Now, he had found me! Amazing!

We sat down and chatted for a long while. What a revelation to discover that he, too, had not been kept. Instead of being adopted into a loving home as I had been, he had been raised in poverty by his paternal grandparents. Shortly after giving birth, our birth mother decided that she was not able to take care of this baby either and had allowed her husband's parents to keep David. All those years of feeling rejected just because I was a girl, not being kept because I wasn't a boy, dissolved before my eyes. Our mother hadn't wanted either of us! But what about our sister? Suddenly I had remembered Sharon, the sister I never knew I had until that day, near the end of my college years, when I had received Grandma's letter. Years had passed. Every so often I had taken out that picture, trying to imagine what Sharon looked like at that time. Should I try to find her? How would I be received? Where was my sister now? Unfortunately, David knew very little about her whereabouts, only that she was married and lived in the South Bend, Indiana area. He promised to forward any new information he was able to obtain. In the meantime, he shared with me his past, troubled journey. He had gotten into trouble during his teenage years and spent some time in jail. Following his release, he married twice and was father to five boys. Currently divorced, he was now engaged and planning a summer wedding which he hoped I could attend. Following that initial visit, David sent me the newspaper article and picture of Sharon's wedding, which helped solidify my deep desire to connect with her someday.

Over the next few years, David and I saw each other frequently and enjoyed sharing our boys during their growing up years. Sadly, David died years later from lingering heart problems. As I spoke at his funeral, I couldn't help but feel a sense of both sadness and encouragement. I had found and now lost that special baby brother; however, I had also laid aside yet another rejection from my past. Not only I, but my brother too, had been rejected. Healing had begun.

Chapter Six:
The Ministerial Journey Begins

---

*I*t was now 1960. My two little boys and I were still living in my family home with my father and Anna, our housekeeper, in Riverside, Illinois across the park from the Presbyterian Church. Coming back home had been a difficult, but necessary decision. My father was alone now since my mother's death and had welcomed us home with much joy. He especially loved spending time with my boys.

The doorbell rang. Two gentlemen were at my doorstep. One I recognized as LaRue Thompson, Dean of Men at my high school. The other was a stranger. As it turned out, these men were from the Presbyterian Church. As I escorted them into my living room, Mr. Thompson introduced his friend, "This is Rev. Harold King, our pastor." After a few moments of "let's get acquainted" talk, they got to the purpose of their visit.

"We understand," began Mr. Thompson, "that you play the piano." I nodded and he continued. "Since you play the piano, we feel confident that you can direct a children's choir for our church." *"Why would you think that?"* I wondered. They carefully explained what they had in mind—a small choir of children, ages first through fifth grade, meeting after school one day a week. Although I was very surprised by this idea, I also found it very challenging. My dad and Anna would watch the boys and I would be able to get back into music. Surprising all three of us, I said "yes". Where was God in all this? Was He leading me back into ministry, this time in an area I dearly loved—music? Might this be a step toward eventual full-time ministry?

My first day at the church I met with Rev. King. He had reviewed my teaching background and also looked at those familiar, descriptive words in my high school yearbook, "Quiet, poised and self-controlled."

"I know that you are not very outgoing," he began, "but I will make you effervescent!" Really? I had just gone through a painful divorce and was not relating very well to the rest of the world. Once again that dreadful word, "reject" had popped up in my mind. Could I really change? Could I be that person that Rev. King envisioned? He felt I could; I was not too sure. What exactly did it mean to be "effervescent"? Because I had agreed to give it a try, I left his office, challenged, but confident that the Lord was leading me one step at a time along a very special journey and this was the first step.

What began as one small children's choir soon became one large choir plus two more choirs, one for middle schoolers and one for high schoolers! I was able to involve the mothers in these programs which included a Bible lesson and refreshments. Soon Sunday School and youth group responsibilities were added. Each time more responsibilities were added to my position, Rev. King would say, "Since you are doing such a great job with...I am sure you can accept this new challenge!" He was probably the greatest encourager I ever had. I especially appreciated his philosophy concerning staff relationships: to everyone outside his office I was always perfect. Any problems we had, which were few, were settled in private. Would that all pastors I later worked with had the same philosophy!

Each Christmas Eve, all three of my choirs sang and soon our program was known throughout our village. One very special Christmas Eve, my brother, David, brought his father to our program, offering him an opportunity to speak to me personally. His father, the man who had demeaned me so much during my early years, who had been the main reason my birth mother had given me up for adoption, wanted to ask for forgiveness. He had become a Christian and was now dying of cancer. He wanted to tell me that I had not been a bad little girl. He had made it all up. He was jealous. He thought my mother loved me more than she loved him. As I look back now, I wonder how this could have been true. After all, she gave me up for adoption because he didn't want me. However, on that Christmas Eve, knowing that death was drawing near, he wanted to set the record straight and ask for forgiveness. As I looked at his troubled face, I realized that forgiveness was certainly possible, but forgetting? That would take time. For years I had been plagued with deep feelings of rejection—rejection caused primarily by this man standing before me and the fact that they had kept my baby brother (or so I thought at the time) and given me away. Yet, knowing the truth that I wasn't the bad little girl I had been led to believe, was one major step in the forgetting process. With tears in my eyes, I forgave him. My healing from past rejections continued.

I truly loved my ministry at the church and soon was working twenty hours a week. One of the tasks I enjoyed most was Vacation Bible School. Mark especially enjoyed his class. This fact alone was a miracle, since the very first time I brought him to the church nursery on a Sunday morning, he screamed the whole time! After a few Sundays he settled down and was a big help when Ronald later joined the nursery group. Both boys were very close to their grandfather. Anna, too, was a big help as she loved and understood children in general and my boys in particular. Since she cooked all the meals I continued to flunk as a cook! However, I really didn't care since I was very busy with my work at the church and my two little boys.

I happily had the perfect job and I loved every minute of it! However, the day came when Rev. King shared with me that he felt called to another position. He would be heading up the stewardship program for the Chicago Presbytery, the church governing body of the area. This was a great personal disappointment for me, as I would now lose my "encourager". What did my future hold? Where would I find another "encourager"?

Finding a new pastor for the church took time. The church Session (the governing body of elders) thought they had picked out the perfect person to assume leadership in Rev. King's place. "He will be just perfect for you!" they exclaimed. That turned out not to be the case. He was there only a few months when he informed me that I would need to leave because he was bringing in his own Director of Christian Education from his former church. This was a real shock both for me and for the congregation. What a disappointment! However, about that same time, I received a phone call from Rev. Donald Gordon from Westminster Presbyterian Church in Grand Rapids, Michigan. They were looking for a full-time Director of Christian Education and asked if I would consider such a position. I had no idea how they had received my name or even knew that I might be available. However, after discussing this with my dad, who was less than enthusiastic about my moving, I agreed to come to Grand Rapids at least for an initial interview. This was a big step for me and I needed to be sure that this was what the Lord wanted for me and also for my boys. Ron and Mark were always my first consideration, since I never wanted them to experience the feelings of rejection that I had felt all those growing-up years.

My visit to Westminster and Grand Rapids was very affirming and I happily accepted the position and soon after we moved to Grand Rapids. I loved Grand Rapids from the very beginning, and the church seemed to be a perfect fit for me. And it was. I spent a delightful year there, directing their Christian Education program for children grades six and under. I also discovered that they had an extensive music program which involved three choirs for children and youth. The adult choir was excellent also. It did not take very long for my two boys and me to adjust to, what was for us, big city life. I still vividly remember my first day at Westminster when Don Gordon showed me a map of the city on the wall and told me to take that day to memorize it! It turned out to be a great suggestion! To this day I can still close my eyes and visualize that map!

While still living in Riverside, I had begun dating Bill Wharton, an architectural engineer from Fairbury, Illinois, who was currently working in Peoria, Illinois. We were introduced by Marge Voris the summer that she was directing Vacation Bible School at our church. She and I had been working closely together on this project and had become good friends. Her husband was part of a five-member group of guys who had all graduated in the same class from Fairbury High School, in Fairbury, Illinois. Marge's husband was a renown neuro-surgeon in Chicago. Our first date was a "group date" with the other men from the group and their wives. We went to an Arabic restaurant for dinner and sat on the floor around small brass tables. It was great fun, especially for me since I loved Arabic food! This was the beginning of a journey which lasted almost two years while we were still residing in Riverside. After I moved to Grand Rapids, Bill managed to make the five-hour trip from Peoria, Illinois to visit me about once every month or so. It was on one of those occasions that Bill asked me to marry him. I had been unsure about remarriage for quite some time; however, while at Westminster, I began to feel that my being divorced was a problem and that my boys needed a father. Carl had not contacted us for quite some time, and when he finally came to Grand Rapids it was to tell me that he had remarried. I was shocked! I had always believed that if Carl was able to overcome his addiction and desired to be married, he would come back to us. I was crushed! Once again, I was experiencing rejection! Now it was because he had chosen another woman. I wondered once again, where was God in all of this? Had I stopped loving Carl and was I now ready to begin a new life with a new partner? Perhaps I should have waited a while to make a decision; however, when Bill proposed I felt led to say "yes" and move on. Bill had worked hard at trying to establish a good relationship with my boys during the years we were dating and I felt that marriage would go a long way in cementing that relationship. Thus, it was with mixed emotions that I announced to the church that I would be leaving Westminster that June. I had loved my work at Westminster and knew I would truly miss the church and also Grand Rapids. Many years later I learned that Carl's marriage had been only one of "friendship", as both he and his wife were ministers of music at their local church. His wife knew of his problem, but wanted to marry him anyway. He had never expressed an interest in pursuing a relationship with his sons, although as they became older, he did spend short periods of time with them, especially in the summer when he and his wife vacationed in Arcadia, Michigan. Interestingly, throughout his life he remained very supportive of me and my ministry. He called from time to time and kept encouraging me to pursue a Ph.D. God had somehow found a new "encourager" for me in a most unlikely place.

Bill and I were married at the Presbyterian Church in Riverside on August 2, 1964. Rev. King returned to perform the service.

Friends came from Michigan and other parts of Illinois to attend. We spent our wedding night at the Water Tower Place on Chicago's Magnificent Mile. The next morning, we were surprised to find my Michigan friends, Marge and Harold Hartger, enjoying breakfast at the same hotel! Later that day I was to have yet another surprise—a few days' stay at a summer cottage on Lake Michigan, a wedding gift from the Hartgers. The rest of our trip found us traveling around Lake Michigan to various spots which were special to both of us. Our honeymoon, unfortunately, ended a few days early because I missed my boys! This became a difficult struggle for me throughout our marriage, as I sincerely tried to accept the role of placing my husband first and my children second. Even with the later addition of two more children, this task was never fully accomplished. Perhaps it was because I could never forget that my birth mother had put her husband's wishes ahead of her obligation for the child she already had and had proceeded to give me away. I knew that, regardless of the circumstances, I would never be able to put my children in second place in my heart and priorities. I knew this was not right and surely not Biblical, but it represented my feelings. My children always came first!

Upon returning from our honeymoon, we gathered up the boys and made our way to Morton, Illinois, a small town a short distance from Peoria where Bill worked. We purchased a ranch-style home with money from our joint savings. While there I continued my children's choir ministry in two churches—the First Methodist and the First Mennonite. We also purchased a piano and I launched into giving lessons. It was on March 18, 1966 that our third son, Jeffrey William, was born. My first two births had been difficult but this one was fast and easy. The doctor examined me and said that since I was not fully dilated, I should plan on several more hours. He was barely out of the room when Jeff arrived! Surprise! I was delighted that we had another boy. Bill, I think, had hoped for a girl. I believe there had actually been a time in my life when I had asked the Lord to please send me five boys—a perfect basketball team! My dad came from Riverside by train to help out those first couple of weeks and of course Mark and Ron were delighted to see him. Dad was a huge, positive, influence on their lives and greatly loved by all of us.

The following fall, the nearby elementary school contacted me to see if I would be willing to share a fifth-grade classroom with another teacher. I would teach English and social studies in the morning and she would teach math and science in the afternoon. What a great opportunity to return to the teaching that I truly loved! I easily found a babysitter and off I went.

After a couple of years, the school system decided it needed a guidance counselor. They approached me with the idea that, if I would be willing to enroll in a master's program in guidance and counseling at Illinois State University in Normal, they would pay my tuition. That seemed like an opportunity too good to pass up. During those two years of part-time study, I switched from teaching 5th grade at the elementary school to teaching social studies at the junior high. As if this were not enough to keep me busy, I also continued directing children's choirs and giving piano lessons.

Our family enjoyed worshiping at the Methodist Church until theological issues arose, centered around the pastor's preaching. When it became apparent that these issues could not be resolved, Bill and I chose to leave. At this point several other members of this church, who had formerly been Presbyterian, decided to also leave and along with us begin the task of organizing a Presbyterian Church in Morton. Our local Presbytery agreed with our project and soon we had, not only an organizing pastor, but a transformed barn as our place of worship. Its construction was so unusual that a picture of our new church was posted in a national architectural magazine.

Following my graduation from Illinois State University in August of 1968 with a master's in Guidance and Counselling, I served as a guidance counselor at the junior high for a year before Bill decided to make a job change. We discussed various possibilities and finally decided to move to Grand Rapids where he accepted a position with Wold, Bowers, DuShane and Covert. We purchased a red-brick English Tudor house with three bedrooms, two small dens, a large living room, dining room and kitchen in Ottawa Hills. Shortly thereafter, my father came to live with us as he was in failing health. We converted one of the dens into a bedroom and were able to enjoy a few months together before he needed to be moved to a nursing home. Because he knew of my great love of teaching piano and of my beautiful memories of my cherished Mason and Hamlin grand piano, my father purchased a Yamaha grand piano from the Grand Rapids Symphony in order for me to continue my playing and teaching.

A highlight of this time was the opportunity to audition for a spot in the Grand Rapids Symphonic Choir, the vocal unit of the Grand Rapids Symphony. I sang the only solo I knew, *"He Shall Feed His Flock"* from the Messiah. Afterwards the accompanist commented that I must be a pianist because my timing on the sight-reading piece was perfect. What a joy it was to be able to sing the major classical works of composers like Bach, Mozart and Beethoven; however, singing in Latin and German proved challenging. I adored Al Smith, the director of the choir. He was truly a "shepherd of the flock." I was in seminary the year "Smitty", as he was fondly called, decided to retire. The Symphony decide to honor him during the intermission of his last concert. As the current president of the choir, I had the honor of presenting him with his retirement gift on stage. After saying a few words of gratitude and giving him his gift, I gently kissed him on the cheek. It was so hard to say goodbye to our beloved director.

Amid the joys of reestablishing our lives in Grand Rapids, came the very sad news of my father's declining health and his untimely death in December of 1969. This was a very difficult time for me. My father had been the pillar of my life. He was always there to advise, but never direct. Throughout my growing up years, he taught me by example how to make wise decisions, although over the years my decisions were not always wise. His love for me and my boys was unending and his absence a huge void in our lives. I can remember the many times he would patiently sit down with me and explain all the various alternatives to solving whatever problem happened to be on my mind on any given day, yet reminding me that the final decision would always be mine. He, of course, maintained my mother's directive that "nice people don't raise their voices." That meant that the first time Bill raised his voice he automatically became a "not nice person!" I was with my father when he took his final breath and as he did so he whispered my mother's name. "Alice" he murmured and I believe at that moment they were reunited.

I have had the great privilege of a lifetime of travel. In the spring of 1970 Bill and I traveled with a group from his former church in Fairbury, Illinois to visit the Holy Land, and Egypt with a stop in Rome along the way. This was very special for me since it was the first time I had returned to Egypt since leaving there in 1957. Although I have since that time made several additional trips to Israel, this first one was the most memorable. Words cannot adequately describe what it was like to literally "walk in the footsteps of Jesus." Visiting sites like Golgotha and the Garden Tomb were spiritually uplifting, especially when guided by a delightful gentleman from England who Biblically narrated each stop along the way.

The Garden Tomb

On this first trip to Israel, while staying in Jerusalem, I had the unexpected privilege of hearing violinist Jascha Heifetz present a recital. It was spectacular! I remember that at the end of the concert, members of the audience, instead of clapping, silently made their way down the aisle toward the stage to honor this great musician. This was an experience I shall never forget.

On later trips to Israel, after I became ordained, groups I led from my various churches would participate in a special service of the Renewal of Baptismal Vows on the banks of the Jordan River near the spot where it is believed that Jesus was baptized. Christian Reformed Church pastors are not allowed to rebaptize individuals; however, a renewal of baptismal vows is permitted. Our groups would form a circle near the river, water would be obtained in a small bowl from the river and would then be passed from member to member as each repeated the words, "Remember your baptism and be grateful.

In November of 1970, our family moved into the new home we built in Cascade. I found the perfect lot in Hidden Hills—yes, on top of a small hill and Bill designed the house to fit the lot. Our home had 4,000 square feet—large enough for an expanding family! We joined the Cascade Christian Church which was about the only mainline church in the area and I became involved with the music program there. After just a few months I became the choir accompanist.

While still living in Grand Rapids, we had applied to the Michigan Children's Aide Society to adopt a baby girl. After three active boys, a little girl seemed to be the perfect addition to our family. The process took two years or so, due to the fact that we wanted a girl and all the available babies were coming up boys! However, that special day finally arrived in March of 1972 when Jennifer Christine was welcomed into our family. She had blue eyes and dark hair (which later became blond) and at five weeks old already was sleeping from 7 to 7. The neighborhood women welcomed her with a lovely shower which was held on our back deck. Her bedroom was perfect for a girl—all in pink with a canopy bed. Her brothers adored her and she became the center of our world. She was both dedicated at the Cascade Christian Church and later baptized at Bill's former church, First Presbyterian, in Fairbury, Illinois. Why both? Because I had been baptized by immersion on my sixteenth birthday, believer baptism was very important to me. When I joined the Presbyterian Church in Riverside I had asked Rev. King if I had to believe in infant baptism to become Presbyterian. He had assured me that both forms of baptism were blessed by the Presbyterian denomination. Mark and Ron had both been dedicated as infants; however, after we joined the Cascade Christian Church they both chose to be baptized by immersion there. However, since Bill had been a life-long Presbyterian, when Jenny came along, she was both dedicated and baptized!

In the summer of 1973, we purchased a camp site at Sandy Pines, a recreational area near our home. We purchased a green and white striped pop-up camper and enjoyed not only camping there, but also at other sites throughout the United States. Camping was a welcome break from a very busy schedule which included thirty piano students.

When our youngest son, Jeff, was in second grade in 1974, our family was invited to attend a friend's wedding in Clitheroe, England, a small town near Manchester. What a memorable experience that was! The men all wore morning suits with top hats and walking sticks; the women wore long dresses and fancy hats. The stone church where the service was held had a very old cemetery nearby. We had roast duck as the main course for the dinner that followed. Yummy! The next day we continued on to Scotland to visit friends in Glasgow. Before returning home, we visited St. Andrews, famous for its golf course, and Edinburgh Castle where, even in June, it was cold and rainy. At other times when Bill and I visited England we enjoyed renting a car and traveling through the English countryside, especially the Lake District. On one of these trips, this time with friends, we included a visit to Wales which was special to Bill because his mother was Welsh. A trip around the coast of Ireland several years later with a group from my church in Florida completed my travels in that area of the world.

It was in the fall of 1974, with a two-year old daughter still at home, that I learned of a new ministry opportunity. The newspaper ad read, "Leighton United Methodist Church is seeking a part-time Director of Christian Education..." I glanced at my four children who were watching TV nearby and then looked back at the ad. Would I accept the challenge to return to a ministry which in the past I had thoroughly enjoyed? What about my children? What about the Cascade Christian Church we loved and I served? Oh yes, aside from my initial application to teach in Egypt, I had never before applied for a job! Opportunities had always been "dropped in my lap" so to speak. Should I follow up with this?

These questions were still very present on my mind as I later sat in the office at Leighton and chatted with Keith Laidler, the pastor. I carefully answered his inquiries as to my past experience and then accompanied him on a brief tour of the church facilities. I noted right away that they used Gospel Light Sunday School materials—a definite plus since that curriculum represented a very conservative, Biblical approach to the presentation of the Gospel! The church also needed a choir director, an additional plus.

Therefore, after briefly discussing this with my family and prayerful consideration, I accepted the position.

It was there that I once again enjoyed a year of ministry. During that time, I had the unexpected opportunity to preach one Sunday morning when the pastor became ill. This was a first for me. I decided to choose a text from Jonah and use my "trying to escape ordained ministry" experience as an example. Jonah and I had a lot in common. I had felt God's call to ordained ministry early in my high school years but circumstances and lack of encouragement had put these plans on hold. Now that call resurfaced. I was about to preach my first sermon. Fortunately, I did not have a disastrous experience like being swallowed up by a whale. Instead, it was just a quiet acknowledgment that at last I had to stop running and seriously consider God's call on my life. Surprisingly, the congregation was very affirming of my preaching, even though I had had no previous experience. However, at this point my situation at Leighton took a serious change. What I had believed was a solid relationship with the senior pastor, turned out to be far from that. I'm not sure what happened. The church was becoming increasingly dissatisfied with Keith's preaching and began making comparisons with mine. This situation continued to cause a problem between the two of us. Things came to a head when Keith decided that I had to leave. I had finally yielded to God's call and made the decision to enter Calvin Theological Seminary in the Fall and I wanted to finish out my year at Leighton as originally planned. This issue was brought to the governing body and the decision was made in my favor. Obviously, the remaining months were filled with tension and ministry suffered as a result. I often wonder how I could have handled the situation differently, but later came to realize that this experience really helped me better prepare for the years of ministry which lay ahead.

My journey toward ordination, therefore, began in the spring of 1975 with an initial interview at Calvin Theological Seminary with Dr. Richard DeRidder, the Seminary Registrar. He was not only accepting but was genuinely committed to my success. He would become a major supporter in my journey toward ordained ministry.

I initially decided to pursue a degree in Christian Education, but later switched to pastoral counselling before finally yielding to God's call to consider ordained ministry. Unfortunately, although I had seriously prayed about this, I had not shared with Bill my deep sense of call. I did not realize until much later that Bill was not one hundred percent on board with my decision.

Since it was necessary for me to have denominational support, I was faced with the decision to choose between becoming Methodist or Presbyterian, my only choices since at that time the Christian Reformed Church was not ordaining women. Reflecting on the placement systems of both denominations, that is, appointment by the denomination (Methodist) or a direct call by a local congregation (Presbyterian) I chose the latter. Being the "control" person that I was, it was a no-brainer for me to decide that I did not want a denominational hierarchy to decide where I would be serving. I preferred a personal call from a congregation along with mutual prayer in making that decision. Lake Michigan Presbytery, therefore, agreed to take me under their care. The program involved being under the care of a local church for six months, becoming an "Inquirer" for a year and finally a "Candidate" for an additional year. During that time, I would be meeting regularly with the Candidacy Committee of the Presbytery who would monitor my Seminary progress.

Soon after that initial interview with Dr. DeRidder, I was informed of my acceptance. Since I did not have the pre-requisite requirement of two years of college Greek, I needed to enroll that summer at Calvin College in order to complete at least the first year of that requirement. I was the only female in summer Greek, taught by Dr. George Harris. Although I was not exactly an A student in Greek, I really did quite well and most of all I enjoyed the class, especially my classmates. Five of my male colleagues from that class became my support group during my four years of Seminary: Jerry Lion, Roger Kraker, Al Hamstra, Tim Douma, and Ed Laarman. Jerry became my "forever friend."

Early in September of 1975 before my classes began, I attended the annual fall Seminary picnic, feeling a bit anxious about this new journey which lay ahead of me. Dr. DeRidder spotted me and immediately ushered me over to meet Dr. Bastiaan VanElderen, professor of New Testament who, Dr.Ridder assured me, would be my "best friend" as, he noted, we had much in common. An hour-long walk around the lake together proved his prediction to be true. Bas and I had very much in common, especially our Middle Eastern experiences. We had several mutual friends but, more importantly, mutual areas of interest, namely Egypt. Bas had been digging for many years at archeological sites at Nag Hammadi in Upper Egypt and later at Wadi el Natrun near Alexandria. During those early months at the Sem, I was able to arrange financial assistance from Amway to support his dig at Nag Hammadi. I also introduced him to my Egyptian family, giving him personal support whenever he was in Cairo. Although Bas was out of the country for a large portion of my four years, we always remained in touch.

Life at Calvin Seminary was like a dream come true for me. Although I was still fighting the idea of becoming an ordained pastor, I did finally yield to the suggestion of Lake Michigan Presbytery that I enroll in the Master of Divinity program. That way I would become more "marketable" or so they thought. Part of the requirement of this program was preaching six times. Well, believe me that's all I did! Not one time more! Each of us had a preaching partner. Mine was my buddy, Jerry Lion. He attended each time I preached and offered helpful advice. I did the same for him. I shocked him by noting on one occasion when he preached that he adjusted his glasses 36 times during the course of his sermon!

The evaluations from the various churches where I preached were usually the same: "She will make a great preacher for someone else's church!" The reality of possible rejection loomed big overhead. Was I really called to pastoral ministry and if so, why was being a male so important? Was I ready to face yet another possible rejection? I also was required to preach one time in front of my preaching class. During the evaluation time that followed, one male student commented that, "I wouldn't mind having a female preacher if I didn't have to look at her legs!" After that and for the duration of my ministerial journey I always wore a robe!

While in Seminary I sang 1st tenor in the Sem Choir and was the only female! When asked about me, the guys would just say, "She's not special. She's just one of the guys!"

The Seminary Choir

Frequently on Sunday evenings we would sing at various Christian Reformed churches. Many times, the services would begin with a half hour of informal singing. Then the regular service would commence. My observation was that this experience was like going to a football game and ending up at a funeral! It obviously took me a while to get used to Christian Reformed worship. It was truly amazing that eventually I became a Christian Reformed pastor!

Part of the Sem choir program was an annual tour during winter break. Our families accompanied us. One year we experienced a frigid ice storm on the East coast, another year a blinding snowstorm at Dort College in Iowa. It was on this trip that Bill and I had a very humorous experience. Each choir member and his or her family were invited into private homes to spend the night following the choir concert. When Dr. B. J. Haan, the president of the college, received word that he would be hosting our family, he at first thought that Bill must be the student; then he decided that Bill must be the bus driver. Never did he imagine that I would be the student. He was strongly opposed to the ordination of women! Graciously, however, he accepted his assignment and spent quite a bit of time showing us around the campus. He made special note of the fact that many of the buildings were a result of his personal input. As we prepared to depart, I decided to purchase a thank-you gift for him. Trudging through the snow and icy wind, I shopped at several stores, looking for the perfect gift. I found just what I wanted: a barbeque apron which read, "It is hard to be humble when you are as great as I am". He accepted the gift in good humor and we all enjoyed a laugh. On the way home we accidentally left one student at a rest stop near Chicago. The Sem had to find a Chicago alum to pick him up and fly him home!

My most unforgettable choir trip experience, however, happened during a visit to a Christian Reformed Church in Elmhurst, Illinois during the winter of 1979. Bill and I sat in the living room of a retired couple, enjoying an evening cup of tea when the conversation turned to the gentleman's job prior to retirement. As it turned out he had been a garbage collector, beginning back in the 40s. When I asked where he worked, he responded, "In Riverside." "And exactly where in Riverside did you work?" I asked. "In the Scottswood-Bloomingbank neighborhood", he replied. I gasped! "You were my garbage collector!" I couldn't believe this! Here I was sitting in the home of a man of whom, as a young child, I had been deathly afraid! Every time he would come to my back door, pick up the garbage can, haul it over his shoulder, and retreat to the truck, I would scurry away and hide.

He never looked at me nor said a word which made it even scarier! When I shared these memories with him, he looked at me and replied, "But you see I couldn't speak to you because I had just immigrated from the Netherlands and could not speak English." What a marvelous reunion this night turned out to be! I also have used this incident several times as a sermon illustration.

Amid the busyness of raising four children, attending seminary full time and teaching my piano students, I managed, along with several others, to participate in an ecumenical Bible study in our home. This group consisted of persons in our neighborhood who came from various denominations. It soon became apparent to us that Cascade needed another church. Most of us were attending the Cascade Christian Church as there were few "mainline" churches in Cascade. We all dearly loved Rev. Ray Gaylord, our pastor at Cascade Christian. I decided to have a chat with him about my idea of starting a Presbyterian Church in Cascade. Because of the absence of other mainline churches in Cascade, Cascade Christian was growing, literally, out of its building. How would Rev. Gaylord feel about another church? Well, he was enthusiastic! He immediately announced to his congregation that all Presbyterians needed to leave! Our mission was to start a new church and he was fully on board. With his affirmation I next approached Lake Michigan Presbytery which was somewhat lukewarm to the idea. They did, however, agree to send us an organizing pastor once we had 200 committed to membership in this new church. It took only one summer to accomplish this goal, as several of us went door to door in our various neighborhoods to recruit potential members. By the fall of 1978 we had reached our goal of 200 and, as promised, Presbytery sent Rev. Tom Keiser to become our organizing pastor. Several Presbyterian churches in Grand Rapids sent us some of their members, especially those living in the Cascade area. In addition, Immanuel Presbyterian Church was closing and graciously offered their support and later on after their building sold, their stained- glass windows. Our first church home was the Thornapple Elementary School in Ada. We soon outgrew that facility and moved into Forest Hills Middle School as our next place of worship.

Meanwhile I was preparing to graduate from Calvin Seminary and sought the Lord's will for my future. Still struggling with the idea of actually serving as a pastor, I jumped at the invitation of the Coptic Evangelical Church of Egypt to teach Greek in their Cairo Evangelical Seminary. The one catch was that my husband needed to find a job there. He spent many months researching the possibility of a position as an architectural engineer in Cairo. In the meantime, Memorial Park Presbyterian Church in Allison Park, Pennsylvania had contacted me in the hope that I would consider accepting a position as an assistant pastor of Christian Education. I was resistant; they were persistent! Even though Bill eventually found a position in Cairo, it became very apparent that God wanted us in Pittsburgh and not in Cairo. Bill had no trouble finding a great position there. Although on the outside it appeared that Bill was now very supportive of my ministerial journey, when it came time to make a final decision as to just where I would serve, Bill's attitude became "I really don't care what you do as long as you are not successful." This was both further rejection and a real eye-opener for me as to just how insecure my husband was concerning his own career. It suddenly dawned on me that through the years Bill had always enjoyed taking secretaries out to lunch, for instance, but never fellowshipped with his bosses who might have been in a position to help him further his career. The possibility of my success now became a potential threat. At that point I could have once again felt rejected. However, by this time the Lord had placed His hands on my life in such a way that, instead of rejection, I felt a strong sense of call. Bill's attitude was both sad and unfortunate. Although this attitude changed somewhat over the years, his sincere support was never there.

Graduation day 1979 came all too soon. I had loved my "nest" at Calvin Sem, but now it was time to take flight. Was I ready? Were any of us ready? I remember crying that day—tears of joy at having completed the task, but also tears of sadness at leaving this loving, supportive "nest". These had been some of the happiest years of my life. As I walked up to receive my diploma from President John Kromminga, I remembered his earlier challenge to me when earlier that year I had given Al Smith, our Symphony Chorus director, a kiss at his retirement ceremony. As it turned out, Dr. Krommenga was a good friend of Smitty's. Following this event, Dr. Krommenga had informed me that I would not get my diploma at graduation unless I also gave *him* a kiss! The moment of decision had arrived! Dr.Krommenga looked at me and whispered, "I am chicken" but I thought he said, "Are you chicken?" so I immediately delivered the required kiss much to his surprise and the amusement of all present.

Having received and accepted a call to Memorial Park, the next step was my ordination. On December 7, 1980 I stood before my professors, colleagues and friends at Central Reformed Church in Grand Rapids and calmly answered the ordination questions. Special that day was the return of Rev. King to bring the Message, professors Andy Bandstra and Bas VanElderen to give the Charges, and both the Grand Rapids Symphonic Choir and Cathy Barrow to sing. I had a total of thirteen pastors, professors and elders participating! They all represented special aspects of my journey. As they gathered around me and laid hands on my head and shoulders, I sincerely felt that God was calling me into pastoral ministry in spite of my many years of resistance and fleeing. This was truly an occasion which I would never forget.

Soon after receiving my Master of Divinity degree, and before leaving for Pittsburgh, I had enrolled in the Master of Theology program, a post-graduate studies program at Calvin Seminary, specializing in New Testament Studies. Happily, Bas had finished his work at the Free University of Amsterdam and had returned to teaching at the Sem. I was able to enroll in several of his classes as well as serve as his graduate assistant, correcting students' Greek examinations. Probably my favorite class was his class on Parables. It was during that fall semester that I was invited to accompany him to the University of Chicago to attend a conference on New Testament studies. There I met Dr. John Dominic Crossan, a New Testament professor from DePaul University, who was an expert on the subject of teaching parables to children. I was fortunate to sit next to him at lunch and was seriously engrossed in this "academic" conversation when laughter erupted from across the table. The man at the center of all this hilarity was sharing with his tablemates nearby about his hometown. Among the thoughts shared was the fact that police drove by each house every twenty minutes, thanks to the large gangster population of his town, and that one of these gangsters was directly involved with organized prostitution in Chicago. Soon the names "Bob Murphy" and "organist of the Presbyterian Church" came up. These comments caught my attention! I interrupted the conversation by asking the speaker, "Just where do you live?" "Riverside" he replied. Startled, I asked, "What does Bob Murphy have to do with a gangster involved in organized prostitution?" To this he responded, "Every so often the gangster's son escapes his home and goes to live with Bob Murphy." I laughed, "Well, that is very interesting because I am from Riverside and used to live across the street from that church and went to school with Bob Murphy's daughter." I also went on to share the tragic story of the Starved Rock murders in the fall of 1959, where Bob's wife and two of her friends (both mothers of classmates of mine) had been murdered. All this information intrigued the gentleman, so after lunch he sought me out.

"Do you ever get back to Riverside?" he asked. "Yes", I said. "I have a class reunion this October." Immediately he took out his date book and noted the exact dates I would be in Riverside. "Good", he said. "I will be home that week-end so you and your husband must come for lunch after church on Sunday." I did not know who he was, and he did not know me either. He jotted down my name and phone number, gave me his address and said he would call me to confirm. It turned out that his home was on Scottswood Rd., just down the street from my childhood home. Meanwhile Bas was standing by in utter astonishment. I turned around and asked him, "So, who is this person with whom my husband and I are having lunch?" "Martin Marty" he replied. Recognizing him as being a very famous professor of church history at the University of Chicago and having read at least one of his books I commented: "You've got to be kidding! Church history was my worst subject! Besides, why would he invite me to lunch? I am a nobody!" Bas replied, "If you were 'somebody' he would never have invited you! You notice he didn't invite me!"

True to his word, a few days before our luncheon date, Marty called me to confirm. What a wonderful man he turned out to be! The luncheon at his home, along with his wife and my husband, was a warm, personal experience. There were beautiful hand-hooked rugs, depicting Riverside scenes, hanging on their walls, artwork which his wife had created. A marvelous Mason and Hamlin grand piano graced their living room. The whole day was a most memorable experience. It was great to have a friend in Riverside. Only one of my high school classmates had chosen to live in Riverside following graduation. Most of us had rebelled in one way or another over the snobbish attitude of most of the villagers. Blacks and Jews, and even for a while, Catholics were not welcome, that is until home owners, desiring to sell their six-bedroom houses, realized that these large Catholic families were ready buyers! Even though our class graduated in the fifties, most of us had the mindset of those who rebelled in the 60s. Riverside's values were not our values!

I later learned that not only had Marty raised his own children but had fostered several others. He was great with kids! On one special trip to Riverside many years later, I was accompanied by my grandson, Cory. I will always treasure the picture of the two of them together.

Following the death of his first wife, Marty eventually remarried and moved to a condo in the John Handcock Building in downtown Chicago. I had also become widowed and remarried about the time Marty had made his move. One reason for the move involved his new wife's work with the

Chicago Symphony Orchestra as a member of the board of directors. They could almost walk from their condo to Orchestra Hall. About a year after my new husband, Syd Cammenga, and I were married, we visited the Martys in their gorgeous apartment which had marvelous views of downtown Chicago and Lake Michigan. Marty had a second condo on another floor to house his very large library of books. I asked him if he ever visited his former home in Riverside, and he said "no". He wasn't interested in any changes they might have made. Of course, since Riverside was on the National Historic Registry, no external changes could be made. I, on the other hand, had visited my former residence several times, each time noting interior changes which had been allowed, some of which surprised me. I learned that after peeling off several layers of paint, marble windowsills were uncovered in the downstairs main bathroom. The family that had originally purchased my home had spent thousands of dollars restoring it to its original condition; however, later owners completely remodeled the interior and all the restoration work was covered over. I had a hard time accepting that, as I much preferred the restoration work. They had, however, spent many hours restoring the lawn to the point where their gardens were highlighted on one annual garden tour of Riverside.

As I think back on those seminary days, I realize that I could not have begun this journey had it not been for the initial encouragement of my family, my church, my professors, and my seminary choir members who were always there to lend support. Now it was time to put all that preparation into practice and begin the ministry to which I had been called.

Chapter Seven:
The Journey Continues Through Pittsburgh and Allegan

---

*O*ur family's journey to Pittsburgh presented a big challenge in many ways: new schools for Jeff and Jenny and a new house in Glenshaw (a small town just outside of Pittsburgh) for our family. Located in the center of a cul-de-sac, our picturesque home was perfect for our transplanted family. Mark and Ron (who had now changed his name to Aaron), were on their own with only Jeff and Jenny left at home. However, it wasn't long before Aaron unexpectantly returned home, enrolled in college, and skillfully added a side porch to our house. It was easy for him to do. I just walked with him down the street, showed him the porch I liked, and a few days later I had my new porch.

We soon found that getting around in Pittsburgh was a real challenge: hills, bridges and tunnels. Then there were all those "belts": blue, red, yellow, green, orange and purple, all designed to help you navigate the city. Perish the thought if you ever took a wrong turn, especially exiting a tunnel or crossing a bridge!

Ministry at Memorial Park Church was also a challenge from the very beginning. Our staff consisted of a senior pastor, an associate pastor, a full-time music director, two secretaries, two custodians, a social hostess and, of course, me. Each Sunday one pastor, usually the senior pastor, preached and a second pastor served as liturgist. Upon my arrival I learned that the church had had women elders for less than six months and had only added them because they were faced with discipline from the United Presbyterian denomination if they did not comply with the rule that all churches had to have at least one female elder. Several in the church had serious concerns, not only about women elders, but certainly about a woman pastor. One couple was outspokenly against my presence and instructed my secretary to let them know whenever I was scheduled to preach so that they could make sure to be absent! The wife confronted me one day with the words, "You will never be my pastor!" I replied, "Well, then, perhaps I could just be your friend." This situation went on for several years. Then one Sunday as I stood in the pulpit preparing to preach, I looked down and there in the front row sat this couple. Had my secretary slipped up? What had happened? Would they get up and leave when they realized I was preaching? The service progressed and they never left! From then on, they were always there when I preached, even smiling. I never knew what changed their minds. I only know that they became good friends and loyal supporters. God is so... good and full of surprises!

Then there was Safwat Habashi. He, as an elder, had been very vocal about opposing my appointment. He was an Egyptian married to Pearl, an American nurse. She had been working in Tanta about the same time that I was teaching in Cairo, yet I had never met her. Being the gracious individual that he was, Safwat came up to personally greet me that first Sunday. In the course of our brief conversation, I asked him if he were related to two of my former students, Wadia and Samia Habashi. They were his sisters! "You were their teacher?" he asked. "Yes" I replied. Wow! What a difference that made! Being a teacher in Egypt is a highly respected position; therefore, at this point everything changed. He became my number one supporter! Many years later he and his wife are still among my dearest friends.

Shortly before my arrival, there had been a split in the congregation. A small group of members wanted to have a more charismatic service, utilizing especially the gift of speaking in tongues and raising hands in worship. This idea did not represent the thinking of the majority of the congregation and therefore was not viewed by the leadership as a possibility. As the Senior Pastor Jerry Landrey was heard to exclaim, "You only raise your hands when you need to use the restroom!" As a result, about thirty members left along with one of the pastors. The hurtful part of this situation was the splitting up of several families. Most of the young adults and youth left; their parents remained at least initially. Several left later to be reunited in worship with their children. The result of this split was a huge decrease in the youth group. As pastor of Christian Education, youth were my responsibility. Instead of twenty-five or more high schoolers, I was left with six: two were the senior pastor's children and one was mine. The six kids and I met together and decided on a new name for the group, "Alpha". Leading this group turned out to be one of the biggest challenges of my entire ministry, yet the most rewarding. These kids recruited their friends and soon the group began to multiply. Each time ten kids were added, one volunteer couple was added as well. Soon we had forty kids and four dedicated couples in leadership! I divided the youth and leaders into four groups, with each group being responsible for the evening program one Sunday a month. We had a small music team that led our worship time each Sunday. Even to this day, my son Jeff looks back on those days as instrumental in shaping his spiritual life and his future walk with the Lord. Today the youth group and its outreach ministry are so large that they have their own building adjacent to the church.

Women's ministry was also under my leadership. It was there that I met Bobbi Anderson, who would soon become one of my dearest friends. Her Bible studies, along with those of Peggy Harris, were deeply inspiring and made a great impact on the women of our church. Years later, after I had left Memorial Park, Bobbi died following a lingering illness. I was privileged to join pastors from not only MPC but also the break-off church (Northway Christian Community) to participate in her memorial service. It turned out to be the beginning of many years of mutual ministry between these two churches.

Another close friend during my Pittsburgh years was Maggie Everett. She was one of those first two women elders. We found that we had much in common and enjoyed working together. One day I learned that she was in the hospital, recovering from surgery. I hastened to the hospital to visit her and was shocked upon entering her room to find Dr. and Mrs. Norman Vincent Peale sitting by her bed. "Excuse me? Am I missing something here?" I inquired. Maggie smiled and said, "I guess I forgot to tell you! Meet my parents!" What a joy! This was the beginning of many years of shared spiritual journeys. In spite of his fame, Dr. Peale would always be just Maggie's dad to me!

As the months progressed, Pastor Jerry and I locked horns! Our relationship had started out a bit rocky. He insisted that I must wear skirts at all times. One cold winter day as we were standing outside waiting for a car to pick us up, he looked down at my bare legs and remarked, "Aren't you cold?" That did it! I informed him that from then on, especially in the winter, I was wearing slacks!

Often, he would be faced with a perplexing problem, ask for my advice, not take it and get into trouble. Then he would be mad at me! One day he was so angry that he suggested that I look elsewhere for a position. My reply was, "I can't do that because if I left you would lose your best friend!" My reply stunned him but also gave him food for thought. Several days later he sat down with me to discuss a new idea. Our shared ministry would now be based upon gifts, not roles. Since I worked well with people, I would be the Executive Associate Pastor with responsibility for the 24 elders, 24 deacons and 7 other staff members. He would continue to preach, work with the singles ministry, and oversee missions. What a great idea! I was thrilled! The plan was that each month I would meet with the elders and deacons in small groups of four to six to discuss their specific ministries in preparation for the monthly Session meeting. Each elder had an area of responsibility. For instance, elders involved in elementary age children, youth, singles and adults would constitute the Christian Education committee. Other elders and the board of deacons were divided up in similar fashion. I would share reports of these meetings with Pastor Jerry as he prepared the agenda for the monthly Session meeting. Because many items had been thoroughly discussed in these small groups prior to the actual Session meeting, the meeting went smoothly and speedily. Weekly I met with the staff in ministry groups (pastors, leaders, maintenance, secretaries) and gave Pastor Jerry a "state of the staff" report each week. Wednesdays over lunch we all met together to critique and discuss the Sunday bulletin, especially the sermon topic. That meant that we pastors had to have our sermons ready by Wednesday. As a result of these discussions, the pastors received valuable sermon feed-back. We also learned to have our sermons ready before Saturday night!

One area of my work which went extremely well was adult education. Since we had two worship services, I designed two sessions of adult classes, nine in each time slot. That way each member could choose to attend worship first, then Sunday School or visa-versa. Unfortunately, some chose to attend two Sunday School classes and omit worship! Our church was very strong on education. Thirteen weeks of classes were required for new members, engaged couples, new church officers and infant baptisms. Following completion of the new members class, participants were encouraged to become a part of our small group ministry. The one I belonged to back in 1981 was still going strong years later.

Early in my ministry in Pittsburgh I began supporting one of my college students, Lisa Anderson, and her Mexican friend, Mirna Sotomeyor, as they pursued God's call to mission work. Lisa, Mirna and I had attended the Urbana (Illinois) Missionary Conference in December of 1981 where Lisa received a call to enter missions following her graduation from Penn State and where we met Dr. Billy Graham and George Beverly Shea. Lisa's ministry involved training men and women in various parts of Mexico for leadership in Christian camping. Eventually that ministry extended throughout

Central and South America. Mirna, along with Diane, an American friend, chose to minister in Chalco, a slum area of Mexico City, and later on at a Christian camp, also in the Mexico City area.

Two years following my arrival, our youth ministry had expanded to the point where a full-time director was needed. We now had over 50 kids. Saleem Ghubril, a young Lebanese gentleman, was selected. We got off to a very difficult start. During his initial interview with me he said, "I know about working with Pastor Jerry, but I have no idea how to work with you!" Too bad! You are stuck with me! The problem, unfortunately, was mine as well. I felt like John the Baptist when he acknowledged that "Jesus must increase and I must decrease." Giving up Alpha was a huge step for me. I wanted to make sure that it was in good hands. It took a while for me to realize that it *was* in good hands with Saleem and that he was, indeed, the person the Lord had selected for the position. In the beginning, however, problems working with him continued as supervision kept being passed back and forth between Jerry and me. Saleem had difficulty accepting authority, even from Jerry. Like it or not he ended up with me. As time went on, however, he became very committed to his work and Alpha continued to grow under his leadership. We eventually became good friends and colleagues. I, too, blossomed as Executive Associate Pastor, as equipping others for ministry was truly my gift. Jethro's advice to Moses in the eighteenth Chapter of Exodus, coupled with Paul's instructions in Ephesians, became my model for ministry. The key to this style of ministry was delegation and support. My goal was to make sure that when I eventually left, ministry would continue to be strong under lay leadership.

One year it became evident that our budget was $40,000 in the red. I instituted an "Operation Paper Cup." Each organization had to pay for its own use of paper products such as cups, plates, and silverware. At first the groups weren't very happy, but when they discovered how quickly the $40,000 deficit disappeared they were astonished! My job also included monitoring Pastor Jerry's expense account. I informed the church officers and Jerry's friends that if they went to lunch with him, they paid the bill! This saved a great deal of money since Jerry was very social and enjoyed lunches with others. Special for our staff were quarterly day-long retreats where we shared ministry goals and experiences. It was through these retreats that I became firmly committed to team ministry.

Two programs which our youth group started were very special to me. The first one was a mission project which involved our youth joining with other Christian youth to rebuild sub-standard houses in Appalachia. We were housed in the dorms at Appalachian State University (Little did I know then that their football team would one day upset my beloved Michigan football team!). What a challenge it was to learn for the first time how to remove tar and feathered interior walls and install dry wall. It was a messy yet rewarding job. It also served to bring the group closer together. The second year of this project, Saleem joined our staff and participated with us. Following that experience he had another idea. Why not do the same thing in Pittsburgh? There were many needy families there and what an opportunity that would be to be able to serve the community where we lived. As a result of that vision, The Pittsburgh Project, as it is called today, was formed which now invites young people from churches throughout the United States to participate. These youth come to Pittsburgh for two-week-long work camps during the summer months. Buildings to support this project were purchased which included dorm space for the participants. What a blessing this project became!

The second program was CSSM, Children's Sand and Surf Mission. For two weeks each summer our youth group traveled to Ottawa Beach State Park in Holland, Michigan to offer a VBS-type program for children enjoying the Lake Michigan beach. We were sponsored by local churches who provided housing and meals. It was a great experience both for the children who attended and for our youth. Leadership skills were developed and several of our young people later went on to serve in full-time ministry positions.

In my spare time I loved participating in the Mendelssohn Choir of Pittsburgh, the choral section of the Pittsburgh Symphony. Bob Page was an exceptional director. He stretched me musically beyond anything I could have ever imagined. What an honor to sing under his leadership! His nickname for me was "Revsy Babe." This choir introduced me to a whole new world of music. The discipline both vocally and otherwise was unbelievable. If you missed a rehearsal for any reason (even being delayed as I was, sitting on a bus, waiting for the police to arrive, after the bus had been robbed!) you had to attend ITS, individual testing session, where you hoped that someone else had missed the same rehearsal as you and could join you in the make-up session. Bob never hesitated to personally call you out during rehearsals if you made a mistake, even if it were simply not being able to whistle! The rewards, however, outweighed the discipline. We had the privilege of traveling with the Symphony to perform concerts in Carnegie Hall, Lincoln Center and Chautauqua, all expenses paid!

Singing the fourth movement of Beethoven's 9th Symphony was a very special experience for me. Having sung it with both the Symphonic Choir in Grand Rapids and Mendelssohn now in Pittsburgh, I knew it well. Even after I left Pittsburgh, I was able to return periodically for fun reunions. Pictured here are some from our group, enjoying what turned out to be our last reunion with Bob.

Years later, following Bob's death, those of us who had sung with him previously had the opportunity to return to Pittsburgh to participate in a memorial concert featuring the choruses from the Fourth Movement of this 9th Symphony. I knew the words by heart since in 1987 I had had the privilege of being part of an international choir, recruited from all over the United States, to perform concerts throughout France with the Symphony of Lyon. All of us had sung this work previously and were prepared to perform it with just a minimum number of rehearsals, all of which took place in Paris. We had our final rehearsal in Lyon and then presented concerts in several small villages like Vichy, Dijon, Rouen, and Strasbourg. It was interesting that as I visited these small villages everyone seemed to understand my French perfectly. That wasn't the case, however, in Paris!

In the fall of 1988, I attended my first University of Michigan football game. One of the college students in my congregation had tickets to the game and whenever she could not attend, she gave me her ticket. This event was the beginning of a lifetime addiction! I had loved all sports growing up, but I had never been a participant in any. Watching college football had always been my favorite, beginning with the University of Illinois. However, when I moved to Michigan in 1969 my loyalty switched, though some of my family remained Illinois fans.

One very special event of 1988 was Jeff's graduation from Calvin. The following year he married his one and only sweetheart, Amy Gulliver, and moved to Edmore, Michigan where he began his teaching career. After a year Jeff was able to obtain a teaching position in Holton, Michigan and bought a home on several acres in the country just outside of Fremont. Journeying with Jeff had been an interesting experience. I never knew until the day he graduated from high school that he was graduating with honors. Early in his senior year, I took a group of young people from Memorial Park on a tour of several Christian Colleges. It was on that trip that Jeff chose Calvin College, back in Grand Rapids. The first week at Calvin he wrote us a letter, informing us that he had a job in the kitchen (where, incidentally, he met Amy) and asking us to please send him $200 a month. He would take care of the rest of his expenses. The amount must have been sufficient because we never heard a word about money after that.

Amid all the joys of my time in Pittsburgh there was one disappointing experience. I had not yet finished my Master of Theology degree at Calvin Seminary when we moved to Pittsburgh. I learned that there was a joint Ph.D. program between Pittsburgh Seminary and the University of Pittsburgh, where I could obtain a degree in Biblical studies. I was eager to explore this possibility. I learned that the first step was taking the Graduate Record Exam. This is usually taken right after one's undergraduate studies have been completed. However, since I graduated from Monmouth with honors, I did not have to take it to enter Illinois State University to pursue my masters in guidance and counseling. Later when I enrolled at Calvin Seminary, I again was exempt because of my grade-point average at ISU. So here I was thirty-two years out of undergraduate school having to take this broadly-based entrance exam. The results were shocking! Since I am a very slow reader and the reading test was timed, my score on that section was not acceptable; however, my score on the non-verbal section was in the 99th percentile! If I wanted to pursue a Ph.D. in math I would be accepted but not in Biblical studies. Really? On one year of college math? That did not make much sense to me, especially since the fact that I was a slow reader had never prevented me from obtaining honors in all my previous school work. In addition, the University of Pittsburgh refused to accept Arabic as the fourth of my four required foreign languages, Greek, Hebrew and French being the other three. I was too busy with my work at Memorial Park to take classes in German which had been their suggestion, after which they might have reconsidered my request for acceptance. I gave up the challenge and have always regretted that choice, although I must admit that the thought of a Ph.D. in math still gives me a chuckle. Instead, in 1987 I completed my Master of Theology degree in Biblical studies from Calvin Seminary, writing my dissertation on the joy passages of Paul's epistle to the Philippians.

Later on, as our children grew older and out of the house, Bill and I began to focus on traveling internationally, just the two of us. For me this usually would begin with return trips to Egypt. Once a congregation I was serving knew that I had lived and taught in Egypt they were anxious to see for themselves the great wonders of this ancient country and more importantly view the mission work there. Fifi, the daughter of my longtime friend, Pastor Menes Abdul Noor, owned a travel agency in Cairo and carefully arranged all these trips for me. We would not only tour all the ancient sites, but also visit various churches, both Coptic Evangelical and Coptic Orthodox, as well as CEOSS (Coptic Evangelical Organization for Social Services) which provides education, health, agricultural assistance and guidance, especially to those in small villages throughout Egypt. It is based in Minya. One year I spent six weeks with Pastor Menes and his wife, Nadia, studying Arabic with a tutor. Spending quality time with Menes and Nadia has always been very special to me. One year, Nadia and I enjoyed a cruise up the Nile together. We flew to Aswan, cruised down the Nile to Luxor, visiting several ancient temples along the way. Often members of my tour groups chose to do this extension after our scheduled time in the Cairo area.

One summer, a group from Memorial Park Church joined me on a work-camp trip to the American College for Girls in Cairo (now called Ramses College) where I had previously taught. We painted walls in the mornings while it was still cool, took mid-day naps and then did some sightseeing in the late afternoons and evenings. That year we were there over the Fourth of July and participated in a festive day of activities and great food in the suburb of Maadi, an event sponsored by the U.S. Embassy. I still proudly wear my "4th of July in Egypt" t-shirt each holiday.

Either combined with trips to Egypt or planned separately were visits to Greece and the Greek Islands. Mykonos was a special favorite of mine. Although we did not have a long visit there, the captive white buildings gracing the hilltops were well worth seeing in the short time there. I remember on one such trip to Greece our plane experienced a terrifying "wind shear" as it was attempting to land in Athens. The plane dropped several hundred feet before finally stabilizing and landing safely. My seatmate was an airline pilot on vacation who did little to reassure me that we would not crash; in fact, he totally expected us to! So did the screaming flight attendants! When we finally landed safely in Athens, there was no electricity at the airport which forced us to find our luggage in the dark. Regardless of the inconvenience, we were grateful to be alive.

In 1989 Pastor Jerry accepted a call to a church in Beaver Falls, Pennsylvania and I was left to ponder my future. As the Executive Associate Pastor, I had the right to remain, but I was not sure if that was the right decision. I did, however, have several months to consider my options.

Following Jerry's departure, Rev. Bob Veitch came to Memorial Park as our interim minister for a year while the church searched for a new senior pastor. During that time, he and I made some changes in leadership responsibilities. Bob felt that it would be difficult to call a Senior Pastor to a church which was basically run by the Associate Pastor. While this plan had worked extremely well for Jerry and me, I had to agree that it probably would not work for most senior pastors. Therefore, I gradually turned over many of my leadership responsibilities to Bob and he, in turn, opened the door for me to preach more often. As a result, I became more confident in my preaching ability and decided to search for a solo pastor position. It was during that search time that I attended a leadership conference in Hershey, Pennsylvania led by Dr. Peale. I was anxious to have some time alone with him to seek his guidance concerning my future. When I told him that there was a church in Allegan, Michigan interested in calling me, he said, "Well, Maggie won't like that!" Dr. Peale was a father first, then a pastor! Yes, leaving Maggie, my best friend, would be difficult. Dr. Peale later agreed that I was, indeed, ready to journey out on my own. The Lord was really stretching me!

Early in 1990 I accepted the call and was installed as the pastor of the 1st Presbyterian Church of Allegan, Michigan. Rev. Harold King, my pastor and colleague from Riverside, came to preach the installation sermon. Ironically, he had also pastored the Allegan church many years before. The congregation was overjoyed to see him again.

About the first thing I did upon returning to Michigan was purchase a season ticket to the University of Michigan football games. I car-pooled with the Perrigo family, members of my church. What fun we had chatting about the prospects and highlights of the games as we traveled back and forth! Eventually their son, Tim, got married and the recessional at his wedding was the Michigan fight song, "Hail to the Victors." Unfortunately, that day was also an away game for Michigan at the University of Illinois. We thought we had planned the timing of the wedding perfectly to make sure we could watch the whole game before the wedding. What we hadn't planned on was the time of the game being changed! As a result, the game began during the wedding! Following the service, I was given the task of watching the game on my office TV downstairs and running upstairs periodically to update those in the receiving line each time Michigan scored. We all arrived at the location for the reception on time, but couldn't begin eating until the game was over. Talk about priorities!! At least Michigan won! On yet another game day, Tim could not attend, so the pastor of the Wisconsin Synod Lutheran Church in Allegan was invited to join us. Since that denomination was firmly against woman pastors it took a bit of convincing for him to make the decision to join us! In the end it was a good experience for both of us.

One summer while in Allegan, we had the opportunity to house-sit for the Rienstra family at their home on Lake Michigan, right outside of Douglas. Marty Rienstra had been a year ahead of me at Calvin Seminary and was a forerunner in the struggle for the ordination of women in the Christian Reformed Church. My dream ever since moving to Michigan had been to own a home on the lake and have a Samoyed. Well, here was my opportunity to give it a try. The house was perfect and so was their dog! It was not long after that that we purchased a Samoyed puppy and at least half of my dream was realized. While at the cottage, I had truly believed that I would spend all my spare time gazing at Lake Michigan's waves and sunsets. This lasted for about two days. After that I really wasn't even aware that Lake Michigan existed except for feeling the gentle evening breezes. Living on Lake Michigan permanently was a dream that I knew I would never realize, but at least it was fun for a time and I would eventually have my Samoyed.

It was this same year that I decided to find my birth mother. My adoptive parents had both gone home to be with the Lord and I felt a need to seek out my birth mother. I had lived my whole life fearing rejection. Every situation, every opportunity was evaluated in terms of the possibility of rejection or failure. On the other hand, I regularly preached on acceptance and forgiveness. The Apostle Paul in the third Chapter of Philippians advised us to *"forget what lies behind and strain forward to what lies ahead."* Had I ever really forgiven my birth mother? I had had a wonderful life with my adoptive parents—all the opportunities that life had to offer. Why did I now feel the need to connect with my birth mother? As I thought more about this, I came to realize that it was really my sister, Sharon, with whom I wanted to connect. I still had all the information that my brother David had given me and knew it would not be difficult to find her. But could I face another possible rejection?

I dialed my sister's number. A voice answered. I tried to remain calm. Slowly I began to unfold my story to my silent listener. "You've made a mistake," she said. "I'm not the person you are looking for. Be more careful next time." I was unprepared for this response. I had expected either spontaneous joy or instant rejection, but not this. How could she deny the very obvious? I knew her name, where she graduated from high school, our grandparents' names, even the fact that she, like I, was a descendant of Clement Clark Moore who wrote "The Night Before Christmas". All those stories about ship building in Delaware... hadn't she heard about all that? I was truly stunned. What next?

Perhaps a letter...yes, I'd write a letter and enclose some pictures. I waited. Weeks. No response. Should I go there? Maybe if she saw me in person...I attempted another call.

Again, I dialed, this time from the home of a close friend who lived in the same town as my sister. No answer. I looked up her married name in the phone book. There was another family with the same last name. Might they know her? I took a chance and dialed the number.

"Sharon might be at her mother's," a cheerful voice volunteered.

"Do you have that number?" I asked.

My birth mother! In my efforts to find my sister I had almost forgotten about her! I wrote down the number. I dialed. An older woman answered. I hesitated. What should I say?

"Mother, this is Gayle."

"Oh, I knew you would call someday," she replied.

She asked a little about me and I shared that I was a pastor. This pleased her and she began to share a bit about herself. She agreed to write, which she did. She mentioned the name of my birth father, Carl Kuntz, but gave little information—only that he had lived in the St. Louis area and had been an airline pilot. They, however, had never married. Years later I made an attempt to find him through Ancestry.com. My efforts led nowhere. I checked with airlines located in St. Louis, changed the spelling of his name, guessed what his age might be, to no avail. I finally gave up. I had had such a marvelous relationship with my adoptive father that I really did not need to investigate further.

Mother and I exchanged several letters and finally agreed to meet. She was a strong University of Notre Dame football fan and selected that campus as our meeting place. A friend drove her to meet me there. I have to say that the meeting was not as emotional as one might have thought. We did not exchange hugs nor touch each other in any way. We merely sat on benches in the park and began with just general conversation. I finally got up the courage to ask, "Why?" Her only comment was that she had done the best she could at the time. She never explained the circumstances of my birth nor the reasons for my adoption. However, having met my stepdad again just before he died, I already knew the answers to those questions. It was interesting to discover that had I not gone to teach in Egypt back in 1956 we would have ended up teaching at the same school in Brookfield, Illinois! This first visit was followed by several more visits, later on in her home where I met her current husband. He knew nothing about me, and I promised to keep it that way. I was just "an old friend".

I continued with my attempts to meet my sister. My birth mother kept telling me that my sister knew all about me and was anxious to meet me. She told me she worked at Gantos in South Bend and suggested I visit her there. My first attempt was just before Christmas. From the one picture David had given me of her she was easy to locate. I did not identify myself but told her I was a friend of her mother's and would like gift suggestions for Christmas. She was very friendly and helpful, and I was able to pick out the perfect gift. I repeated this process in January prior to my birth mother's birthday. This time, however, at checkout I revealed my identity. She took one look at me, turned around and fled to the shoe department's storeroom. Anxious to meet me she was not! I tried a phone call again in response to which she threatened to call the police if I ever called her again. I let the matter drop but continued to keep in touch with my birth mother. She became ill and was admitted to a nursing home for treatment and then to the hospital. It was there that I met her doctor. I was startled when she introduced me to him as her daughter! After he left the room, I suggested to her that it was time for us to tell her husband who I really was. Surprisingly she agreed. I left the hospital and went immediately to her home where I found Roman, her husband watching TV. He was delighted to see me and especially delighted to learn who I really was. He said, "I'm so glad that Betty has at least one sane child!" referring, I guess, to my sister. Before leaving I did notice a picture on the table of two boys. I inquired as to their names and learned that they were Sharon's boys, Jeff and Steve Cooley. Years later I would be very grateful to have remembered their names.

In June of 1990 my son Mark married Tracy Beyer in the backyard of her home near St. Paul, Minnesota. Mark and Tracy had met on Mackinac

Island a couple of years before when both were working at the Mission Point Resort. I had fond memories of St. Paul having gone there many times to visit my grandparents on my father's side. I was their only grandchild. I still remembered kneeling by my chair following breakfast each morning for those long morning prayers by Grandpa Copeland. I remember, too, the trips outside in the frigid weather to use the outhouse! What a great joy it was when they finally got indoor plumbing.

Mark and Tracy's wedding service was perfect until the final benediction. At that moment a policeman suddenly arrived at Tracy's home to warn us to take cover immediately because a tornado was coming! The entire wedding group quickly crammed inside their small house where we huddled for more than an hour before it was safe to return outside for the reception.

Later that month, Aaron graduated from Slippery Rock University with a degree in physics. Aaron's educational journey had been difficult to say the least. He had quit school at sixteen because he was bored. I was not really surprised. He had been bored before. He had threatened to quit school while in the second grade. The very wise principal at his school spent many of his lunch hours taking Aaron around the school to make repairs. It was during that same time, as a second grader, that Aaron managed to fix the overhead lighting in his bedroom, a task which Bill had been unable to do. Of course, there was one hitch. Aaron neglected to turn off the electricity! Now in his twenties, he finally decided to return to school and earn his GED. While working for his GED, his physics professor gave him an A before he even took the class, saying that Aaron knew as much about physics as he did and didn't need the class! I was delighted Aaron chose Slippery Rock University to complete his education, following two years of study locally in Pittsburgh. I had remembered Slippery Rock from my childhood when my Uncle Leonard Duncan had been Vice-President there. Visiting his family and teasing my two cousins, Stan and Don, had been great fun. I also remembered the steep hills. Returning for a visit many years later, I noticed that those hills were now filled with many new buildings as Slippery Rock had really grown.

In late June of 1990, Bill and I took a fantastic cruise through the fjords of Alaska. During our trip home I received a phone call from our daughter, Jenny. She had just learned that she was pregnant. What a shock! How could I ever accept the fact that my daughter could have sex outside of wedlock, much less get pregnant? I remembered when I was facing the temptation to have premarital sex at her age, my concerns were two-fold: bringing shame on my family and disappointing the Lord. How could she do this to herself? How could she do this to me? I was humiliated. How would I tell my church? I loved my daughter with all my heart and knew that, regardless of the circumstances, she would always have my support. But again, what about the church? Once I returned home, I finally found the courage to tell my Session the truth. What was their response? "What's wrong. Don't you want to be a grandma?" That response was certainly not what I expected! However, their acceptance of the situation was a huge relief for me. I knew that I had their unconditional support and I was very grateful.

March 5, 1991 turned out to be a very special day in the life of our family. Cory Andrew Wharton was born to daughter Jenny and her boyfriend, Tony Moore. His middle name was Andrew, honoring my beloved Seminary professor, Dr. Andrew Bandstra. I was there for the birth of my first grandchild. Jenny did a fantastic job but was exhausted when Cory was finally born. The nurse handed Cory to me and it was love at first sight. All my previous concerns and fears disappeared in that instant. From that day on Cory had two moms and loved them both equally.

I became the school and sports mom; Jenny handled the personal stuff. Cory became the center of my life, especially when it came to sports—basketball, football and baseball. He never went through an awkward stage. He began with basketball while we were still in Allegan and continued in all three sports while we lived in Florida. He was seriously involved by the time we moved to Grand Rapids and joined me as a super University of Michigan sports fan!

During our years in Allegan, I became very involved in our local ministerial association and eventually became president. Allegan's 24 churches were too many for a town that size; however, the ministers, rather than feeling competitive, became very supportive of each other. Together we introduced a "Carols by Candlelight" service, with most church choirs participating. We as pastors also met once a month for lunch and fellowship. Since the Roman Catholic priest was not available at that time, he and I met for lunch on a different day. On those occasions I learned a lot about his church. We regularly discussed theological issues. I asked him if I would have had to believe in the perpetual virginity of Mary to become a Catholic. He said that that was not a major theological doctrine and not supported by many Catholics. Those lunches were memorable learning experiences for me. He became a close friend and confidant. He genuinely understood my deep concerns about life in Allegan: gossip and prejudice. I shared with him that when I preached from the Epistle of James concerning the use of the tongue, my parishioners commented that they were not gossiping, only expressing "prayerful concern." When I had asked them to please not refer to persons of color as "colored people" they informed me that I really didn't understand life in a small town. Evidently, the Chicago suburb of Riverside did not qualify as a small town. We lived in the church-owned one hundred-year-old manse. When some church members objected to Jenny's Afro-American college friends visiting in what they considered "their house" we decided to buy a nearby condo overlooking the river and move. Yet in spite of these problems, I still loved the people in my congregation and enjoyed serving them. I also came to realize that they were right: Allegan was not Riverside!

We needed an event to jumpstart our Christian witness in Allegan. The perfect person to do this was my friend from Pittsburgh, Rev. John Guest. He was pastor of a very conservative Episcopal Church in nearby Sewickley. His church and Memorial Park had fellowshipped together regularly during the time I lived in Pittsburgh. His few days with us were life-changing for all of us.

Rev. Guest's appearance in Allegan was followed by a city-wide rally in the summer of 1992, featuring Evangelist Tony Campolo, an event once again sponsored by the Ministerial Association. I had the privilege of picking him up at the airport and taking him out to dinner that first night. He chose McDonald's because he wanted to get a "free" toy for his grandson! The rally was a huge success and it gave additional encouragement to some of our struggling churches.

After my house-sitting experience at the Rienstra's cottage on Lake Michigan and having had the joy of caring for their Samoyed, as I mentioned before, I finally got my own Samoyed. Heidi was a beautiful, loving addition to our family. We hadn't had her very long when we were gifted with yet another addition, Buffy, a Shih Tzu puppy.

Another highlight of 1992 was the birth of grandson number two, Mitch Reid, on December 5th. It isn't always fun to travel to Minnesota in the winter, but we did it in order to welcome this new grandson into our family. Two more grandsons, Kelvin Wharton and Daniel Wharton, would soon follow. Will we ever have a granddaughter, I wondered?

Michigan football season continued to be great. On one occasion Bill and I traveled to Florida to attend the New Year's Day Outback Bowl game. Michigan defeated North Carolina State, 42-7. We also met with friends from Allegan who had retired to Leesburg. While there we looked over various possibilities for purchasing a winter home in that area. Bill was hoping to retire soon and our becoming "snowbirds" was high on his "bucket list".

We already had our summer home at Sandy Pines which we had enjoyed since 1972. We ended up choosing a fully furnished new home at Lakes of Leesburg, a retirement community in Leesburg.

Ever since moving to Grand Rapids in 1969, I had been a member of the Grand Rapids Symphonic Choir. Through the years there had been many memorable concerts, but one that really stands out occurred in December of 1995. One of the musical selections for the Holiday Pops was a dramatization of the "Twelve Days of Christmas". What fun it was to glide across the stage at DeVos Hall as one of the "nine ladies dancing." I have a DVD of this which Cory and I enjoy watching. Symphonic Choir was a much-needed outlet for, not only my musical interest, but also for my personal life. Ministry was very demanding of my time and energy and Symphonic Choir provided my needed respite.

In December of 1995 I participated in our West Michigan Friendship Force Club exchange to Mexico where we spent one week each with families in Altotonga (in the mountains near Veracruz), and Tuxtla Gutierrez in Chiapas. Friendship Force is an international organization whereby local clubs are formed with the purpose of exchanging visits with similar clubs in other states or countries. This was my first exchange visit. I hadn't used my Spanish since my sophomore year in high school, but by living with families that spoke no English it began to come back. My only problem was that my new hosts would ask me questions in Spanish and I would reply in French! They would laugh, correct me, and we would move on. Eventually I managed to do better with my Spanish!

At the conclusion of our home stays, I had the privilege of visiting Mirna for a few days. I was awed by her love and dedication to the poverty-stricken people of Chalco where she served. One day during my visit she drove me to Taxco, the city of my third-grade dreams! It was everything that I had hoped it would be. Since Taxco is the silver capital of Mexico, I took advantage of the opportunity to buy several pieces of silver jewelry for friends, family, and, of course, myself! One highlight of this 1995 trip to Mexico was watching Northwestern play in the Rose Bowl on New Year's Day 1996 while in Altotonga. Imagine! United States football in the mountains of Mexico!

Chapter Eight:
The Journey Continues
From 1996-2009

Early in the winter of 1996 Bill and I spent two weeks at our new home in Leesburg, Florida. During our time there, three churches approached me with invitations to join their staffs. Moving to Florida was a difficult decision, especially for me since I hated hot weather! Bill seriously wanted to retire and I was open to moving. Ministry in Allegan had been challenging, yet I had grown enormously through that experience. My preaching and administrative skills had greatly improved. I now had experienced the role of solo pastor and I realized that my gifts lay mainly in multiple staff ministry. I loved being part of a team. Therefore, after prayerful consideration, I chose North Lake Presbyterian Church located in Lady Lake, adjacent to The Villages, a large retirement community. Our family, including Jenny and Cory, moved to Florida that fall, in time for Cory to start school. I was installed as Associate Pastor with Rev. Harold King, as always, preaching the sermon. He had already retired and was living in Sun City Center just south of Leesburg. Everything seemed perfect, except for the Michigan football season which I was going to miss!

My Installation

As soon as the moving van pulled into the driveway of our new home that first day, the little boy next door came to greet Cory. He invited Cory to attend a special program for kids at his church that night and off they went! The two immediately became best friends. Soon Cory was a three-sport athlete. He especially excelled in baseball where he teamed up with a young girl, switching with her from pitching to first base and back for the entire season. The score for most games was around 25-3 in our favor! One particular game stands out in my memory however. The two referees who were scheduled to officiate failed to show up for the game; thus, the two coaches took turns refereeing at first base and home plate. It was the last half of the last inning and our team was ahead by one run. Their team was at bat. One little guy struck out, then the second, and finally the third player came up to bat. The outcome of the game was held in the balance. He hit the ball and ran to first base. It was too close to call. We all held our breath. Then his own coach, who was at first base, declared, "out". What a tough decision for a coach to make! We had won the game, but more importantly, we had learned a valuable lesson: integrity is more important than winning a game. Good sermon illustration!

While serving North Lake Church in Lady Lake, I joined several friends on a three-week tour of Australia and New Zealand. Of course, the scenery was great and the people delightful, but the highlight of the trip for me was having the opportunity to hold a koala. They live on leaves from the eucalypt tree, are largely sedentary and sleep up to 20 hours a day. While awake they tolerate being held by tourists like me, but work in rotated shifts because of their nervous disposition and dislike of human contact. Trips to see sheep herded and sheered, and dances by the Aboriginal tribes were especially interesting. I mention this trip because it was a learning experience for me in more ways than one. This was the first time I had been with a group where I had not been the leader since that first trip Bill and I made to Israel. In spite of being with friends, I was definitely out of place. The group's priorities were not mine. I did not want to spend my free time gambling, drinking or both. As a result, I spent much of my time alone, resolving that in the future I would learn more about a group and its goals before making a commitment to join. Was my not doing certain activities a way of witnessing to my faith, or was it a way of isolating myself from the group and missing an opportunity to witness in more positive ways?

In the fall of 1997 Ruth Peale, Dr. Norman Vincent Peale's wife, came as my guest to Lady Lake to do a women's conference at the Villages. I was driving her to one event when my car phone rang. Great news! At last, I had a granddaughter! Janice Wharton was born to Jeff and Amy! It would be a few months, however, before we would meet her, but in the meantime my heart was filled with great joy! A Wharton girl! Imagine that! Early in 1998 we did get to meet her when all of our kids and grandkids came to Florida to visit us and, of course, enjoy Disney World. Their coming made me a bit homesick as I realized just how far from Michigan we were and how much I missed the rest of my family and I might add, Michigan football games! But since I refused to give up my season tickets, I had to use my vacation time each year to attend both home and away games. Conveniently we had sons in Minnesota, Michigan and Pennsylvania! I would fly to Detroit, Bill would drive to Detroit, pick me up and our football journey would begin. The fall of 1997 Michigan won the Big Ten championship and went on to beat Washington State in the Rose Bowl on January 1, 1998 and claim the National Championship. "It's great to be a Michigan Wolverine!" I put a stuffed wolverine on the pulpit the next Sunday to celebrate! My loyalty to Michigan football was no secret to my congregation. I had purchased a golf cart, painted maize and blue and decorated with Michigan football stickers. Most of my parishioners, however, were either University of Florida or Florida State fans and their golf carts identified their schools as well. I soon learned that football in the South is just as important as it is in the North, maybe even more so. When living in Illinois I had been an Illini fan, but switched to Michigan when moving there. I did not, however, switch to a Florida team!

In the Spring of 1998 Gavin Wharton was born. Another boy! The score was now 4 to 1. Later that fall, Jenny decided to return to Michigan and wanted to take Cory with her. She had been teaching at the local Montessori school where Cory attended. She had never really been happy in Florida. This was a huge decision for all of us. All I could think of was how difficult it must have been for my grandparents to give me up for adoption when I was just a bit younger than Cory. I just couldn't give him back! He was the center of my world. Cory was very happy with his life in Florida and wanted to stay with us. Jenny reluctantly agreed to let him stay and returned to Michigan alone. It was there that she met the man who would become her future husband, Steve Starks, and in April of the following year they gave us another grandson, Cameron. More boys!

In the spring of 1999, Jenny asked us to return Cory. Cory did not want to return unless all three of us moved. I really loved North Lake Presbyterian, but I did not want to force Cory to move back alone against his wishes. Again, I was unwilling to give up Cory. How could I? Also, the situation at North Lake was changing. Prior to my coming, Pastor Gary Lester had assured me countless times by phone that we would have "lots of fun together." This "fun" did not last very long! Over the ensuing months I became aware of Gary's increased interest and involvement with the Villages and its leadership. His motive, he said, was to win Gary Morris, Village CEO, to Christ. Many lunch dates and exotic vacations between the two of them and their families followed. I could see what was happening, but others either didn't see it or chose not to. I said nothing to Gary nor anyone else for that matter; yet, Gary became increasingly hostile towards me. He managed to find fault in much of my ministry efforts. Therefore, because of my family situation with regard to Cory, in addition to the troublesome, seemingly unresolvable problem at North Lake, we made the difficult decision to leave North Lake and return to Michigan. What had gone wrong? Had I failed in not communicating my concerns to Gary? Just as we were on the road, making our way back to Grand Rapids, I received a phone call from one of the church leaders. Gary had just announced that he was leaving North Lake to become a vice-president of the Villages! How sad for a church that truly loved him and had supported him in good faith, even when circumstances did not warrant it! Thankfully, in the coming years, North Lake not only survived, but grew in membership, buildings, and most of all spiritually. I'm not sure exactly what I learned from that experience nor what I would have done differently given a second chance. What I had initially felt as rejection by Gary and lack of response to my concerns by the congregation, now became more understandable. I also knew that the Lord had other plans for me and new doors were about to open.

Before returning to Michigan, I had accepted calls to two part-time positions: one as a Parish Associate in Pastoral Care for Eastminster Presbyterian Church in Grand Rapids and one as Director of Women's Ministry at Calvin Seminary. The women at the Seminary had been having a very difficult time feeling fully accepted amid flak from some of the male students. Some men would actually walk out of class if a woman were preaching. One male student refused to go on the annual choir trip because a woman in the choir had been scheduled to preach at one of the churches the choir would be visiting.

Most of the seminary professors were very supportive of women; however, not much changed until Dr. Neal Plantinga took over as president. He immediately met with the women, listened to their concerns, and dealt with the problem. He announced to the student body that if anyone left a preaching class because a woman was preaching, that student would receive a 0 for the day. In his words Calvin was to be an "accepting and hospitable" seminary. This plan worked, although many male students remained unhappy.

Every ten years a Passion Play is performed in Oberammergau, Germany. This tradition dates back to 1622 when the village was afflicted by a great plague which carried off many inhabitants in a short period of time. In peril of their very lives, the people turned to their faith in Christ. The Village Council vowed to perform a Passion Play every ten years if God spared their village. God did spare their lives and thus in 1634 the townspeople performed this play for the very first time. The day-long performance is held on an open-air stage with a covered auditorium seating 5,000 against a beautiful Alpine backdrop. All participants must have either been born in Oberammergau or have lived there at least 20 years. The man who portrays Jesus must be known for his exceptional character and deep spiritual life. The music of a choir of hundreds is beyond description. I was very privileged to escort groups to performances both in 1990 and 2000. In 1990 we visited areas in Central Europe, beginning in Spain and traveling through France and Italy on our way to Germany. In 2000 we chose to add to our Oberammergau trip visits to the capitols of Eastern Europe. Included in that trip was an extra excursion to Salzburg, Austria, which was highlighted by a Sound of Music tour to all the places where the movie had been filmed and a visit to the home of Mozart. As always, the scenery was magnificent and the food delicious! On these trips, as well as on all of my church group trips, we closed each day with a time of sharing the happenings of the day, reviewing the agenda for the following day and spending time in prayer.

Early in 2002, Bill and I traveled to Sherman, Connecticut to visit Maggie and Paul Everett, our friends from our Pittsburgh days. The tragedy of 911 was behind us, yet the after-effects were still present. Maggie and Paul took us to visit Ground Zero in New York City, which was a very moving experience. This trip included a visit to Trinity Church where my distant relative, Dr. Benjamin Moore, had once served as the first Episcopal bishop of New York City. We also visited Riverside Cemetery where his famous son and my great-great grandfather, Dr. Clement Clark Moore, was buried.

During that summer Aaron and I took Cory to the 76ers basketball camp in Pennsylvania. Aaron and I spent the week sailing on Chesapeake Bay. The weather was so hot that on July 4th we gave up sailing and spent the night in an air-conditioned motel! On that same day, Jenny, who had since married Steve Starks, added another granddaughter to our family, Lindsey Christine. Now the score was 6 to 2! Visiting baby Lindsey was our first stop upon arriving home.

Not only was Cory very involved with basketball, he was also active in football. I would often take him to Michigan home games with me where a friendly "scalper" would take my ticket and $50 in exchange for two seats together elsewhere. A highlight of 2002 for Cory and me was another visit to Minneapolis to visit Mark and Mitch and attend a Michigan game with the University of Minnesota. We won big and Minnesota learned how to spell Biakabutuka, the name of Michigan's star running back!

In the summer of 2003 while on the staff at Calvin Seminary, I had the privilege of accompanying thirty high school students, mostly seniors from all over the United States, on a trip to Turkey to visit the sites of Paul's missionary journeys. I was truly amazed at the spiritual depth of these students. At so many of the sites where we stopped, they would spontaneously quote a passage of Scripture followed by the singing of an appropriate hymn. I was further amazed at how helpful they all were when I accidentally fell pool-side at one of our hotels and broke my wrist. I soon learned, as I was whisked away to the hospital in Izmir along with a translator, that persons in Turkey basically only speak Turkish. Neither English, French nor Arabic worked! Nonetheless, my wrist was set perfectly and I was able to navigate my way through the rest of the trip, especially with the assistance of members of the group.

One highlight of this trip was a private meeting with the Patriarch of Antioch who shared with us information about the Antiochian Orthodox Church and presented each of us with a small cross. This meeting had been arranged by Professor Bastiaan VanElderen, who, unfortunately, could not accompany us due to a serious illness. This was disappointing as he had planned to do most of the lecturing which would have provided us with valuable information gleaned from his many trips to Turkey. As an alternative, our leaders used his notes and took turns sharing the lectures with the group. I was overjoyed to learn sometime later that one of the girls from Grand Rapids had made a decision on that trip to pursue ordained ministry.

I had the privilege of accompanying a group from my church on yet another trip to Turkey. My group was combined with two other groups, both led by Roman Catholic priests. Together we shared daily devotions, alternating between Protestant and Catholic liturgy. I was even invited to read the Gospel during the Catholic services. In addition, when the Catholics went forward to receive the communion elements, our group joined them, receiving a blessing as we crossed our arms over our chests in lieu of receiving the elements. This made all of us feel a part of this blended group. As always, a visit to Ephesus was a highlight of our trip. This is the best preserved of all the sites Paul visited on his missionary journey. My cousin Elaine Orr accompanied us.

Ephesus

Our 1990 Oberammergau group followed up that experience with a trip to Norway, Denmark, Sweden, Finland and Russia in 1994. While in Denmark I noticed that most of the churches appeared to be empty. When I questioned our guide about this he said, "We don't need the church. The government takes care of us." I then asked, "But what about death? Don't you need the church when someone dies?" His reply was simply that he

159

had not yet experienced a death in his family. The lack of religious participation unfortunately appeared to be the norm throughout Scandinavia.

Norway, because of its magnificent scenery, was my favorite stop on
this trip. We traveled by boat from Sweden to Finland. While on board
I decided to risk 25 cents and play a slot machine, something I had
never done before. When I won $2.50, I decided that my gambling days
were over!

I was amazed at how easy it was to cross the border into Russia. The
crossing guards were friendly and welcoming. The highlight for me while
in Saint Petersburg was attending a performance by the Mariinsky Ballet,
one of the world's leading ballet companies, founded in the 18th century.
In spite of their great reputation, the male dancer almost dropped his
female partner! The Hermitage was huge and thus we could only cover a
small portion on this visit. I managed to buy a t-shirt honoring the Good
Will Games being held there at the time. When I returned to the bus with
my t-shirt, several others wanted me to go back and buy them one too.
This turned out to be quite a task as no one vendor had a very large quan-
tity of shirts, necessitating my visiting several vendors in order to purchase
the required amount.

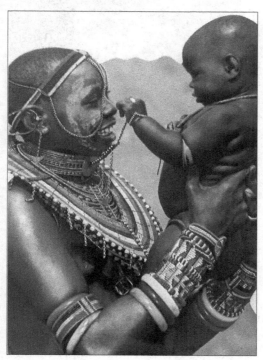

Highlighting my years at
Eastminster were two mission
trips to Nairobi, Kenya. David
Andrus, one of our elders,
accompanied me on the first
trip. Day Star University in
Nairobi had invited us to come
there to visit, not just their
school, but their outreach
ministry into the countryside
as well. The extreme poverty
we witnessed was depressing.
Many families lived in homes
of cardboard and straw.
Indoor plumbing was not
available. Trips to villages
in the outskirts of Nairobi
helped us get a firsthand view
of women cooking and caring
for their children.

One bright spot was our visit to the Kinyago-Dandora Christian Elementary School on the outskirts of Nairobi. As a result of this trip, many members from Eastminster felt led to sponsor one of these students through financial support, periodic letters and pictures. I chose two girls and was delighted by the regular letters and pictures they sent me over the years.

Because of our daily exposure to these poverty-stricken conditions in and around Nairobi, it was decided that we needed a break. This break took the form of a five-day safari at the Masai Mara National Reserve. It was exactly like what you see in the movies: tents with nets over your beds, safari vehicles, and close-up views of all sorts of wild life. One morning I woke up as a monkey was unzipping our tent! The safari vehicles did not carry guns nor other protective weapons. The experienced drivers knew the eating habits of the animals and planned their rides accordingly. Only once did we have a close call. We journeyed too close to a baby elephant and the mother became a bit anxious! We escaped fast!

Our trip home turned out to be rather eventful. David and I passed easily through security and were seated in our plane ready for take-off from Nairobi Airport when we were notified that there was a terrorist threat in the control tower. As a result, our flight was delayed four hours, causing us to miss our connecting flight to Amsterdam. David looked at me nervously.

"What are we going to do?"

"Just follow me," I replied.

David did just that, without another question nor complaint.

I went immediately to the transfer counter and shared our problem with the attendant. Her reply was great news for us.

"We are required to put you on the next available flight. The only seats we have are in business class, so enjoy your upgrade!"

We surely did! Neither David nor I had ever flown business class before and we were thrilled with the upgraded service, especially the food.

Our second trip to Kenya was very similar except that this time Loie, David's soon to be fiancé, accompanied us and David was the leader. He had learned to be a good follower on the previous trip so now he was prepared to be the leader on this one. It was delightful to reconnect with the children we were sponsoring. We brought the children soccer balls to replace the tied-together plastic bags which they had been using as balls for their game. We also brought clothes and school supplies. This time we were invited to visit their homes and meet their families. Viewing their living conditions up close was shocking! Yet these families, most of them Christians, appeared to be very happy and content despite their deplorable conditions.

On this trip, we spent a few days at the Ark where we were the "animals" inside the structure and the wild beasts were the "tourists" outside! If we chose, we could be awakened in the night if an unusual animal appeared at the salt lick.

Although we thoroughly enjoyed our safari trips, our strongest memories would always be of the extreme poverty which existed there and the strong witness of the Christians in the churches, schools and families we visited.

Unfortunately, about this time trouble was brewing at Eastminster. I had known Bob Funk, the pastor, for many years, as we had previously served together in the Presbytery of Pittsburgh. As I previously mentioned, I had accepted his invitation to serve as his Parish Associate. He had come to Eastminster while I was serving the Presbyterian Church in Allegan. I remember when his call was announced I had made the comment to a group of pastors that, "This marriage was not made in heaven." I knew Bob and I knew Eastminster, having worked there part-time while in seminary. They were definitely not on the same page theologically. He was much more conservative than they were. Before Bob came, the worship services had always been traditional. From the beginning of his ministry there, Bob had wanted to add a contemporary service. The Session finally agreed to give it a try; however, after some time the Session realized that this plan was not working. Neither service was growing. After much discussion, the Session decided to return to a one-service format. Bob's heart and soul were with the contemporary service and he was not in favor of merging the two in spite of the decline in attendance; however, the Session insisted on returning to the one service format and voted accordingly. This was an unfortunate move. During the worship service on the Sunday before this merger was to begin, Bob announced that "The third point of my sermon is that this is my last sermon, and my last Sunday. I am leaving this church, the Presbyterian denomination and starting my own church." What a shock it was for me to hear this for the first time as I sat at the lectern, having been the liturgist for the service! Where did that leave the church? Where did that leave me? Why had Bob not shared this with me? Immediately following the service, I called our Presbytery Executive and by 4:00 p.m. that day Bob and all his belongings were out of the church. About thirty members left with him to begin this new church. This was a devastating experience for the church. They had already experienced a difficult split several years before and were not prepared for this one. This event appeared on the front page of the Grand Rapids Press the next day. Upon returning to my office that day, I had an unexpected visitor—Rev. Steve DeVries, pastor of the Plymouth Heights Christian Reformed Church, located just a few blocks away. He had read the paper and had come to offer encouragement and support. What a blessing he was! Knowing he was nearby helped me adjust to pastoring alone for the next six weeks while the Presbytery searched for an Interim Pastor. I enjoyed the opportunity to preach regularly and the church began to heal. However, following interim Roger Grandia's arrival, it became apparent that I would have to leave. According to the Presbyterian Book of Order, a Parish Associate is "attached" to the parish pastor under whom she served and once that pastor leaves, the Parish Associate must depart also. I did not want to leave. The church did not want me to leave, but Presbytery would not compromise. Their point was that I loved the church too much and it would be difficult to call another pastor if I were still there. How can a pastor love a church too much? I was devastated. My forced departure was a very sad event for both the church and for me. I appealed this decision to Presbytery but lost. I was to have no contact with the church for a year, yet even after that year of "shunning" Presbytery extended my penalty for another year. Both the church and I were disappointed and shocked.

Understanding my situation at Eastminster, my friend Jan Strand mentioned to me that her church, Trinity Lutheran, was looking for an associate pastor. Although I did not know a great deal about the Lutheran denomination, it seemed like an opportunity worth pursuing. I met several times with the pastor and eventually with the search committee. They unanimously affirmed my call to their church and began planning for my arrival. However, when word came to them about the situation at Eastminster, without even consulting with me, they withdrew their call. I was crushed. I felt I was an innocent victim of an unfortunate situation at Eastminster and did not deserve to be punished yet again. Why was this happening to me? Where were You in all this, God? More rejection? Yet, through it all, I knew that God still had a special plan for my life. He had just not revealed it all to me yet.

Following our return to Grand Rapids in 1999, Cory had been attending Cadets at Plymouth Heights Christian Reformed Church. Cory encouraged us to visit this church following our departure from Eastminster. I had remembered Pastor Steve's incredible visit following the split at Eastminster and looked forward to visiting his church. Although I had originally believed that this was to be the first stop on our "church searching" journey, as it turned out it became our one and only stop. This was the perfect fit for us and, better yet, it marked the beginning of my entrance into the Christian Reformed Church.

A short time after my departure from Eastminster, I received a call from the head chaplain at Spectrum Health, asking if I would consider a part-time chaplaincy position at Blodgett Hospital. They needed a temporary chaplain to fill that position, which was vacant because one of the chaplains had been called to serve in the military for eighteen months. I had had one unit of Clinical Pastoral Education at Pine Rest the summer of 1978 which qualified me for this temporary position. Needing a church to support my ministry at Blodgett Hospital, I chatted with Pastor Steve and along with the approval of Council (the leadership body of the church) and Classis Grand Rapids East (the regional governing body), I was re-ordained in the CRC. I officially left the Presbyterian Church USA with this move and therefore my "shunning" by the Presbytery was cancelled. Happily, I was able to renew relationships with my friends at Eastminster and support them in their continued journey toward healing.

My reordination procedure included an oral exam by Classis Grand Rapids East. Classis informed me in advance that the exam would be on the Heidelberg Catechism. Having preached many sermons on the contents of this document, I felt confident that I would pass. It was fun to be questioned along with several of my students from the Seminary who were also preparing for ordination! We all passed. My ordination service, held at Plymouth Heights, included participation by several of my grandchildren, a message by my seminary colleague, Rev. Howard Vanderwell, and music by my close friend, Cathy Barrow. Rev. Vanderwell joked that this was the first time he had preached at an ordination where the pastor's grandchildren participated. The congregation joined me in singing hymns of commitment: "May the Mind of Christ my Savior" and "The Servant Song."

Plymouth Height's Ordination

The "Servant Song" had always been a challenge for me, especially the words, "let you be my servant, too". For me it had always been easier to serve than to receive service. This was an important lesson for me to learn and a continual challenge.

Son Mark had always been interested in my heritage connection with Dr. Clement Clark Moore and was busily engaged in research. He felt this research could benefit by my reconnecting with my birth family. My attempts at connecting with my birth sister had been unsuccessful to say the least; however, I had remembered the names of her two sons, Jeff and Steve Cooley. Mark went online and found a Jeff Cooley who lived in Osceola, Indiana, near South Bend. Could this be my nephew?

After considering this possibility for a few days, Mark decided to make the call to Jeff. When he answered, Mark explained his mission without identifying himself or a possible family connection. Jeff eagerly responded and informed Mark that his dad, Bob Cooley, was also investigating the family genealogy. It was decided that the four of us would meet for lunch on May 4, 2005 in South Bend. Great!

The designated day finally arrived. After formal introductions we chatted a bit about our current lives. Bob was retired and Jeff was a banker and, I might add, a strong Notre Dame fan. Jeff mentioned that his brother, Steve, who was a high school teacher and football coach, was an equally strong Michigan fan! So...that's where my interest in football came from! I not only "adopted" it; I was "birthed" with it!

As our conversation continued, Mark began to talk about family connections to Dr. Moore. Jeff began to pick up on this connection. We mentioned my brother, David, to which Bob replied that he knew about his ex-wife, my sister, having a brother, but she had not had contact with her brother in many years. In fact, I soon learned that Sharon had not connected with any of her family, including her sons, for quite some time. She appeared to be dysfunctional in that regard, but still a loyal Notre Dame fan! At this point Jeff figured out the possible family connection, looked at Mark and said, "You must be my cousin!" After which he turned to me with great joy and exclaimed, "And you must be my aunt!" Amazing! What had I expected? Certainly not this great joy at recognition! Surprise maybe, but not such great joy! Both Bob and Jeff were stunned to know of my existence. I had come prepared with letters and pictures which they later took home to share with their wives. Realizing that my sister had little or no relationship with her sons helped me mark another "rejection" off my list. I wasn't the only one my sister had chosen to ignore! Before we left our meeting, Bob insisted that we all get together soon. We agreed on the date of June 26th, a gathering to be held at Bob and Nancy, his wife's, house in St. Joseph, Michigan. We later learned that when Jeff returned home following our lunch, he immediately told his wife, Lynette, that he had something special to share. She replied that she had special news to share also, but wanted Jeff to share his news first. She was delighted with his news. She then gave him the equally exciting news that she was pregnant! It was a great day for all of us! What a joy it has been to have this very special relationship through the years. In October of that year Kenna Grace was born to Jeff and Lynette. After that, every year our family joined Jeff's family for Kenna's birthday and for a celebration sometime during the Christmas season. We also had a tradition: whichever of our teams lost our annual rivalry game, that person had to make a congratulatory phone call to the other. This was painful when you lost!

Several years later we invited Jeff's family to visit us at Sandy Pines. It took only a short time before their family decided to purchase a place of their own there. We now see them frequently during the summer along with Steve, my other nephew, and his family who visit from time to time. Connecting with my birth family has been one of the greatest joys of my life! In this photo we have Jeff, Lynette, Kenna, Steve, his wife Heather and daughter, Bentley, Mark and I.

Of the many trips that Bill and I made together two really stand out. The first was the last trip we made—a cruise around the Straits of Magellan. As interesting as this trip along the coast of South America was, what I remember most was walking with the penguins on the Falkland Islands. We were told to walk only on the designated path; however, the penguins were free to walk anywhere and sometimes journeyed very close to us.

At other places along the water, we saw penguins clustered together by the thousands. I understand that they mate for life.

The second memorable trip was a cruise along the coast of Norway. We traveled to Bergen the day before the cruise began so that I could visit the museum of Edvard Grieg in nearby Troldhaugen. I had played his A Minor Piano Concerto while in high school and was delighted to hear it played as background music in his home. That is the composition for which he is most famous.

Also on this trip we especially loved the views of the midnight sun and the magnificent fjords. The cruise itself was exceptional as our ship stopped to drop off mail at many small villages along the fjords where we could leave the ship and visit.

My ministry at Blodgett had been very different from pastoral care ministry in my former churches. Hospital patients only remained in the hospital for a short time, thus long-term ministry with individuals was usually not possible. It soon became apparent that my gifts and desires were more clearly directed toward ministry in a parish rather than in a hospital setting; thus, it was that God opened the door for my return to church ministry early in 2006.

The full-time Associate Pastor of Pastoral Care at Plymouth Heights had accepted a call to a chaplaincy position in Jenison and the church decided to downsize the position to half-time. This was the perfect fit for me! Happily, Pastor Steve and the Council readily agreed, and I soon began my work there.

One of the first things I did was to locate parishioners who had once been Stephen Ministers. This was a program for which I had been trained while serving North Lake Presbyterian Church and had continued during my time at Eastminster. This time around, however, I used a program called "Caregiving as Way of Life" as a review for these former Stephen Ministers. Having this program utilized by the congregation was initially a challenge, but soon the church members began to appreciate the value of one-on-one caregiving and eventually were willing to participate.

2006 was the 50th anniversary of my Monmouth College graduation. It was celebrated with a very special reunion on campus which both Bill and I attended.

At my 60th reunion in 2016, only six from my class of over 200 were able to make the trip.

What made both of these reunions special was the variety of classes offered, appealing to both the alum and the spouse. I took a refresher course on computers as well as a travel seminar. The campus had changed considerably since 1956 and it was interesting to tour not only the campus, but also the town of Monmouth. The town had changed very little. I remember how it looked as I walked to the high school the winter of my senior year to do my student teaching in English. I had a great teacher as my supervisor and thoroughly enjoyed my semester with her. I had begun to realize that my parents' insistence that I get a teaching certificate had not been a bad idea at all!

For several years I volunteered as a night chaplain at Butterworth Hospital and upon retiring was honored for having completed 1,000 volunteer hours. I gained a lot through this experience. Each night I would rest in a comfortable room, try to catch a few winks of sleep before being called, usually by trauma bay, to give pastoral care to either the injured individual or his or her family. This was a challenge for me since I had routinely avoided even so much as placing a bandage on one of my children's wounds! Also, my duties as a chaplain at Blodgett had not included trauma care. Now at Butterworth I learned firsthand how to place catheters in patients! Night chaplaincy was a good experience for me, but certainly not my cup of tea long term!

A highlight during my ministry at Plymouth Heights Christian Reformed Church was a mission trip to Uganda. Our group members were guests of Tim and Angie Sliedrecht, who served with Good Shepherd's Fold in Soroti. Several from our group spent time each day working with babies in a nearby orphanage. I spent several days conducting training seminars for local pastors. The final seminar was held in the "bush" where the only toilet was a hole in the ground! How grateful we should be for the little things in life like indoor plumbing.

We spent several days enjoying a safari, which was a first experience for most of the group. I also had the privilege of leading a worship service, with, of course, an interpretor.

Before leaving I, too, was able to spend some time cuddling babies at the orphanage

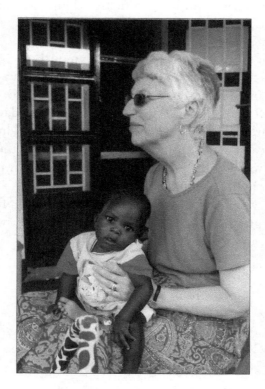

I have always considered leading mission trips to be a very special privilege and this one was no exception. The group not only learned a great deal about mission work in Uganda but bonded over this shared experience. We also had the opportunity to bring back this mission challenge to our congregation through pictures and testimonies.

In June of 2009 Cory graduated from Grand Rapids Christian High, having participated in both football and basketball all four years. I had had great fun, not only attending the games, but also traveling with the basketball team to videotape the games. I would then convert the video into a DVD and present it to the coach each Monday morning. The parents of the players became like a "family" and it was hard to lose that connection when all the players graduated. It was especially hard to lose this special relationship with Cory. Someday I would have to let him go, but I kept hoping it would be later rather than sooner.

Asian travels for Bill and me included a three-week tour of China with Grand Circle Tours. What was special about this trip were the number of occasions when we were able to mingle with Chinese families: enjoying meals in their homes, watching them do Tai Chi in the park or listening to pre-school children sing selections from the "Sound of Music."

Seeing pandas in Xi'an brought back childhood memories of Mae Lin and Sue Lin, pandas at the Brookfield Zoo. Relatives would come to visit us in Riverside from all over the United States just to catch a glimpse of these two pandas and of course, get free housing! Viewing the Terracotta soldiers and the Great Wall were highlights for me.

Bill and I at the Great Wall

Perhaps one disappointment with the entire trip was not receiving information about Buddhism. Although we visited several temples, our guide could tell us only one thing about Buddhism—worshippers held a great respect for deceased relatives. Our guide's mom was a Buddhist, her father an atheist, and she had no idea what she was. This was a special opportunity for witness, but I am not sure that I was very successful. To be a Christian in China is not socially acceptable and often one who does convert feels ostracized from his or her family. The culture in China is one of sameness: haircuts, clothing, life-style. Becoming a Christian challenges that culture.

The other special Asian trip which I made was to Japan with one of my seminary students, Hitomi Urushizaki, and her fiancé Peter Kotnilov. Her father was a pastor in their hometown, and she invited me to visit Japan and preach at her father's church. Little did I know that I would be the only woman who had ever preached at that church let alone at any church in the entire denomination and also that the service was being recorded!

Copies of the tape were then sent to other churches for their viewing. What the response was I never knew.

Most of my time in Japan, however, was spent enjoying the rest of the country, especially Tokyo. The food was delicious, but very expensive. The flowers were unbelievably lovely; the people gracious and kind. They were also very tidy. I accidentally dropped a gum wrapper on the sidewalk and all surrounding activity ceased while my onlookers made sure I picked up the paper! Visits to a tea house

and lovely Japanese gardens, as well as learning to eat with chop sticks, added to the charm of my visit.

Chapter Nine:
The Final Leg of the Journey: 2010 and Beyond

---

*I*n the spring of 2010 Cory returned home to Michigan following a year at Ohio Dominican University in Columbus, Ohio. Although he had had a football scholarship, as a freshman he had seen very little playing time. It turned out that Columbus was not a safe place for Michigan fans. He had had his car broken into twice during his first month there, even though the only evidence that he was from the state of Michigan was his license plate. He also found the environment at ODU too socially active and therefore his grades suffered. He decided that he would enroll at Grand Rapids Community College and remain at home for a couple of years. When I went on line to help him sign up for his classes, I discovered that GRCC was offering two semesters of Classical Arabic. Wow! I had waited a long time for this. I had studied for a time both with Father John from St. George's Orthodox Church and with a Seminary student from Egypt, but neither lasted very long. I enrolled in the class at GRCC immediately!

I was initially a bit concerned about how I would be accepted by my classmates, especially since most of the students were my grandson's age. The first day the teacher asked each of us to explain why we were taking the class. When I explained that I wanted to learn to read and write Arabic so I could better help Arabic-speaking students in the English as a Second Language Class I was teaching, the class was very affirming and supportive of their seventy-four-year- old classmate! They were even more supportive when we were asked to choose partners for special projects and they realized I was making A's! It was good for me to have a bit of a break from my rather demanding work as a pastor. It gave me a better perspective on real life—life outside the church setting. Even meeting fellow students on the elevator was refreshing.

My ministry at Plymouth Heights held many special moments. Once again being a member of a ministry staff was very affirming for me. Although my experience in Allegan as a solo pastor had been in some sense rewarding, it had made me realize that I preferred being involved with a multiple-staff. Working with Pastor Steve was very enjoyable. I often said that "God saved the best for last." It was also fun working with Doug DeVries, Minister of Music, and being part of both the adult choir and the bells. My work with Stephen Ministry required a large part of my time, but was also very rewarding in that it involved working with many caring volunteers who reached out to emotionally and spiritually needy members of the congregation. In addition, my four-year experience with seminary student intern, Phillip Westra, was fantastic. We operated like two peas in a pod. When Pastor Steve initially spoke with me about hiring him, I said, "Congratulations! You now have two of me!"

The summer of 2010 Pastor Steve decided to take a sabbatical. This afforded Phillip and me the opportunity to plan together our summer of preaching and leadership. Each Sunday we would trade off with one of us preaching and the other serving as liturgist. We had a guest preacher about once a month. As one could easily imagine, we worked together very well, and the summer passed quickly and uneventfully. Phillip was an exceptional student and intern. He was also president of the Seminary Senate and exemplified quality leadership.

The spring of 2011 Bill and I made a trip to Fairbury to visit his brother, Bob, who had been hospitalized for some time with Alzheimer's. This turned out to be their last time together as Bill died later that summer. He had been ill for several years, both with cancer and bladder problems. Six weeks of hospitalization and special treatments that summer had not been successful, and he peacefully passed away on August 31st. Cathy Barrows sang for his memorial service just as she had sung for so many important occasions in my life. She made heaven sound very real! I was now widowed, living alone once again and looking to the Lord for what might lie ahead. Bill's death was especially difficult for Jenny who had always been very close to her dad, and he with her. Bill, I think, had always related better to Jenny than to the boys. I'm not sure exactly why. Perhaps it was because our boys could excel in so many areas in which Bill struggled. Bill always said that he knew how to fix things in his head but the message never reached his hands! After he was retired, however, he managed to have a super relationship with Cory and admitted that he was a much better grandfather than he had ever been as a father.

In June of 2011 Mark's son, Mitch, had graduated from high school in Minnesota and left for college in Los Angeles that fall. In order to save money on tuition costs, Mark accepted a job and moved to San Francisco to establish residency. He knew that Mitch would soon be transferring to Berkley to complete his education. Since housing costs in San Francisco were outrageous, Mark bought a used boat and lived on that for the next five years! It was a great sacrifice made for the son he loved very much!

In March of 2012, I had a phone call from Jenny. She asked, "So, how are you doing, Mom?"

"I'm a bit lonely," I replied, hoping she might invite me to dinner. Instead, I received a second phone call from Jenny.

"A friend of mine just called and asked how you were doing. She has a friend that she thought you might be interested in dating."

"Don't you think it is a bit early?" I replied. "After all it has been only six months since Daddy died."

"Daddy told me before he died that he wanted me to make sure that you didn't wait too long to start dating again," she replied.

This surprised me as Bill had never communicated that thought to me. "What's he like?" I asked cautiously.

"I understand he is tall, good-looking and rich!"

I wasn't sure that really made a difference, but anyway I somewhat reluctantly replied in the affirmative. I'd at least give it a try.

A week later Sydney Cammenga called and asked to take me to dinner. That was fast! I agreed and the date was set. When he arrived, I was pleasantly surprised that he was not just tall, but very tall! That was a real plus, since I was over 5'8" tall. I had had to wear flats most of my years with Bill because he was barely 5'8".

For our first date we went for dinner at his favorite country club, even though he doesn't play golf. We both ordered salmon. We repeated this choice of destination and meal every Friday evening for several weeks. It wasn't too long before I met his family. His son, David, and his wife, Sandra lived in Zeeland. She, I learned, was preparing for the ordained ministry in the Reformed Church of America. On this first visit I also met their son, Zach and his fiancé, Joanna, both of whom would soon graduate from U of M. They were planning to be married following graduation and wanted us to be sure to come. They also mentioned dancing. Did we dance? No. Would we try? "Yes," I volunteered, "we would." And we did. I bought a recording of the Platters singing "Only You" and "The Great Pretender", the two songs I had danced to in Cairo on the rooftop of the Semiramis Hotel.

We practiced at my house regularly for the next few weeks. At the wedding Syd announced that we would only do one dance. Ok. We ended up dancing every slow dance the entire evening!

In June I retired from Plymouth Heights Church and again, Cathy sang for the service. I had loved every minute there. Phil Westra graduated from Seminary that same month and accepted a call to a church in Vermont. He will make a great pastor! He had been a wonderful intern and friend.

Following my retirement, it was decided that I would begin attending Syd's church as I felt it was important for me to be away from Plymouth Heights for a time. They would soon be calling someone to take my place and my not being there would make it easier for that new person to bond with the congregation. As it turned out, Sara Albers became the new Associate Pastor and she was the perfect fit for the church. She was young, pregnant with her first child, and very capable of relating to the younger generation at the church. My working through the transition to East Paris, Syd's church, was not that easy. There were no women in key leadership positions and I sensed that this would not likely change. Yet for Syd's sake and to give me a brief break from active ministry this was the right choice.

Sometime that July Syd and I attended his family's annual Camperee, this time at Ludington State Park. I camped in Syd's trailer; he camped out in a borrowed tent. This was my first opportunity to meet about half of his family, 57 persons to be exact. Syd was the eldest of eight children, six of whom were still living. They, their spouses, children and grandchildren would meet each year at a different campground along the shores of Lake Michigan. Some came from as far away as California. I never learned all their names but had fun anyway. One small problem was Syd's brother, Andy, who was a pastor in the United Reformed Church, a break-off from the CRC over the controversy concerning the ordination of women. He was shocked that Syd would be dating a female minister and openly expressed his feelings to everyone present. He took every opportunity to remind Syd that, he, too, had once been strongly opposed to women in leadership. Most of the family, however, were very supportive of both Sandra and me and the whole issue of females in ordained ministry. Andy's strong feelings on this issue were demonstrated repeatedly until shortly before his death when he softened up a bit and decided to love and accept me as his sister-in-law even if he could not affirm my calling as a pastor.

That Fall, Syd attended his first Michigan football game. I will never forget that first game. Syd entered the stadium, looked around and asked, "Why is everyone wearing yellow?"

"It's maize, Syd! Remember maize and blue?"

That began a one-game yearly tradition that lasted throughout our years together. We jokingly told others that this had been our prenuptial agreement!

Go Blue!

Also, that Fall, Jenny went with me to purchase a new place at Sandy Pines. We had had places there off and on since 1972. Sandy Pines consisted of several "phases". Our camping experience began in Phase 1, then in Phase 2, and now we were looking in Phase 4. We found just what we wanted as to location, but we knew at the time that the old trailer there would have to be replaced eventually. The new location was N78 in Phase 4, on a hill with a gorgeous view of the lake.

Also, that year I traveled with a Friendship Force club from the Boston Massachusetts area to Trajulio, Peru. Members of the chub assured me that if I were ever in their area, they would make sure I attended a Patriot's game to see Tom Brady play! I had followed his career as a quarterback during his years at Michigan and had continued to cheer him on as a New England Patriot.

Before traveling to Trajulio, our group made a special stop to visit the ancient ruins of Manchu Picchu, an Incan citadel set high in the Andes Mountains above the Urubamba River valley. Built in the 15th century and later abandoned, it's famous for its sophisticated dry-stone walls that fused huge blocks without the use of mortar. Its exact former use is unknown. Because of its high elevation, 7,972', we had to take special medications in preparation for our trip. We even encountered an alpaca which inspired me to later on purchase an alpaca cape, delightfully soft and perfect for a chilly day.

On January 28, 2013 I accompanied Cory on a cross-country trip to Los Angeles. Cousin Mitch was in school in Los Angeles and Cory had decided to join him, hoping to find work there as an athletic trainer. The plan was for me to travel with him to L.A., help get him settled and then take Amtrak home. We made a fantastic side trip to the Grand Canyon. Cory took one look over the canyon and remarked, "Well, now I know why it is called 'grand'!"

We spent our first few days in L.A. furnishing their new apartment and getting acquainted with the big city. Time flew by and soon it was time for me to return home. This time it was even more difficult for me to say goodbye than seeing him off to Ohio Dominican. L.A. was just too far away from home and I was too attached to Cory! How long would it take for me to adjust to this change? I really didn't know; but what I did know was that a huge piece of my heart would remain in California.

I traveled back to Grand Rapids by train, stopping for a few days to visit my friend, Bob Bulten, in Albuquerque, New Mexico. We had a wonderful couple of days together, especially enjoying a tram ride up the nearby mountain.

Bob had been widowed for several years and was now a confirmed bachelor. He continued to be a great friend and a much-needed counselor as I struggled through the next few years without Cory. This separation anxiety was a new experience for me as I had not experienced this when my four children had left home. My relationship with Cory had always been different. He was the only one of my "children" who excelled in sports and with whom I had a special "bond" while supporting him in all his endeavors.

Upon my return to Michigan I noted that Syd and I had been dating now for almost a year. Syd had had an auto accident in October and had begun to wonder if he should move from his condo off 68th street in Caledonia to a more convenient location, closer to stores, etc. in case he might lose his driver's license. On the recommendation of a friend, we visited Breton Terrace, a retirement complex which was part of Holland Home here in Grand Rapids. I helped him decide on an apartment and even helped him make the decorating choices. I had remembered the colors of the furnishings in his condo and chose accordingly. I also had been planning to move to a condo and had put my house on the market shortly after returning from California. Meanwhile, people at East Paris were beginning to wonder just how serious our relationship was. We had a standard answer, "We are enjoying the journey." One day our friend, Elaine Helmus, asked Syd if we were going to get married. Instead of giving the usual reply he said, "No, we're not." Later that evening he shared this conversation with me.

"Why did you say that?" I asked.

"Well, you don't want to marry me, do you?"

"Well, you never asked!" I replied.

"Well, do you?"

"Yes, but do you love me?"

"Yes, of course I do," he replied firmly, like a true Dutchman.

Thus, with this rather unromantic proposal, we became engaged.

Since both our homes were on the market, we immediately began making plans for a May wedding to be held at East Paris Church. Jenny would be my matron of honor, granddaughter Lindsey my bridesmaid, and granddaughter Anna Wharton my flower girl. Cory would come home and give me away.

You know what they say about "the best laid plans". Well, our plans took a sudden turn for the worst when two nights before our wedding Syd fell and broke his femur. The morning of our wedding found him having surgery at Blodgett Hospital. He was barely out of surgery before the decision had to be made as to where the wedding would be held. We took the advice of Syd's doctor which was to hold the wedding in the lovely atrium of the hospital, move the time up an hour, and put a notice of the location change on the door of the church. Others were to be called. We found an electric piano for our organist to play and enjoyed the natural flowers that graced the atrium. It was a perfect setting. The Wiersmas, my friends from Eastminster, provided the music with Christy playing the violin and Ray accompanying on the piano. She played my favorite, "Meditation from Thais", which I had already informed her she would be playing at my funeral! Cathy, of course, sang; this time it was "My Tribute" with the appropriate words, "How can I give thanks for the things You have done for me?"

The hospital provided a room for the reception and although we did not have linen tablecloths nor fancy dishes, everyone had a great time and Syd even managed to stay throughout most of the reception.

Syd's room was on the third floor of the hospital in a unit where I had previously served as chaplain. Some of the nurses remembered me. They decorated Syd's room, helped him dress, and accompanied him to the service. They even provided a bed in his room for me to spend our wedding night. Not very romantic! After several days in the hospital Syd was moved to the Breton Rehab Center, right next to the Terrace, where at least I could visit him for the next week or so. Our planned honeymoon to Chicago had to be postponed.

Because my house closed before his did, I moved into our place at Breton Terrace a month before our wedding. We both had to do considerable downsizing in order to jointly furnish our apartment. My first day there I was surprised to meet my neighbor across the hall, Barb Morgan, a friend from years ago at Westminster Presbyterian. That helped considerably in transitioning to a new location. I did miss my grand piano, which I sent to Aaron in Pittsburgh. He placed it in the new addition he had just built onto his house.

My new life at Breton Terrace included preaching at the 6:00 p.m. service the third Sunday of every other month. I had always worked with a liturgist and happily Syd became that person for me at these services. That was a huge step for him since he had previously been very opposed to women in ministry. Obviously, his attitude had softened a bit. In addition to my preaching opportunities, I learned that some residents played bridge on Monday nights and soon I became part of that group. Wanting to work on improving my playing skills, I joined three guys for a Wednesday afternoon group. We were very competitive, but that helped keep us on our toes and not allow age to diminish our game. We turned out to be great friends through this experience.

We had not been married very long when I realized that Syd spent very little time in our living room. I had sold most of my furniture because I thought Syd would enjoy having his own furniture grace our living room. Boy was I wrong! When questioned about why he spent so little time in our living room his response was "I hate that furniture!" He, as it turns out, had preferred his den furniture and only agreed to keeping his living room furniture because it had been my idea. That did it! The next day I shopped at New 2 You, a consignment shop, bought new chairs and donated our old ones. Later on, the couch was replaced as well. Now we were able to happily watched TV together, although we did not always share the same tastes. I preferred sports; Syd preferred the stock market and Fox news. The solution was purchasing two TVs, one of which was placed in Syd's den for his morning check on the stock market. That solved the problem of program preference, but put us back to square one on togetherness, although since the stock market closed late afternoon, Syd did join me for the news and game shows after that. Fortunately, we also found other ways to enjoy life together and our marriage was blessed.

Syd and I decided that we would continue to attend East Paris Church, following our marriage. As I mentioned before, I realized from the beginning that this church did not allow women to serve as elders or preachers. Therefore, I became active in pastoral care, which included recruiting and training Care Givers and a team of Visitors who regularly visited our many shut-ins. I also continued to teach seminars on "Islam and Christianity", not only at East Paris, but at other churches as well. The final class in this series always involved a trip to Al-Tawheed Mosque near our church. Our time there would begin with a brief introduction to Islam by an assistant to the Imam, an Arabic meal, followed by attendance at their afternoon service. Following the service, Imam Morsy would join us to answer any questions the group might have. If later on the group posed questions to me which I could not answer, Imam Morsi was always more than willing to sit down and discuss these issues with me. Whenever I expressed doubts or fears concerning the troubling world situation, he would always say, "Carolyn, can't you trust the One who created you for your future? Have you forgotten how much He cares for you?" He became a special, trusted friend. He was also Egyptian. Since Arabic is very dialectic, it was fun being able to use the Egyptian words for "how are you" (izzaek) with him. Although many of us would have liked to have been able to express our appreciation or at least greet with a hug, this practice was forbidden. "Too tempting" Imam Morsy said. Instead, we just crossed arms over our chests as a greeting.

Several years later the mosque had an unfortunate incident with a disturbed Moslem woman who entered the mosque and made terrorist threats, which fortunately she was not able to carry out. The Kaufman Institute at Grand Valley State University received word of this and felt that the area churches needed to organize a support system for the five mosques in Grand Rapids. Our church became a support group for Al-Tawheed. At one particular meeting of representatives from the supporting churches, the president of Tawheed, looked directly at me and said, "We always welcome you

The Hussein Children

to visit us. Why don't you ever invite us to visit you?" What a surprise! What a challenge! I was totally unprepared for this. Immediately I met with Imam Morsy and plans began. Almost thirty of their members joined us for worship the Sunday after Easter, including Imam Morsy and stayed to have dinner and fellowship with thirty of our designated leaders. I thought they would never leave! We were all having a great time!

Just before my arrival at East Paris the church had decided to sponsor an Iraqi refugee family through Bethany Christian Services. At that time, they had never considered the fact that no one in the congregation spoke Arabic! That's when I entered the picture. They asked for my help. I immediately bonded with this beautiful family, the Husseins, who had recently arrived from Iraq. Their experience there had been very traumatic, having witnessed the deaths of relatives and friends. Anhar (the mother), Joseph (the father) and children, Narjus, Wharda, and Yakoob, and later on their third daughter, Sally and I bonded immediately. Anhar began attending my English as a Second Language class at the Church of the Servant and soon, she not only completed classes there, but also earned her US citizenship. Her husband later became a citizen as well. Helpful in this process was a government textbook which had all the questions and answers in English but gave the explanations in Arabic. Both of them passed their written exams with high marks!

Early in 2014, Cory was recruited by MTV to appear on their Real World series. He next appeared on the Challenge, an athletic and endurance competition which definitely lived up to its name! On one series Cory was joined by cousin Mitch and together they managed to place second and win a bunch of money. Fortunately, both of them escaped injury and had a great time. I, on the other hand, was plagued with worry most of the time. Fortunately, I really didn't know the extent of their activities until I saw the show later on TV. Still missing him!

The highlight of 2014 was the wedding of Jenny to Adam Mercer on July 27th. Jenny and Steve Starks had had a very troublesome marriage. Bi-racial relationships are difficult enough, but Steve's background, not only as a person of color, but also as a child in a dysfunctional family, complicated the situation. He was repeatedly unfaithful and neglectful in keeping other commitments. Jenny had tried very hard to keep their family together, but it just didn't work out and they divorced. I remember back when we lived in Pittsburgh and she began dating Cory's father, Tony, also a person of color, that all of our family were very supportive. I was amazed at how easily this worked out for me, especially considering my hometown's attitude toward persons of color. I had hoped at the time that perhaps eventually Tony and Jenny would marry, but that was not to be. Now Jenny had another chance for happiness. Adam was the perfect match for Jenny, except for the fact that he was an Ohio State fan!

Later that year Syd and I enjoyed a delightful Amtrak trip to visit Mark, Cory and Mitch, and Syd's brother, Andy in various spots in California. We began with the northern train route, Chicago to San Francisco, visited Mark there, and then rented a car for a trip down the coast to Los Angeles. Along the way we stopped in Santa Barbara to visit my childhood best friend, Patsy

Nelson. I recognized her right away even though I hadn't seen her in over 50 years. While growing up, she had always been the "beautiful one." She had been our homecoming queen at Riverside-Brookfield High School and repeated that honor at Knox College. Now we were just two "old" friends! It was interesting, though, how the years had somewhat changed our situation. I was healthy and happy and she was not in good health, widowed, and had a son suffering from cancer. Seeing each other again brought back so many happy memories of our childhood days in Riverside.

Since Syd also enjoyed travel, we joined several couples from Breton Woods for a Netherlands Waterway Cruise in the Spring of 2015. For me, the best part of the trip was an extra bus tour through parts of the Netherlands, Germany and Switzerland. While in Switzerland we had an opportunity to take two trains and a bus for the fifteen-mile journey from the small village where we were staying, to visit Frutigen, the delightful small village where I had wintered following my evacuation from Egypt in 1956. Even though the two villages were only fifteen miles apart, this was "as the crow flies", not navigable distance. As a result, our trip included two trains and a bus. The ownership of the Sieber-Mueller Pension had remained in the same family all these years and so, according to tradition, I signed the special guest book reserved for those who had been their evacuation guests.

While fellowshipping at East Paris Church, I joined friends, Bob and Deb Reitsma, in their mission work in Mazatlan, Mexico. For two weeks each February, beginning in 2015, I worked with them as they ministered to children in an orphanage, run by the Salvation Army and also participated in a food ministry for children who lived in the impoverished "colonias". Two mornings each week would find us making sandwiches and packing lunches at the Vineyard Church downtown.

The lunches were then loaded on trucks and delivered to remote colonias, some located in garbage dumps. We went along to help distribute the food. Then later in the afternoon, when the children from the orphanage returned from school, we would conduct a "vacation Bible school type" program of songs, Bible stories and crafts.

These occasions gave me opportunities to use my Spanish. Fortunately, I was no longer responding to questions in French!

In our spare time Bob, Deb, and I always enjoyed walking up and down the beach, viewing gorgeous sunsets, eating coconut shrimp at a local beach restaurant

and shopping at a bazaar located just down the beach from the resort where we were staying. One of the owners of a shop there made weekly trips to Taxco to buy jewelry. Each year before I came, I would send the owner a note, via Deb, to let him know what I would like him to purchase for me. He always was ready with a wide selection. One year I found myself there during Super Bowl week. The Patriots were playing and being a Patriot fan (as in Tom Brady), I was really looking forward to the game. Two days after the teams were announced, Super Bowl T shirts were available at the local bazaar! At first, I thought I would have to miss seeing the game since I was not at home in the States; however, I soon learned, much to my surprise, that this game was very popular in Mexico and screens were available outside and inside restaurants all over downtown Mazatlan. Tourists, especially from Canada, had decorated their golf carts in Seattle Sea Hawks colors (the opposing team). Patriot fans were obviously in the minority. On game day Deb, Bob and I participated in a fund-raising dinner at the Vineyard Church to benefit their food ministry. We enjoyed watching the game on their big screen TV. Most of the guests were Sea Hawk fans. Unfortunately for the Sea Hawks, but great for the Patriots, the Sea Hawks made a huge mistake on the last play of the game, allowing victory for the Patriots! There was only one person from among the 60 present who joined me in celebrating!

My physical energy was challenged in the spring of 2017 when a friend, Flo Mitchell, and I went on a hiking trip to Tuscany, a hilly section of Italy. Each day we hiked at least eight miles, four miles up to a remote village, enjoyed an interesting tour around the town and then hiked four miles down to our waiting bus. There were no smooth paths and often when we hit "pot holes" we felt right at home! The scenery, however, was spectacular, the weather perfect, and the food delicious. Italian ice cream was especially delicious, as noted in this picture!

We were made very much aware of the threat of terrorism while departing from the airport in Rome. Arriving in Florence had been very easy, but here in Rome things were very different.

Soldiers and police with guns handy were everywhere, yet as always, God was good and we made it home safely. These trips were special to me in that they afforded me the opportunity, not only to relax, but to expand my horizons to include opportunties that normally I would not have been able to experience. As the years passed, I realized more and more just how very sheltered my childhood had been: no persons of color, few Catholics, no Jews, minimal need for a car. It was almost like what I had experienced in China and Japan: in Riverside almost everyone looked and acted the same, and had the same values.

In October Cory learned that he was a father! Ryder K. had been born the previous April to Cheyenne Floyd, the result of a "one-night-stand" at a New York MTV reunion event. Cory was so happy that he was literally in tears as he simultaneously shared the news with his mom and me. I was happy for him but troubled. I remembered when his mom became pregnant with him how difficult it was for me to accept, especially in the beginning. However, in the years that followed, Cory had brought much joy into my life. He had made a profession of faith while we were at Eastminster and maintained his walk with the Lord through his four years at Grand Rapids Christian High. Now he was going to be a father! Selfishly, I realized that that probably meant that he would be spending the rest of his life in California, so very far away from Michigan. How would my friends feel when I shared the news with them? What about my Christian testimony? Was there any way that I could use this event to grow in my faith and in my ministry? That would be the challenge I would have to face in the days ahead. The truth was that many of my friends were experiencing the same thing, but reluctant, as I was, to share. It was freeing and a comfort now to begin to open up to others and allow them to do the same. God always seems to bring good out of seemingly difficult situations.

Life continued on as usual at the Terrace. Then one bright day in December, I received a phone call from my friend, Pat, whose dog I simply adored.

"Carolyn, the Helmuses, who live on the third floor, adopted a cute dog, a Shih Tzu-Lasa Apso mix named Billy, a few weeks ago and find that they are not able to take care of him. They asked me if I knew of anyone who might want him and, of course, I thought of you. What do you think?"

I didn't have to think long. Syd had made it clear from the very beginning that having a dog would never be an option. When I moved into the Terrace, I had made the difficult decision to have Jasmine, my cocker spaniel, adopted out, as I felt that I could not manage two animals in our small apartment. However, what I did not realize was how our cat, Toby, would react. He was inconsolable. He missed the mommy dog that had raised him. Here was a possible way to remedy that situation, in addition to the fact that I, too, missed my dog! It didn't take long, however, for me to give Pat my answer.

"You know that Syd has said that he will never have a dog in our apartment!" I replied

"Could you ask him?"

"I could try, but I am sure the answer will be 'no'"

I hung up and cautiously approached Syd. Sure enough, the answer was 'no', just as I had expected.

A few minutes later Syd walked into the living room.

"So, what does this dog look like?" he asked.

I quickly showed him a picture of one from the internet.

"Well, ok, but I'm not picking up any shit!"

I was shocked, but quickly made a call to the Helmuses and they came right down to introduce Billy to us. It was love at first sight. Since I had to adjust my schedule a bit to make sure I would be home on the day of his arrival, it was two days before he could join us. I was ecstatic. So was Toby!

February 2018 was a month which I would never forget. As I mentioned earlier, East Paris had never had a woman elder nor heard a woman preach. I knew when I married Syd that he had not been in favor of female leadership in the church, but he had always accompanied me whenever I preached at other churches. As I mentioned earlier, he had even served as my liturgist on many occasions. In January of 2017 Syd met with the elders and challenged them to come up with a Biblical reason why I could not preach. He had obviously changed his position on the subject! After studying this issue for a year, the elders made the decision that the church would not have women elders, nor would any other woman ever preach, but I could! I'm not sure from where the Biblical basis for this decision came! But in any case, I was delighted and preached for the first time in February. Six people did not attend, two of whom were, and still are, Bob and Deb Reitsma, my best friends. In general, it was well-received and I preached frequently thereafter, especially following the departure of Pastor James who accepted a call to a church in Montreal in July. Bob always read my sermons and would comment, "A great sermon for a guy to preach!" yet he still calls me his "favorite pastor!"

April arrived and so did Ryder's first birthday. I accompanied members of Jen's family to California to participate in the festivities. The party was on a Saturday with over 150 guests present. Activities for the children and lots of great food were enjoyed by all. Then on Sunday I had the privilege of baptizing Ryder in a special service held at her grandfather's home in Pasadena. Miraculously she did not even cry when I baptized her! I spent time with her parents, making sure they both understood the commitment they were making to raise Ryder in such a way that one day she would make her own commitment to Jesus Christ as her personal Savior. We all sang "Jesus Loves Me" to close.

Later that month I traveled to Egypt to visit friends. I discovered that travelling from Chicago is much cheaper than from Grand Rapids. Not only that, but by flying on an United Arab Emirates airline I could add another country to my list of countries visited and enjoy a stop at Abu Dhabi. I couldn't leave the airport but at least I got a brief flavor of the country.

While in Egypt I joined Nadia Menes on a church women's retreat at a Coptic Orthodox Church center on the Red Sea. The trip through the spacious farmlands reminded me of other times when I had had the opportunity to actually walk among the fields and get acquainted with a fellah, a member of the fellaheen (farmers), and his son. It's not often that you can enjoy this close of a contact; however, this fellah probably did not even realize that I was a tourist.

Fellaheen

My time at the retreat center provided. a welcome time of relaxation.

Prior to attending the retreat, I spent several days with my close friend and former piano student, Suzie Greiss. I was amazed to see how Cairo had changed. Not only did the city now have supermarkets, but large malls as well. Suzie had established a program for the women of the Zabbaleen (garbage collectors) called "The Association for the Protection of the Environment." I was so very interested in how the program operated. Each day began with the collection of garbage. The men from the Zabbaleen would travel through the wealthy sections of Cairo, collecting whatever garbage was available. Who knew what jewels might lie in this trash? Pile upon pile overflowed their small carts, as did the recognizable smells. Discarded treasures often lay among rotting waste.

Zabbaleen Father and Son

Soon the collection would be over and the Zabbaleen would journey back to their village in the Mokattam hills, an area adjacent to Cairo's largest cemetery. Garbage scents now blended with other refuse which seeped from the homeless who sought refuge among the dead. The smells only intensified, as we visited one of the shabby homes of a Zabbaleen family. This family, like many of the others, lived among the garbage they collected. Mothers sat outside, gathered around piles and piles of garbage, diligently searching for recyclable goods. What could not be recycled was fed to the pigs, whose presence on the scene added to the ever-increasing foul smell. Most of these families were Christian. Moslems would not have wanted to be a part of this lifestyle, partly because they did not have pigs nor did they eat pork.

There were, however, positives among the overwhelming negatives in this Zabbaleen village. These inevitable scents brought forth future opportunities, opportunities made available through the Association that Suzie founded. She began this project by constructing a building where women could come and learn how to make marketable products from the recycled materials their husbands collected. These products included purses, jewelry, rugs, quilts, stuffed animals and tablecloths to name only a few. Next, she financed housing so that at least some of these families could find some measure of escape from the putrid smells of discarded garbage. But what about their children? Most had never attended school. Recognizing this situation, Suzie built a school which included a nursery and a daycare center for the younger children. What an amazing transformation of an area where I had initially visited during my tenure as a teacher in Cairo back in 1956. Scents had become cents! And children, regardless of their environment, will always be special.

Zabbaleen Children

As products were developing so was the market. What began as small and local, soon developed into an international market. Suzie was able to travel all over the world with her message of hope for these disadvantaged people. She brought her message to Grand Rapids during Calvin's January Series in 2010. What was the result? The negative scent of extreme poverty had now become the positive scent of hope.

Before I returned home, Suzie and I attended church at Kasra Dubara where my friend Menes had served. One thing special about this church was the fact that tourists can enjoy instant translation of the service. What was very special about this particular Sunday was a surprise and treat for me when they sang my favorite hymn, "Jesu oo hyoon feeya", speaking of the risen Christ. It brought tears to my eyes as I joyfully join the congregation in song. I knew all the words by heart.

For a time of relaxation after church, Suzie took me to the Gezira Sporting Club for lunch. There I watched a woman bake pita bread, one of my favorite foods.

Before coming on this trip, Suzie had asked me what I liked to eat. She and her husband lived in a gated community outside of Cairo and had a large staff of house servants, cooks, grounds keepers and chauffeurs. Her cooks were anxious to minister to my tastes. My choices were very basic: tameya (Egyptian falafel), lentils soup and pita bread. The cooks were amazed at my choices. That would be like serving a steady diet of hot dogs and chips in the States! Nevertheless, morning, noon and night I had tameya, along with other dishes as well. One nice thing—they never serve liver in Egypt!

Returning to Egypt always brings back so many memories: memories of tragic circumstances, unfulfilled love, life-long friendships, incomplete mission. What would my story have been like had I remained in Egypt? Here it is sixty-four years later and I still have no answer. Why is it that every time I come to Egypt and then have to return home I always shed tears? Egypt will always have a deep place in my heart that nothing nor no one will ever reach. It is much more than just remembering Mike and the brief time we had together. It is the feeling that I left something behind, perhaps an unfinished task that will never be completed no matter how many times I return to Egypt. Part of me will always be there.

But on a much lighter note, as I look back over my life, this story would not be complete without mentioning my favorite pastime: Michigan football. This relationship began back in 1970 when our family moved to Hidden Hills in Cascade, Michigan. Everyone there appeared to be either a Michigan State fan or a University of Michigan fan. I chose the University of Michigan for no apparent reason. I wasn't able to attend any games, however, until 1981 when our family moved to Allison Park, PA while serving on the staff at Memorial Park Presbyterian Church. One of my college students, who attended Michigan, had season tickets to the football games and, as I already mentioned, occasionally gave me hers when she was unable to attend. When we moved to Allegan in 1990, I was able to obtain a season ticket. When Cory turned six, he went along too. We always managed to find a scalper who would take my ticket and $50 or so and give us two tickets together. As Cory grew older, however, this practice was not that easy, but he still faithfully came with me. Over the years he has attended at least one game with me each year, even since moving to California.

Mark moved back to Michigan in 2019 and subsequently accompanied me to games as well, especially when we played an away game with his favorite team, Illinois.

Wherever we play, it is always a thrill to sing "Hail to the Victors" with 110,000 plus fans! And when we win, we march out of the stadium chanting, "It's Great to be a Michigan Wolverine!"

Why is Michigan football so important to me? Is it just winning the game? Actually, it probably is more than that. I have come to realize that I have a very competitive spirit. For that reason, as a pastor, I stopped playing bridge for a season. I was not a very good loser. Becoming a Michigan football fan gave me an opportunity to compete vicariously. During the late 1900s Michigan usually won big, but since then Michigan has not done that well. Bragging rights have been limited. What was the answer? Support basketball as well!

In the fall of 2018, Michigan football was in full swing. Mark and I made a special trip to attend an away game at Northwestern. We arrived early and were delighted to discover that not only was parking free, but so was the shuttle service to Ryan Field (the former Dyke's Stadium). Neither is free at Michigan! As we wandered around prior to the start of the game, we encountered the Northwestern wildcat. There he was—right before my eyes! I looked at Mark and said, "I need a picture." Clothed in my Michigan sweatshirt I approached the Purple and White Wildcat. "Can I please have a picture with you?" I pleaded. He looked a bit puzzled but nodded his consent. "You see," I continued, "I used to be a Northwestern fan growing up and I still treasure those special memories." He smiled at me, put his arm around me for a photo and said, "Be happy. I forgive you!" and gave me a big hug. That picture has never left my refrigerator.

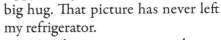

2019 began on a very sad note. Syd had been in failing health for quite some time, but insisted that I participate in my annual mission trip with the Reitsmas to Mazatlan, Mexico. When I left, Syd was in rehab at Breton Woods, awaiting an available spot in the Extended Care facility. He appeared to be stable. I returned on Friday, January 31st in the late evening and visited him the next morning. Things had changed drastically during my absence. He was now in hospice care and declining rapidly. Monday morning Syd went peacefully home to be with the Lord, his entire family by his side. His funeral the following Saturday was attended by many friends from both his family and mine. It was held here at the Terrace with our friend, Rev. Jerry DeVries, officiating. We all will miss him very much. During our years together I had increasingly felt his genuine support of my ministry and I had especially appreciated his willingness to serve as liturgist whenever I preached. He was great at it and many commented that he, too, should have been a minister! As we parted that day, I expressed the hope to Syd's family that I would not be losing them as well. I had become very attached to his family, especially his great-grandkids. I didn't want to miss them, too!

As I began my journey through that next year alone, I was very blessed to have family nearby. Mark had a great new job with New Holland Brewery; Aaron and Ann had moved back to Michigan where Aaron started a home remodeling business. Being self-employed offered Aaron the opportunity to spend long summer days on his sailboat, harbored in Muskegon. Jenny welcomed me into their home every Thursday evening for dinner and Jeff and Amy afforded me many opportunities to relax at their home in Fremont. Syd always loved going there to spend time with Amy and keep track of her gardening endeavors. He had had to give up his garden plot in Caledonia the year before which saddened him greatly. Over the years we had enjoyed all the delicious, fresh vegetables he had grown there.

2019 was filled with added stress, however, as I tried to give pastoral care to our aging and dwindling congregation in the absence of a pastor. Several of our dear members went home to be with the Lord and I had the honor of doing their funerals. Toward the end of May I was, however, able to get away with my friend, Carol Stark, to enjoy a Viking River Cruise on both the Rhine and the Mosel Rivers in Europe. I had visited most of these places before, but they were new to her and I enjoyed revisiting them, especially Bernkastel, Germany, and their attractive 17th century gabled timber-framed houses, my favorite form of architecture.

Our last stop was in Paris, her favorite, but not exactly mine. I had been there several times before and found the people to be not very friendly. Yet

this occasion was different. As we visited the site of the Notre Dame Cathedral, I was moved by the emotion displayed by the French people who were joining us in viewing the remains of the tragic fire that had recently destroyed a large part of the structure. I wondered at their tears since it had been my experience that not many Parisians attended church. Perhaps Notre Dame was more than a church to them; it was a landmark, representing their very existence.

July and August were filled with relaxing times at Sandy Pines. Each time I would retreat to Sandy Pines I would say to myself, "This is mine!" It is my only real home. I am grateful for my place at Breton Terrace, but it basically belongs to Syd's family, with my having the right to live there until I die. My family has grown up with Sandy Pines and they consider it their home, too. This summer we missed the use of our pontoon boat as it had been in the repair shop for most of the summer. Hopefully before football season begins, we will be able to take it out for a spin. I have always treasured my moments at Sandy Pines with its many outdoor activities and countless opportunities for long walks and quiet sails. One of the special lessons that all pastors must learn is the difficult task of finding the time and opportunity to relax. Jesus gave us the perfect example when He often left the crowds and went off alone to pray.

Our dear Hussein family added another girl in 2016! Unfortunately, Sally was born deaf. It occurred to me that it might have happened because Anhar and Joseph were first cousins. I remembered in Egypt that we had a class at the College for special needs children, many of whom were there because their parents were cousins. I never mentioned this to Anhar; however, after the doctor questioned her about that possibility, she asked me if I had suspected that and of course I told her the truth. We prayed together and I think she was at peace with the situation. Sally was, fortunately, able to have a cochlear implant which made a decided difference in both her ability to communicate and in her behavior. Special education became available for Sally and as a result all four children were enrolled in school full-time. That made it possible for Anhar to return to school to work on her GED and prepare to take college courses. She would like to own her own grocery store someday. What a joy it has been for me to be able to work with this family! I am really the only "grandmother" they have. One special blessing has been the opportunities God has granted us to share our faith. I remember on one special occasion following Sally's birth when I was invited to a family gathering. I asked one gentleman who was present if there was some special ritual which was practiced at the time of a baby's birth. He said that the "shahada", the confession of belief in the One God and Mohammed as his prophet, was whispered in each ear. Then he asked me what we did with our babies and I had a wonderful opportunity to share, not only with him, but with the whole group, our rite of infant dedication or baptism. Another time Anhar and I talked about Abraham's willingness to sacrifice his son. I realized as I spoke with her that it really didn't matter, at least not initially, if that son were Ishmael or Isaac. What was important was Abraham's faith in offering his son. This, in turn, led to a discussion concerning the reason for a sacrifice in the first place. What a wonderful opportunity to share the Gospel truth of why the shed blood of a sacrificial lamb, Jesus, was necessary for the forgiveness of our sins and the salvation of our souls! God is good...all the time!

Our Senior Pastor at East Paris had left during the summer of 2017. Prior to his leaving our church had gone through a renewal program at the Seminary in the hope of bringing new life to our congregation. This had not been met with the needed support of the congregation in many areas of projected change. As a result, the congregation continued to decline. I continued to assist the church with pastoral care for the following year; however, in November of 2018 I informed them that I would be retiring from my volunteer pastoral duties the following November. This became more difficult than I had imagined it would be. I truly loved the people of this congregation; however, the responsibility of being available to them 24/7 had become too much for me. The congregation was declining and therefore faced some difficult decisions. A transition committee was formed and after many months of discussion a decision was made to pursue the possibility of a joint ministry with Living Waters CRC, a church plant nearby, which consisted mainly of Koreans and Calvin University students. Their worship style was very contemporary, which was a rather wide departure from the worship style at East Paris.

When that last Sunday in October arrived with my departure at hand, I was saddened by the fact that there was no note of thanks or appreciation in the bulletin nor in my box. What really hurt, too, was the failure of the leadership to even acknowledge emails I had sent to them during those latter months, offering suggestions as to how some of the merger problems might be resolved. I knew that the majority of members were not really comfortable with contemporary music, yet had a strong desire to remain together as a church. Many had expressed the hope that the church would still be there when the time came for their funerals! I had spent time sharing these thoughts with others and received very positive feedback; however, the Council did not so much as acknowledge having received these emails. I'm not sure I handled this situation well. Was it wrong for me to feel unappreciated? Did any of them realize what a sacrifice seven years of 24/7 volunteer pastoral care coverage involved? As one close friend with whom I confided remarked, "Well, the Lord noticed and that is what counts!"

For years many of us from East Paris had gone to LaGrave CRC at Christmas and Easter to enjoy their very traditional services, especially their music. I had hoped that these worship times would fulfill my traditional yearnings and provide spiritual satisfaction for the rest of the year; however, that turned out not to be the case. It just wasn't enough. Prior to entering the ordained ministry, I had been totally immersed in classical music (piano, violin and vocal) and traditional worship. I needed to return to my roots, but LaGrave was downtown and not really accessible to me. Also, they were fully staffed and I wondered if there would be significant opportunities for me to participate in ministry there. Thus it was that, following my departure from East Paris, I returned to Plymouth Heights CRC from where I had retired in 2012. This was the perfect answer for me. As Pastor Steve put it, "welcome home!". The second Sunday there I joined the choir and the following Sunday the Bell Choir was reestablished. Soon I was invited to join the seasonal orchestra which was preparing to play on December 22nd. This I now was able to do because, early in November, I had taken a major step and joined the Bretonnaires orchestra here at Breton Woods. I hadn't played the violin in 64 years, but miraculously it came back! I had the old violin which had belonged to my grandfather and I began with that; however, I soon learned that it would cost $2000 to restore it and even after repair, it would not produce excellent sound. God provided. I had submitted a reference for a couple from East Paris to purchase a residence here at Breton Woods. When they did so, I was rewarded with a referral fee that more than covered the cost of a new violin. What a joy it was to now have the time to engage is so many musical activities, especially the violin!

My friends with whom I played bridge here at the Terrace were all aging—most over 90! Several of our bridge partners had either passed away, or were now residing in our assisted living facilities or rehab center. As a result, there were only three of us left to play, and it takes four to have even one table. Now in retirement, when I have time to make new friends, I find that these friendships tend to be short-lived. As the years go by, I realize that I have more friends enjoying heaven, than I have walking beside me here on earth. Regardless of the circumstances I am pledged to maintain an "Attitude of Gratitude" in all phases of my life. This pledge I shared with the Breton Woods congregation on one occasion when I preached. I reminded them that Paul had shared with the Christians in Philippi that in Christ he had learned to have joy and be content regardless of the circumstances.

As I look back over 2019, I realize that these years were a mixture of sorrow and joy. In many ways it was hard to once again be widowed. Perhaps having been raised an only child made it a bit easier. I tried to join some of my friends for dinner on Tuesday evening when fish was on the menu. It had been a year now that I had avoided red meat and as a result, I had felt much better. My family had been very supportive, especially son Mark, who spent much of his free time with me, not only accompanying me to all the Michigan football games, but also joining me frequently to watch Michigan and Illinois basketball games on TV.

Attending a CALL class at Calvin on creative writing tremendously helped in writing my life story. As a result, I was able to put more of myself and my innermost thoughts into my writing. This became a bit easier now that I was back at Plymouth Heights and relieved of the responsibility of 24/7 pastoral care at East Paris.

Also, in 2019, I joined Ancestry.com to learn or confirm my genetic heritage. I was not surprised to discover that I am mostly English with the rest being German, Norwegian, and Swedish. I had hoped to find a match with my birth father, but so far that has not been possible. It did affirm, however, my genetic connection to Clement Clark Moore as a grandparent several generations removed.

A week after Christmas 2019, I left to join other Michigan fans for the New Year's game against Alabama in Orlando. The few days before the game I spent with a friend in the Villages. This trip almost began with disaster! I never realized until I got on Rt.75 from the Tampa airport that this was the first time that I had ever rented a car and driven on my own anywhere. Everyone knows how I still hate driving! The trip from the airport began with a huge mistake: I headed south instead of north on Rt.75. Thank goodness for the GPS that got me back on track. I reached my destination a bit late, but at least I arrived safely! I loved my visit with friends, but, unfortunately, Alabama won the game. Coming back from the game which was in Orlando, there was a huge traffic jam what with all the traffic from Disney added to our already busy crowd coming from the game. I had problems with my cell phone GPS and had to make the return journey by memory. And it worked! God is so...good!

The day after New Year's while still in the Villages I had lunch with Jerry and Donna Lyon. Jerry and I, as you may recall, had been preaching partners during our seminary days. His words to me upon my graduation were "remember I am only a phone call away." I was blessed! Jerry had retired from his church in Connecticut and was serving part-time on the staff at North Lake Presbyterian, the church where I had formerly served.

My last day in Florida, Karen (the friend with whom I was staying) and I journeyed to Tarpon Springs, my favorite spot in Florida. There we had a delicious Greek lunch and enjoyed the bright sunshine as we ventured in and out of all the little shops this delightful Greek fishing village had to offer. Returning home, I realized that, yes, the sunshine in Florida was great, but being near my family, including my dog and cat, were much more important!

My next journey, still in January, was with Jenny and Adam to see my great-granddaughter, Ryder. We picked a very busy time in the life of Cory and his family. MTV was at his apartment almost every day filming. Jenny and Adam stayed at a bed and breakfast, but I stayed with Cory. It was hard for two-year-old Ryder to renew a relationship with relatives whom she had only seen occasionally, yet Jenny and Adam, who had her most of the time, had lots of fun with her. Cory had become a real celebrity and had a huge fan base.

The purpose of this trip was to witness the "Reveal" celebration where a large group of friends and relatives gathered to learn whether Cory's and current girlfriend, Taylor's, yet-to-be-born baby would be a boy or a girl. Yes, Cory was going to be a father again, but this time with a different mother. He and Taylor had been dating for quite a while and had decided to start a family—California style without a prior marriage. At the "Reveal" celebration only one friend knew the sex of the unborn child (not even Cory and Taylor knew) and had prepared for the revelation, giving each of us confetti pops, which would turn out to be blue or pink when popped. At the designated time everyone popped his/her confetti pop and were surrounded by pink confetti. A girl it was! Everyone appeared to be delighted and much hugging followed. Upon my return to Michigan, I purchased a cross-stitch birth announcement kit, which hopefully would be finished shortly after the new baby arrived. In the midst of Cory's joy over having another girl, my feelings were once again mixed. The values and traditions upon which I was raised affirm that one gets engaged, marries, and then has kids—in that order. That does not appear to be today's progression, especially not in California. The bottom line, however, is that I love Cory deeply and am committed to supporting him, regardless of his choice of life style. He knows where I stand as a Christian pastor and loves me unconditionally.

After a delightful 2019 Christmas season filled with lots of music, both at church and at the Terrace, I was looking forward to our annual Bretonnaires spring concert. I made my usual trip to Mexico and returned toward the end of February. Suddenly in March life as we knew it changed dramatically with the onset of the Covid 19 virus. No more music either at church nor at the Terrace. Church services from Plymouth Heights were streamed and in person services at the Terrace canceled. The months which followed were filled with isolation and disconnect with friends and church activities. I especially missed my musical involvement which I had so recently enjoyed. On the positive side, however, later in the year, services at Breton Woods were resumed (masks and spacing observed) and once again I was able to preach here at the Terrace, at the Ridge, and at Raybrook. Although on the surface the negatives appeared to outweigh the positives, I committed myself to focus on the positives: the wonderful blessings of family and ministry opportunities which the Lord continued to pour out daily. One day this year of isolation would pass and we would be able to look back and say, "We survived. God is good—all the time!"

As I write this now, the tense changes to the present. I miss my friends. If I see them at all, I have to stay at least six feet apart from them and wear a mask. One bright spot: I received two masks with Michigan emblems on them! Fortunately, the weather is warm, which makes daily walks, with or without the dog, very enjoyable. Apart from working on my cross-stitch, I do not find very much else to do. I tend to be quite neat, so there are no drawers nor cabinets to rearrange nor clean. I do find time to edit what I had already written in this, my autobiography. My Creative Writing group here at Breton Woods shares manuscripts via email which greatly help me in the editing process.

I missed my kids! Even though we can take walks, six feet apart, I still miss our hugs! The dog is thriving with the nice weather and my constant availability to take more walks.

My bridge friend, Howard Postma, is confined to his apartment due to recurring health problems. His family is not allowed to visit, so I have made it a point to be with him as often as possible, usually sharing our evening meals, either ordering them from Breton Dining, cooking them myself, or enjoying those provided by his family. Two "visiting angels" from the organization by that name cover two shifts each day and I take the afternoon-to-early-evening shift. I am learning the commitment and joy of sharing time with someone who is very grateful for every moment given. At 94 he still has a sharp mind and enjoys watching Wheel of Fortune and Jeopardy with me each night. In many ways I am gaining more than I am giving. I am truly blessed to have this special friend.

Before the pandemic hit, I had planned to visit the last country on my "bucket list", Croatia, with my friend, Judy King. We were to fly to Venice, Italy for a day or two and then embark on a cruise along the coast of Croatia, ending with a visit to two Greek Islands. Unfortunately, that all changed when the virus hit and our trip had to be cancelled. As an alternative, I am now planning a trip alone for the spring of 2021 to travel to Croatia, Montenegro, Bosnia, Herzegovina and Slovenia with Grand Circle Tours. Bill and I traveled with this agency when we went to China and loved the personal visits to homes and events which were included. I feel blessed to have had opportunities to visit so many countries and meet so many delightful people. I have learned that persons from around the world have much in common; however, few have a personal relationship with Christ.

For example, our guide in Japan had no idea about Buddhism even though most in her country were Buddhist. In China we were told that the temples were only visited when families were honoring their deceased. Many wept at the ruins of the Notre Dame Cathedral in Paris, yet each time I had attended services there in the past the Cathedral was largely empty. On the other hand, there is great visible evidence of Islamic followers in countries such as Egypt. Many of the Moslem faithful in Cairo, for example, daily stop what they are doing when the call to prayer sounds, kneel, face Mecca and pray. Common in their everyday conversations are the words "insha Allah" meaning "if God wills" or "Alhamdulila", "thanks be to God". These are just a few of the challenges facing Christians throughout the world today as we try by our words and actions to witness to the saving knowledge of Jesus Christ which will hopefully make a huge difference in the lives of persons everywhere.

It is now April and we have been further confined. My family contacts are now limited to one member. Mark, having been laid off work because all restaurants have been closed, stops by almost every afternoon to take a "six-foot-apart" walk with me outside. I am not allowed to go out of my apartment into the hallway or common areas. If I order food from the dining room it is brought to the hall door of my apartment along with my daily mail. Garbage is picked up twice a week, also from my hall door. I sneeze a lot because I cannot have anyone come in and clean for me. My animals cannot figure out why I am always at home. They must sense that something is wrong because they seldom leave my lap. The dog even sleeps with me! The cat, although very close and super friendly during the day, prefers to sleep in his cage at night. I spend time finishing the counted cross-stitch for my soon-to-be great granddaughter, knitting, reading, working on this book and practicing the violin and piano. It is sad, though, that after I retired to enjoy my music, it all came to an abrupt end in March. With my extra time I even began writing poetry! I'm not sure why I continue to practice the violin as our spring concert has been cancelled and no future plans have been set. I generally do not watch TV much, but lately I have indulged in this because it gets lonely not hearing human voices on a regular basis. They say that we might not have college football in the fall. That would probably mean that schools would not be open either. Although I am not in school myself, both my son, Jeff, and daughter, Jenny, are school teachers and Lindsey is still in high school. Closing school would not, therefore, affect me personally, but not going to Michigan football games would be drastic!!! I also miss not being able to attend worship in person. Since I had just recently rejoined Plymouth Heights CRC, I miss the personal fellowship very much. Fortunately, the services are streamed each Sunday and I can watch them on my tablet, in my pjs with a cup of coffee!

I love listening to music, especially classical as I sit alone. One exception to that is the Platters, a singing group that goes way back to the 1950s. I first heard them when I was teaching in Egypt and dating Mike, my Egyptian doctor friend. I have loved that group ever since. I turn on my Home Google and say "Platters please" and receive two hours of their songs! "Only You" is their most famous song. Every time I hear it, I am reminded of those days in Egypt when Mike and I used to dance to this tune atop the roof of the Semiramis Hotel. It brings back mixed emotions. I loved my time in Egypt and wish that Egypt were closer so I could visit more often or possibly move my whole family to Egypt! That would be a dream come true! The only thing I would miss would be Michigan football!

The special event of April was the birth of my second great-granddaughter, Mila Mae Wharton to Cory and Taylor. She weighed 9 lbs. 8 oz. and was over 21 inches long. She looks just like Cory! I sent an "I'm a Big Sister" teddy bear to Ryder and some matching outfits I purchased in Mexico along with several items I knit for Mila Mae. The cross-stitch is finished, but I will have to wait a bit to have it framed. I plan to give it to them when they visit in the fall. Cory usually flies in to attend a football game with me each year, but things may be different this fall. We still do not know if there will be games and if there are, whether or not fans will be present. What a low blow to my most special annual event!

May 2020 has arrived and we are still observing the "stay at home order" because of the Covid19 virus. Having so much time available each day has given me lots of "thinking" time. I keep looking back over my life and wondering why I made some of the decisions I made. Why was having an imaginary friend so important to me when I was very young? Was it because I was an only child and felt lonesome much of the time? That certainly was not my parents' fault as they spent countless hours enriching my life with piano lessons, violin lessons, art lessons, community concerts, trips to Orchestra Hall in Chicago to hear performances by great artists, travelogues, vacation trips to various parts of our country, and much, much more. Why was it then that I was so driven to finish school early? Actually, I loved school. As I look back, I wonder why I skipped my senior year of high school to attend college early. Was I bored? What did I ultimately gain by shortening my time in high school and repeating the same three-year escape plan in college? Was it really an escape? Was I in a hurry to finish "the program"? When I accepted God's call during my last year of college to teach in Egypt, why did I not follow through on my obligation to complete my three-year commitment? When after my evacuation and return to Egypt I was faced with three options for my future, why didn't I wait a year or so to make such an important decision as marriage? There was Ken at home, Mike in Egypt and Carl in Germany. Could I not have given my decision a bit more time? Would permanently living in Egypt have really been a bad choice? Today I am still challenged by these questions. I have made many trips back to Egypt and as I already mentioned I shed tears each time I leave. Does that mean that God's call to teach in Egypt was a stronger call than His later call to ordained ministry? Why did it take so long for me to acknowledge that call? I can surely identify with Jonah. At least I did not have to endure the physical punishment that he did. As I look back over forty years of ordained ministry, I have to admit that there were many times when I questioned God's call. There were many disappointments and failed opportunities amid the successes and challenges. It has been difficult being a female pastor. Yet in spite of that fact, after much thought, I decided to change the title of this book. Originally it was titled "A Box Marked Reject". Although "rejection" characterized much of my life: my birth mother's decision to give me away but keep my baby brother, my initial rejection by my Great Uncle George in my attempt to attend seminary following college, my rejection by my first husband as he sought intimacy elsewhere, the difficult task of seeking pastoral positions in a male-dominated profession, and my rejection by my sister, Sharon, once I yielded to God's call on my life, one by one those rejections began to heal. When I am honest, I have to admit that the blessings over the years have totally outweighed the disappointments and failures. I have tried to live by the Apostle Paul's advice to the church in Philippi to forget the past. That has not always been easy. Forgiveness is immediate, but forgetting takes time, sometimes a whole lifetime. As I journey through these difficult days of semi-isolation, I grieve each day as I look in the mirror at my hair which is long overdue for a cut. Unfortunately, I have not forgotten my mother's angry words on one occasion, "the only thing pretty about you is your hair." All of us are guilty, however, of saying things when we are upset which we later regret. That's why we have the gift of forgiveness.

This has also been a time of acknowledging my advancing age. Too much sitting has taken its toll. It is hard to get out of bed in the morning, even with arthritis medicine taken the night before. I don't walk as fast as I used to; however, I can still walk faster than all my kids! I am especially grateful to my son, Mark, who walks my dog each day and does my grocery shopping. I have had to learn to live with a less than a perfectly clean house as our housekeeping department here is still closed. I miss the fellowship of attending worship each Sunday but am grateful for the technology that makes streaming services possible. I also enjoy the times I am able to preach at Raybrook, which streams their services throughout their facilities.

Sunday is Mother's Day and although my family cannot take me out to dinner, they have all shown their love in other ways. Sandy Pines is cleaned up inside and out thanks to sons Mark and Aaron and soon flowers will grace my patio here at Breton Terrace, a gift from my daughter. Additional unexpected gifts arrived on Mother's Day: breakfast prepared on my patio by son Aaron, flowers from son Mark, a new Michigan flag from Robin, Mark's girlfriend, and a hanging basket of flowers from Nick, Syd's son. The sun is shining in spite of the cold and it is good to enjoy once again my children and their love gifts. God is good—all the time!

Now is the season to open windows. Six years ago, I pleaded with Breton Woods to fix at least one of my bedroom windows. The answer always was, "These are crappy windows, the manufacturer has gone bankrupt, they can't be fixed and we won't replace them." At various times they did make an attempt to fix them. In May they promised me that, at last, at least one window was fixed and I could have fresh Spring air. I made an attempt at opening one. The top fell down as always and I was injured. At first the doctors thought it was a shoulder injury but later on it was decided that it had been my spine that was injured. Months of therapy followed. Aaron developed an apparatus that allowed me to open the window with my foot which was a temporary fix. Finally, after several discussions with facility, it was decided to replace not just one, but all four of my windows since none of them were operational. This was accomplished in October right before the cold weather set in! Hopefully by next Spring I can enjoy the benefits of fresh air!

June is almost over and here I sit again at my laptop. Things here have let up a bit. I can now go out to visit family and enjoy extended walks. I continue to write poems! I try to write one every other day, reflecting upon the unique situation we all are in right now. Next Monday, June 29th, we will finally be able to have visitors in our apartments.

Very special during this time have been visits with Howard and his family at their cottage on Silver Lake in Rockford. All of his kids and grandkids, except one, came to celebrate his 95th birthday. It was a beautiful day and Howard was delighted to be back at his summer home. This lovely event was followed by a similar time together to celebrate Father's Day. We had steak, baked potatoes, and asparagus! What a treat! Sadly, on August 12th,

Howard went home to be with the Lord, peacefully in his sleep. I had the privilege of conducting his service which was a family-only event at their summer home. He will be greatly missed by all of us. He was a very special father, grandfather and friend.

Throughout my ministry I had always shared with caregivers who had lost loved ones that now there would be two voids in their lives: their loved one and their care-giving responsibility. This became a reality for me when Howard died. I never realized how much of my daily life was spent caring for him and just enjoying our time together. I think of him every day, especially when I drink my morning coffee from one of the mugs his family gave me following his death. Howard and I had identical dinnerware. The only difference was that his set included two coffee mugs. When his family wondered what to give me to thank me for doing his service, they decided that giving me the two mugs plus lots of already prepared frozen homemade meals would be perfect. I agreed!

Mark has Sandy Pines in full operation and it is such a joy to spend week-ends there. I am now on the Chapel Committee which oversees the Sunday services. Because of the pandemic, we have to practice safe distancing. Therefore, we have developed a two-service plan to help alleviate the highly congested services we usually have under the pavilion. On June 21 we enjoyed our first live service. We shifted the platform to the parking lot where we spaced golf carts six feet apart and offered face masks as needed. The residents were very cooperative and both services went off smoothly. It was good to get back to face-to-face worship. At first, we were worried about rain, but God was good. He answered our prayers and brought us bright sunshine every week. We haven't scheduled evening services yet, but hope to be able to very soon. These services always attract a large number of non-residents from nearby communities. The highlight of each summer is the Collingsworth Family, who have been coming to Sandy Pines for years. Hopefully they will be able to return this year. The preachers are always male. I preached there once back in 1978 when I was still in seminary, but no women have preached there since. Perhaps now that I am on the Chapel Committee, I can encourage them to invite one of our gifted area females to preach.

Things continue here on a very limited basis due to the Covid-19 pandemic. I miss not being able to do water aerobics, attend travelogs, pursue my music, volunteer for the symphony, and freely visit all my friends. The biggest lost, however, will be Michigan football if, indeed, the season is canceled or postponed. I always look forward to joining Mark each fall for these home games and am having difficulty adjusting to the fact that, although there may be games, there will be no fans—only family members of the players. Hopefully we will be able to see the games on TV. I feel guilty about my feelings on this issue because so many others are suffering in many more serious ways. Some families in our community are without food, adequate housing, or jobs with little hope of things changing in the immediate future. Many have so little and by comparison we, especially those who are fortunate enough to live where I do, have so much. This must grieve the Lord even more than it does us.

It is now September and I am spending my mornings assisting my Hussein family children, especially Yakoob, do schoolwork on line, since schools are closed. Hopefully, after two weeks on line at home they will be able to return to face-to-face instruction in school. I know the teachers are doing their very best, but it is still difficult, especially for young children like Yakoob. Seeing the family on a daily basis has afforded me the opportunity to talk with them about spiritual things. Anhar, the mother, is very open and interested in learning more about Christianity, yet firmly grounded in her Islamic faith. I believe she was exposed to both faiths while living in Iraq.

Labor Day week-end was very special in that all my children and their "significant others" joined me at Sandy Pines for a family celebration. Sunday was Aaron's birthday which we celebrated on Saturday with a delicious barbeque and a pontoon boat ride on our newly refurbished boat. Aaron had purchased a new transmission, installed it, and we were now ready to launch. Later on in the summer Aaron took Mark, Robin and me on a "dinner cruise" on his sail boat on Lake Michigan. I still wonder at the grandeur of Lake Michigan.

Fall is in full-bloom with trees transformed into beautiful colors and noticeable changes in the weather as well. Some days are sunny, others feel like winter is approaching. Michigan football games are at least on TV, but actual attendance is still limited to the family members of players. I need to be reminded daily to keep this loss in perspective. Hopefully, there will always be next year.

As an alternative to attending Michigan games, Mark, Robin and I have a "watch the game on TV" party here on Saturdays. Since I have two TVs, Mark can watch the Illinois game (he's still an Illini fan!) on one and Robin and I can watch Michigan on the other if necessary. It is great that the visitor ban has at last been lifted even though the virus, unfortunately, continues to spread.

2020 is not ending on a positive note, at least as far as the pandemic is concerned. Many deaths, grieving families, limited holiday travel—everything seems dismal. Is there any light at the end of the tunnel?

Zooming has become very popular. On one occasion I was part of a zoom meeting where the topic of conversation was "What has been the greatest challenge for you during this time of crisis?" I listened as others shared concerning those things they *didn't* have and things they *couldn't* do. When it came to be my turn, I decided to focus on what I *still* had and what I *could* do. I began by remembering the Apostle Paul's words to the church at Philippi, *"For I have learned, in whatever state I am, to be content."* *(4:11)*. I remembered, too, that the following week I was to preach here at the Terrace. Since I had already preached on that text before, I turned to another passage, I Thessalonians 5:16-18, which reads, *"Rejoice always, pray constantly, give thanks in all circumstances."* These verses encouraged me to share with my zoom group my journey over the past year, not just the last eight months, and to emphasize the things for which I was truly grateful.

When I retired in November of 2019 the Lord gave me the wonderful opportunity to return to my roots: music. Then the pandemic happened. No more music at any level. No more in person Michigan football games. Could I still experience gratitude? Could I still share gratitude through my preaching?

My answer came from the theme of my graduate dissertation on the joy passages of Philippians: "Joy Transcends Circumstances." I also remembered the advice I had previously shared with my zoom group to follow what Paul shared with the Thessalonian Christians to "rejoiced always", every day, in every way, in everything. Then I was to "pray constantly", not just in words but in actions, in attitude. Finally, I was to "give thanks in all circumstances." Not "for" all circumstances but "in" all circumstances. I was able to give thanks for my secure home, my abundance of food, and most of all my family. No, I couldn't hug and kiss them, but I could at least visit with them. I could relinquish my total life of independence and allow my family to run errands for me! I found time to finish this autobiography, and finish the T-shirt quilt for son Mark. Happily, I still have monthly opportunities to preach, even at age 84! Thus, in spite of the limitations of my life right now due to the pandemic, I can still affirm that God is not only good all the time, but He is still saving the "best for last."

No autobiography would be complete without special recognition of the love and support I have received from my children and their families. I'll begin with my oldest, Mark, his son Mitch, Cory and I

next comes Aaron, his wife, Anne, and their sons Kelvin and Gavin

then my youngest son, Jeff, his wife, Amy and their three children Daniel, Janice and her husband Sam, and Anna.

Jenny, her husband, Adam, and their three children who remain at home: Cameron, Trenton and Lindsey;

and finally, Jenny's son, Cory, with Taylor and his two daughters, Ryder and Mila Mae. I owe each of them a ton of gratitude for their patience, love, and support during the many months I concentrated on completing this project.

After over sixty years of ministry in missions, Christian Education, and as a pastor, I have learned the importance of establishing and keeping priorities. My first priority has always been the Lord: trusting in Him, leaning on Him, accepting guidance and forgiveness from Him, growing daily in my relationship with Him. In second place has been my family. Initially I was worried that I might be like my birth mother and reject those I was called to love. I had two children close in age because I did not want a child to experience the loneliness I had felt as an only child. Initially I had hoped my children would all be boys, just to make sure I would never be tempted to reject them. Adopting Jenny turned out to be one of the most important decisions in my life. Through the years I was able to realize that I could have just as close a relationship with a daughter as I had had with my sons. Now that I was a mother of a daughter, my life was truly complete. My third priority has always been my work whether it was teaching, counselling, serving as a chaplain, or ministering as a pastor. I had to learn the valuable lesson of making sure that this was in third place and not in first or second place. I also had to learn the importance of taking care of myself. That's where priority four comes in—having fun. Supporting Cory in all his sports activities, attending Michigan football games and participating in various musical opportunities went a long way in fulfilling this task. I had to be careful concerning the latter. I secretly worried that when the going became too challenging in my work as a pastor, I would try to "escape" back into the world of music full time. Perhaps that is why it was not a major step to finally, for the fifth time, retire. I knew that music was waiting, almost as a reward for years of faithful service to the Lord. Spending time with friends should also be on my priority list. This year of pandemic has revealed to me that basically I still am that girl whose high school yearbook labeled her as "quiet, poised and self-controlled." I don't require a huge number of friends. One best friend, male or female, is usually sufficient. I feel like I have failed miserably during these pandemic days in not reaching out to other residents where I live. I have a car; I am able to be somewhat independent. Many where I live are not so privileged. I found myself spending all my time either writing this autobiography, quilting or spending quality time with my family. As I look forward to the completion of this book, I also look forward to having the time and making the effort to live out the message I find myself frequently preaching—-love your neighbor as you love the Lord. I do pray for others regularly; now I must find time to love and visit them too.

It is my sincere hope that now that I have rewritten what was originally a book for my children only, new readers, especially women engaged in ministry, will benefit from my experiences and will grow, as I have, in their spiritual journey, remembering always Apostle Paul's words in Philippians 1:6 that *"He who began a good work in you will bring it to completion at the day of Jesus Christ."*

In closing I'd like to share with you a poem I wrote in 1954 to a friend who was facing a challenging future:

"Today is just the beginning on the road that lies ahead—
a path of bright tomorrows trod with gladness you have spread.
And though the road be rocky, and you stumble along the way,
His hand will ever guide you as you live for him each day.

No fears or doubts can move you when your eyes are fixed on Him
for His way brings only gladness to a soul He's cleansed from sin.
His love is all sufficient—t'will see you through each day,
And keep you ever close to Him though hardships come your way
And so friend as you travel along the road He's planned,
May His love and peace go with you as you serve at His command."

Chapter Ten:
Acknowledgments and Dedication

*W*ithout the support and encouragement of a number of persons, this book would not have been possible. I begin with my family who supported me throughout my journey. They showered me with love and encouragement as I accepted God's call to ministry, studied at Calvin Seminary, and relocated them several times as God moved in different directions. They journeyed with me as I juggled thirty piano pupils, four kids and a husband around my hectic study schedule. They enthusiastically embraced new schools and new jobs as we traveled from church to church.

Visiting Jerry in Florida

During my years at Calvin Seminary, I was blessed to have professors who were supportive and always fair, even if they had questions about female pastors. Especially helpful were my New Testament Professors Bastiaan VanElderen, Andrew Bandstra, and David Holwerda. This was especially true during the years when I was working on my dissertation on the joy passages of Paul's epistle to the Philippians, in preparation for my Master of Theology degree.

The students, especially those in the Seminary Choir,

were also on my support team. They made sure that, in spite of the fact that I was the only woman in the choir, I was accepted, particularly by the churches we visited on tour. Outstanding among other supporters was my preaching partner, Jerry Lion. Each time either of us preached the other listened and offered helpful suggestions. We have remained life-long friends. I will always remember his parting words, "I'm only a phone call away."

Words cannot adequately describe my love and appreciation for my birth grandparents and especially my adoptive parents who took a small, rejected child and set her on a journey toward wholeness. It is in deep gratitude for them that I dedicate this book to their memory.

And finally, I am eternally grateful for a God who took a young girl who considered herself in "a box marked reject", and along with her parents, loved, accepted, forgave, redeemed, guided her to wholeness and gave her a life of unimaginable joy. As previously mentioned, the title of this book was originally "A Box Marked Reject", but later, realizing the change that God had made in my life, the title became "What Others Reject, God Accepts."

Egypt has been and will always be a very special part of my life. I can truly affirm the famous saying that "He who drinks of the waters of the Nile will surely return to drink again."

A Memorable Nile Sunset

About the Author

*R*ev. **Carolyn Cammenga** was born in Oak Park, Illinois and at the age of 4 ½ given up for adoption. "Given up" does not adequately define the emotional turmoil experienced by a young child who had no idea why she was not wanted, what she had done wrong and why her loving grandparents had been forced to "give her up." She came to her new adoptive parents with the word "reject" written all over her. Despite the tremendous amount of love, she experienced from these new parents, the threat of further rejection dominated her ensuing years. She continually feared failure, in school or elsewhere. If she were to fail, would she be given away again? She was never "given up" again, but she did experience several more incidents of rejection. Why did her birth mother give her away and keep her baby brother? Did that mean we only keep boys? Then there was the discovery of a sister who soundly rejected even her very existence.

Running away from the Lord's call for many years, she finally accepted the challenge of attending Calvin Theological Seminary as one of only two female ministerial students in her class. Although almost all of the students and professors welcomed her with open arms, this was not true of the churches she visited as part of the Seminary Choir; nor was it the case when she was searching for a call to a church upon graduation. "You will make a great pastor for someone else's church" was their unspoken message. Even after receiving calls to several churches during her forty years of ministry, rejection was still on the horizon. However, now at this stage of her life, she was able to acknowledge that, although the initial possibility of rejection had played a major part in her life's decisions in the past, all that had changed once she began to trust in the Lord and soundly affirm His call in her life.

This book describes her journey from initial rejection to spiritual wholeness and triumph through prayer and courage, often in the face of challenging professional and personal situations.

CPSIA information can be obtained
at www.ICGtesting.com
Printed in the USA
LVHW011249230721
693278LV00008B/359